# HENRY VIII
## AND HIS QUEENS

# HENRY VIII
## AND HIS QUEENS

*David Loades*

SUTTON PUBLISHING

First published in the United Kingdom in 1994 by
Alan Sutton Publishing Limited, an imprint of Sutton Publishing Limited
Phoenix Mill · Thrupp · Stroud · Gloucestershire · GL 52BU

Reprinted 1998

British Library Cataloguing in Publication Data
A catalogue record for this book is available from the British Library

ISBN 0 7509 0029 6

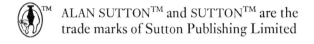 ALAN SUTTON™ and SUTTON™ are the
trade marks of Sutton Publishing Limited

Typeset in 11/12 Ehrhardt.
Typesetting and origination by
Sutton Publishing Limited.
Printed in Great Britain by
WBC Limited, Bridgend.

# Contents

# List of Illustrations

Portraits and illustrations are reproduced by kind permission of the following copyright holders (page numbers in brackets): The Society of Antiquaries of London (4, 19, 152); The Royal Collection © 1994 Her Majesty The Queen (5, 23, 24, 32, 74, 75, 87, 96, 122, 143, 145); Kunsthistorisches Museum, Vienna (12, 93); Syndics of the University of Cambridge Library (18); The Hulton Deutsch Collection (20, 52, 105); Board of Trustees of the Royal Armouries (21); the Marquess of Salisbury (26, 70); Mansell Collection (28, 39, 65, 97, 98, 137); the President and Fellows of Magdalen College, University of Oxford (ref. MCA photo B/1/14) (30); Royal College of Physicians (31); Private Collection/photograph courtesy of Lane Fine Art Gallery, London (33); Fitzwilliam Museum, Cambridge (38); British Library (43, 64, 151); National Portrait Gallery, London (45, 47, 81, 88, 139, 141, 142); Trustees of the British Museum (53, 148, 161); Bodleian Library, University of Oxford, MS Douce 363, fol. 71R (56); Huntingdon Record Office (67); the Dean and Canons of Windsor (77); Ashmolean Museum, Oxford (85, 99, 119, 138); Victoria & Albert Museum, London (102); the Trustees of The National Gallery, London (108); The President and Fellows of St John's College, Oxford (117); Elmbridge Museum (125); Crown copyright material in the Public Record Office is reproduced by permission of the Controller of Her Majesty's Stationery Office, SP 1/167 f.14 (128).

# Preface

This is a book about a king. It is not about six women, although they are very important to the story. Henry VIII married all but one of his wives because that was what he wanted to do at the time. Only once did he marry for purely political reasons, and that was the briefest and least successful of his unions. Each marriage created a political climate of its own, and that climate changed as the nature of the relationship changed. There was nothing particularly remarkable about that in a personal monarchy, except for Henry's unique determination to have his own way. It was not that he suffered from unbridled lust. Contrary to what is sometimes believed, he was not promiscuous, and his known mistresses can be counted on the fingers of one hand. In that respect he was outdone by both his major contemporaries; not only the notorious Francis I of France, but also the sober and pious Holy Roman Emperor, Charles V. The remarkable things about Henry VIII were his unpredictability and his compulsive self-righteousness. He had to believe that if he wanted to do anything, then it was legally and morally right to follow that course. Four of his marriages were dissolved, with incalculable political consequences, and each for a different reason. In each case, however, the king convinced himself that he was the wronged and aggrieved party, a conviction which gave ruthlessness, and even malice, to his actions. Each of Henry's marriages is therefore a case study, both in politics and in royal psychology. Together they constitute the most important element in the history of his reign. They also represent his most enduring, and most misunderstood, claim to fame.

I have therefore written this book not to celebrate the wives of Henry VIII, and certainly not to celebrate the king himself, but to examine the relationship between human nature, sexuality and politics in a period when the importance of such a relationship was not merely acknowledged but self-evident. During the Renaissance power was deemed to come, not from the people, but from God by way of the king. How the king behaved, and how he kept his relationship with God in good repair, was therefore fundamental to the well-being of his subjects. Not only the security of an hereditary succession, but also the quality of the harvests and the stability of the social order could depend upon his getting it right. It is not surprising that Englishmen were fascinated, and not infrequently alarmed, by the performance of one of their most notorious kings.

# Acknowledgements

My first thanks are due to Alan Sutton for inviting me to write this book. My students in Bangor have sustained my interest in Henry VIII by their interest and curiosity, and I have discussed the foibles of that wayward prince with many colleagues in a variety of places. I am grateful to Sophie Goldsworthy for preparing the index, and to my wife Judith for her constant encouragement and support. To her, as is appropriate for such a subject, this work is affectionately dedicated.

DL
University of Wales, Bangor
April 1994

# INTRODUCTION

# Dynastic Politics during the Renaissance

Royal marriages were the very essence of high politics in medieval and early modern Europe. The fortunes of states depended upon the fertility of monarchs and their consorts, and upon the accidents of infant mortality. It is not surprising that princes and peoples alike accepted their helplessness in the face of God when the best efforts of their policies could be reduced to the status of genetic gambling. The chief purpose of such marriages was, of course, the begetting of male heirs, but other children were also valuable diplomatic assets, and the marriages themselves might create significant political patterns. At a time when the distinction between a state and a private lordship was not clearly made, an heiress might convey to her husband lands which had hitherto enjoyed autonomy. When the Duchess Anne of Brittany married King Charles VIII of France in 1491, she created a personal union which resulted in the permanent absorption of her duchy into the kingdom.[1] Even more dramatic consequences followed from the marriage of Mary of Burgundy to Maximilian of Habsburg in August 1477. Such dynastic unions far transcended the importance of mere temporary alliances, but those too had their significance. Without the relationship created by the marriage of his sister, Margaret, to Duke Charles of Burgundy, King Edward IV of England might never have recovered his Crown in 1471. Royal marriages were used to seal treaties of peace, as happened between England and France in 1514, or to foreclose other options in foreign policy, as seems to have been Henry VII's intention when he married his daughter, Margaret, to James IV of Scotland in August 1503.[2] A marriage might signal a dramatic change of policy – for example, the union of Germaine de Foix with Ferdinand of Aragon in 1505 – or even the ascendancy of one domestic faction over another, demonstrated by the marriage of Henry VI to Margaret of Anjou in 1445.

For a ruling prince, or for the heir to a throne, marriage was consequently a very serious business, not to be undertaken without much thought and counsel. Not only did the immediate political circumstances have to be taken into account, but also the long-term dynastic possibilities. The empire of Charles V was assembled as the result of a series of such unions, and could hardly have been planned, but the Habsburg marriage brokers could certainly feel that the Almighty had smiled upon their efforts. A domestic marriage, of course, carried neither the risks nor the opportunities of a foreign match, but was fraught with equal hazards of a rather different kind. Edward IV chose to marry the widow of one of his barons rather than seal a dynastic alliance with France. It is very unlikely that this was a mere romantic gesture. Edward urgently needed to demonstrate that he was capable of making his own decisions, and particularly that he was not in tutelage to the Earl of Warwick, who was busily promoting the French negotiation.[3] He may, or may not, have planned to create a new political faction out of his wife's kindred, but that was the predictable outcome. The gesture was clumsily handled, perhaps because of the king's inexperience, and other counsellors apart from Warwick were offended at not having been consulted. Major rebellions in 1469 and 1470 were partly caused by this discontent, but a decade of effective and stable government followed as the queen's Grey and Woodville kindred inter-married with the existing peerage. It was hardly Edward's fault that his premature death in 1483 should have prompted his hitherto loyal brother, Richard of Gloucester, to wage war on that kindred, and to destroy the house of York in the process. In retrospect Edward's marriage seems to have been neither more nor less mistaken than that of his predecessor, Henry VI. By contrast the marriage of the insecure Henry VII to Elizabeth of York in 1486 was an unequivocal success. It was presented as a reconciliation of the houses of York and Lancaster, and effectively prevented the young princess from being used against her uncle's supplanter. Henry was unable to secure matrimonial recognition abroad at the outset of his reign, but the price proved to be well worth paying.

Between 1415 and 1603 only one monarch of England came to the throne married. Of the remaining nine, three (Edward V, Edward VI and Elizabeth) died unmarried. Henry V, Henry VI and Mary chose their partners abroad, Edward IV and Henry VII married at home, and Henry VIII alone married more than once, taking two brides from other princely families and four from among his own subjects. In spite of this variety of practice there were nevertheless certain well-defined conventions, and a ruler's freedom of choice was not usually as wide as it might appear. To make an honourable match a foreign bride needed to come from a powerful and well-established dynasty, and although such a marriage was not expected to create permanent affinities, the bride's kindred might continue to have an inhibiting effect upon the groom's freedom of action. Similarly a consort from a great noble house at home could create undesirable pressures, while to marry at a lower social level was to invite both jealousy and disparagement. Edward IV created serious difficulties for himself by marrying an alleged upstart as well as by making his decision in private, and a lack of noble ancestry was one of the innumerable charges hurled at Anne Boleyn.[4] Few kings expected or sought a helpmate. Margaret of Anjou provided something of the stiffening which Henry VI so notoriously lacked, but that was an altogether exceptional situation, and not one which anybody wished to repeat. It was no part of a consort's normal responsibilities to play an active part in government, and consequently the ability to do so was no particular commendation. Piety was more useful, not only because it helped to improve the image of the Crown, but also because it might attract some much needed Divine favour. Beauty, too, was a much appreciated asset. According to Castiglione '. . . much is lacking to a woman who lacks beauty', because she then lacked the chief means of persuading men to overlook her faults.[5] Fertility, however, was the most desired quality of all, and the one about which there was the most ingenious speculation. After the death of

Elizabeth of York, Henry VII contemplated with apparent seriousness marrying the notoriously deranged Juana, the widowed Archduchess of Burgundy, because she had succeeded in presenting her late husband with two healthy sons and several daughters.[6]

Henry also caused his agents to appraise the widowed queen of Naples for the same purpose, and their frank report leaves little to the imagination. However, it should not be deduced from this somewhat clinical approach that royal marriages were devoid of natural affection. Few monarchs could afford to marry for love, but there is plenty of evidence that these political unions frequently blossomed into genuine relationships which proved satisfying to both parties. A warm relationship might encourage procreation, and discourage the consort from dangerous political intrigues, but for everyone apart from the partners themselves it was a marginal irrelevance, and might even become an obstacle should it be necessary for any reason to bring the marriage to an end. Divorce in the modern sense was virtually impossible, but annulments could be obtained on a variety of grounds, such as non-consummation or undisclosed consanguinity. Sometimes these pretexts were a thin disguise for political convenience. In 1499, for example, Louis XII of France succeeded in discarding his consort, Jeanne, in order to marry Anne of Brittany, the widow of his predecessor, and thus preserve the personal union of their respective dominions. The canon law of marriage was a jungle, and the late medieval Church was not always quite scrupulous in traversing it, but no king of England had ever found it necessary to seek the annulment of an unsatisfactory union. This was partly because the Plantagenets had never suffered from a shortage of offspring. Henry VI and Richard III could manage only one son apiece, but Edward IV left two sons and four daughters; his brother, George, Duke of Clarence, was also survived by a son and a daughter. At first it seemed that the Tudors would be equally fortunate. At one point Henry VII and Elizabeth had three sons and two daughters;[7] but by the time Elizabeth died in 1503 only one son survived, and the succession hung by a thread.

This not only prompted the king's search for a second wife, it also highlighted the fact that the succession in England was governed not by law but by custom. When Richard of York claimed the Crown in the teeth of King Henry VI in 1460, the judges and sergeants-at-law had declared themselves incompetent to adjudicate upon so high a mystery. Instead they had suggested resort to 'dyvers wrytings and cronicles', in the hope that history would provide the necessary precedent.[8] The issue at that point was between the heir general, with a senior claim transmitted through the female line, and their heir male with a junior claim transmitted direct from father to son. No law had decided whether the Crown was a title or a property, and the issue had to be resolved by wager of battle. An unchallenged succession could not be assumed, even when the incumbent monarch had a legitimate son. Henry VI had a son of undoubted legitimacy when York was eventually recognized as his heir. Moreover, legitimacy could be a fragile prop. There had been whispers, but no one had seriously doubted the legitimacy of Edward IV's sons until Richard of Gloucester challenged them in the summer of 1483. Rejecting the superior claim of the Earl of Warwick upon a technicality, he then seized the throne himself. He was a prince of the royal blood,

*Henry VII (1457–1509) (anon. artist, c. 1515)*

of full age and proven competence, and that was sufficient for most of the peers of England. It was not Yorkist legitimacy which overthrew him two years later, but a revival of the Lancastrian claim with French support. The future Henry VIII was about eleven years old, and of unimpeachable lawfulness, when his father fell sick and certain 'great personages',

> . . . fell into communication of the King's grace and of the world that should be after him if his grace happened to depart. Then [Sir Hugh Conway] said that some of them spake of my lord of Buckingham, saying that he was a noble man and would be a royal ruler. Other there were that spake, he said, in like wise of your traitor, Edmund de la Pole, but none of them, he said, spake of my lord prince. . . .[9]

Nothing could be taken for granted in this constitutional vacuum, because there had not been an undisputed succession since 1422, and only three since 1327. It is not surprising that Henry VII became somewhat paranoid on the subject in the last years of his life, nor that fears and uncertainties survived the unchallenged accession of his son in 1509.

The marriage of a ruler was the highest level of the matrimonial game, and carried the biggest stakes, but it was not the only level. Both sons and daughters

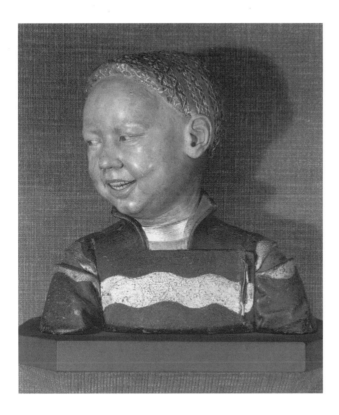

*Bust of a child believed to be Henry VIII as a boy (attributed to Guido Mazzoni, c. 1500)*

were pieces to be moved in the diplomatic game, which usually began while they were still in their cradles. A daughter, particularly, might undergo half a dozen betrothals in the interest of shifting policies before her destiny eventually caught up with her. Some contemporaries believed that young women were being unduly indulged in their choice of partners, but that was seldom the case with a royal princess. Edward IV's youngest daughter, Bridget, did succeed in escaping into a nunnery, but only after her father's death. Because he died young, none of Edward's children were married by 1483, and it is impossible to say with whom his daughters might have been matched in due course,[10] but there appears to have been a marked contrast between Yorkist and Tudor attitudes to marriage. Not only did Edward himself marry within the realm, but so did his brothers, George and Richard. Only his sister, Margaret, was exported. Henry VII, by contrast, married his eldest son in Spain and his eldest daughter in Scotland. Unusually, Arthur's union with Catherine, the youngest daughter of Ferdinand and Isabella, was pursued with unwavering tenacity for over ten years. This was not because there was any prospect of a matrimonial conquest of Castile, but simply because the young Princess of Wales represented the recognition of Europe's newest ruling family by one of the oldest. Margaret Tudor was sent north with a similar consistency of purpose as soon as she was old enough to co-habit with her husband, for the main purpose of counteracting French influence in Scotland and securing England's northern marches. Henry's younger daughter, Mary, was similarly used by her brother to neutralize Louis XII of France, but when he died after a few months she took the unprecedented step of foreclosing further options by insisting upon a union with Charles Brandon, the newly created Duke of Suffolk. Her niece, Princess Mary, was used relentlessly in the same game by Henry VIII, possibly because she was his only legitimate child until 1533. Mary was betrothed to the Dauphin Francis, and to Charles, the young Holy Roman Emperor, before she was five, and further betrothals were mooted, to James V of Scotland and to Francis I (who was only two years younger than her father, as well as being a notorious lecher). Mary's usefulness was heavily reduced by the rumours, eventually confirmed, that she would be declared illegitimate.

Royal bastards had their own usefulness in the marriage market, but were not usually welcomed by other royal families. The Habsburgs used them to anchor the allegiance of powerful but untrustworthy vassals, and the Valois bestowed them upon aspiring noble houses. The Tudors had too few to support generalization, and Mary, of course, remained unmarried until she chose her own partner when queen. In bestowing his daughters every Renaissance prince had to bear in mind that one day his son-in-law might inherit his Crown. Henry VII, Francis I and Ferdinand of Aragon all lost their eldest sons in their lifetime. Henry and Francis had second sons who eventually succeeded, but Ferdinand was left with a complicated dilemma when his wife, Isabella, died in 1504. As Queen of Castile in her own right, she had been forced to concede her husband equal status, but she had no intention of allowing him to retain the crown matrimonial after her death; the death of their son, Juan, in 1499 had left the succession in the hands of their eldest daughter, Juana, and her husband, Philip of Habsburg. Juana would probably never have become an effective ruler, but Philip showed every sign of imposing himself when untimely death removed him from the scene in 1506. This enabled Ferdinand to cling on to power, and when he died in 1516 he was succeeded in both kingdoms by Juana's eldest son, Charles. Dynastically this may have been satisfactory, but it provoked rebellion in Spain, and it was to be many years before the people there finally accepted their alien and often absent monarch. The simplest remedy for this type of problem was to adopt the Salic law (which barred all women from the succession), but that was not the custom in either Castile or England. Every time Henry VIII used his daughter in a matrimonial gambit he was acutely aware that his choice might one day become England's king, and it seems to have been for that reason as much as any other that the options with Francis I and James V were not pursued. Henry's reluctance to face the prospect of leaving a female heir was to become one of the most important factors in the story which follows, and it is important to remember that that reluctance was shared by his subjects. The anonymous nobleman who declared after the Field of Cloth of Gold that if he had any French blood in him he would cut it out with a knife was no more xenophobic than most of his fellow countrymen.

The problem with a female heir lay partly in the prevailing culture of male superiority, and partly in the uncertainties of the law. The conventional view, framed by men but also accepted by most women, was that the human female was weak both in body and intellect, susceptible to temptation, and herself a source of moral corruption to men. The undoubted fact that the Church recognized many female saints, and that recent history could show in Isabella of Castile a queen as formidable as any king, did nothing to undermine the stereotype. Even a humanist educator like Juan Luis Vives, who believed in the schooling of girls, did not make any kind of a case for equality. And Isabella herself gave her daughters an excellent education but did not train them to rule. It was expected that if a woman inherited a crown, her husband would govern. He would receive the crown matrimonial, and his authority would automatically be equal to hers. What would happen in the event of her death was unclear. If there was an heir of full age, his role would cease; if there was an heir under age, he could reasonably expect to receive the Regency. But if there was a disputed succession he might well continue in power, as Ferdinand did in Castile. Some English lawyers, who were prone to be particularly alarmist about female succession, even argued that the realm would belong to the queen's consort in full ownership for the duration of his own lifetime before passing to the next heir.[11] When so important an issue was exposed to such radical uncertainty, it is not surprising that great efforts were made to avoid the contingency. The Scots fought tooth and nail to avoid a marriage between their young Queen Mary and Prince Edward of England in the 1540s, fearing absorption by their more powerful neighbour. They succeeded at the price of becoming briefly a dependency of France, and were then torn by domestic strife when Mary chose her second husband nearer home. Scotland, in short, was to provide a very good example of why Henry VIII was prepared to go to such lengths to secure a male heir.

Matrimony being a sacrament of the Church, the adjudication of disputes was reserved to the ecclesiastical courts, and unfortunately the canon law on the subject was neither simple nor clear. There were, for example, several ways of creating a binding contract. A betrothal *per verba de futuro* was not irrevocable, and was the normal approach used in diplomatic matches, when both parties wished to preserve their freedom of action, and when the principals were probably infants. A betrothal *per verba de praesenti*, on the other hand, was an altogether more serious matter, and would certainly be sufficient to inhibit any subsequent contract, unless it had been dissolved by consent. Such a betrothal, followed by consummation, was held to be a full and lawful marriage, even if no wedding ceremony had taken place. Where there had been a ceremony, but no consummation, the marriage was lawful, but relatively easy to dissolve. Given the complicated and often repetitive nature of royal marriage negotiations, it was normal to resort to the ecclesiastical jurisdiction to clear away the detritus of former diplomacy when the time came to make an irrevocable commitment. Carelessness in this respect could have the most serious consequences, as was demonstrated when Edward IV's alleged pre-contract with Lady Eleanor Butler was used as a pretext for the bastardization of both his sons in 1483. There was also the tricky question of consanguinity to be considered. Many degrees of kindred were clearly forbidden to marry, but cousins inhabited a grey area of huge dimensions, and in an age when most royal families were related to some extent, they created many hazards. The usual rule was, if in doubt, get a dispensation.

However, even resort to the highest ecclesiastical court could not guarantee security. Certain degrees of consanguinity were prohibited by the law of God, and against such law no dispensation could prevail. Unfortunately canon lawyers did not agree exactly where the demarcation line ran, so certain types of dispensation were always liable to be disputed. Moreover, it was absolutely essential to get the terms of the dispensation correctly matched to the case, because if the issue became contentious, invalidation upon a technicality was a constant risk. When it is appreciated that extra-marital liaisons also created impediments of consanguinity, whether they had been acknowledged or not, it may be understood what a jungle the law could be. Since the legal foresters were worthy of their hire, they were not likely to connive at any simplification.

Although few men were more obviously political animals than medieval kings, it must also be remembered that they were human beings. Royal marriages were political arrangements, just as aristocratic marriages were business arrangements, but both required men and women to live together in some degree of harmony if they were to fulfil their basic purpose. The contemporary theory was that love followed marriage, rather than preceding it, and that was probably as realistic a view as any, but matrimonial breakdowns could and did occur. However, female consorts were in a very weak position. Very seldom would their own kin risk a political clash with their husbands by supporting them in the event of a conflict. Princesses became accustomed to being treated like brood mares, and the culture of the period offered them no escape except through the consolations of religion. A queen was not entitled to object to her lord's infidelities (although she often did) and if she risked an adventure of her own faced repudiation and imprisonment or death. The reason for this unequal treatment was perfectly logical. A king's bastards did no harm to anyone, and provided evidence of his potency; but any doubt over the legitimacy of a child borne by his queen could disrupt the succession to the kingdom. Henry VIII concentrated the whole range of matrimonial experience into his not particularly long lifetime, and the story is to some extent one of human whims, foibles and weaknesses. But it is principally a story of constitutional manipulation and political rivalries; a classic, if rather extreme, example of the functioning of personal monarchy during the Renaissance.

# ONE

# The Renaissance Prince: Henry and Catherine, 1504–25

Catherine had originally come to England as a pledge of friendship between England and Spain, and to signify the recognition of the Tudor dynasty by the ancient royal house of Trastamara. She was sixteen and had been betrothed to Arthur, Prince of Wales, for as long as she could remember.[1] As the youngest daughter, her parents had felt entitled to take a gamble on her future which they might not have taken with a child closer to the succession. By 1501 her brother, Juan, was already dead. Her sister Isabella, married first to Alfonso of Portugal and then to his cousin and successor Manuel, had died in childbirth three years before. Manuel had then married another sister, Maria, in a mood of grim dynastic determination. Only her favourite sister, Juana, seemed to have been smiled upon by fortune. She was married to Philip, the Archduke of Burgundy, and was already the mother of one healthy son. Catherine consequently knew what was expected of a royal princess, and understood the risks. She had been carefully educated, not to rule, but to be the consort of a ruler. Unlike Portugal, England was a distant and alien land, and unlike the Habsburgs, the Tudors offered no great dynastic prizes. But by 1501 Ferdinand and Isabella were satisfied that Catherine's future was as well secured as human prudence could make it. The English may have lived in a foggy island and spoken a strange and barbarous tongue, but they were almost as famous for their piety as the Castilians themselves, and that was a powerful consideration. Catherine's mother, Isabella, had become a wife and a ruler by force of circumstances, but the rigour of her piety caused her to be known as 'the crowned nun'. Catherine inherited some of that rigour, partly by nature and partly by education. Together with the pride of ancient royal blood, this was to give the gentle-seeming girl who rode into London to the plaudits of the crowd in October 1501 that steely determination which was to be her chief characteristic, and one of the most potent political facts of English history.

Henry VII was inordinately proud of his new daughter-in-law,

> . . . and sent divers great lordes and knyghtes to convey her with triumphe towards her spouse & husband. And upon the xii daye of November, she was conveyed from Lambeth thorough London with all triumphe and honoure that coulde be devised or ymagened, to the Bishops paleys, by the Cathedrall churche of s. Paules.[2]

The pageantry was the most splendid and sophisticated that the city had ever seen, or was to see for many years. A stage, or mount was then erected in the nave of St Pauls, and,

> Upon the daye of saynct Erkenwald, then beynge Sundaye the sayde ladye was ledde to the same mount, and there prynce Arthur openly espoused her, bothe beynge cladde in whyte, both lusty and amorous. . . .

The Prince of Wales may have looked lusty and amorous upon his wedding day, but in fact he was a fragile youth just past his fifteenth birthday. This fact was well enough appreciated by some of his father's advisers, but unfortunately the question of immediate co-habitation became a political issue. The king was uncharacteristically indecisive, and the Spaniards were divided, some remembering the fate of Prince Juan in similar circumstances. However, Catherine's confessor, assuming an authority which he probably did not possess, announced that it was the express wish of their Catholic Majesties that the young couple should live together at once, and no one felt confident enough to gainsay him.[3] Before Christmas, therefore, Arthur and Catherine set off for Ludlow, where he had been symbolizing his father's authority for several months, and a much enhanced household, both English and Spanish, went with them.

*Ludlow Castle, home to Prince Arthur and Catherine of Aragon during their four months of married life in 1502*

Little is known about their lives during the next four months, leaving ample room for imaginative reconstructions of what went on within the somewhat grim castle where the prince's council endeavoured to establish the realities of peace and good order within the marches. Catherine as yet spoke no English and little French, but Arthur's Latin was probably up to basic communication, and both would have found the Welsh generally spoken by the local people entirely incomprehensible. Quite apart from the attentions which her husband may have paid her, the princess was well cared for, not only by her formidable duenna, Dona Elvira Manuel, but also by Arthur's chamberlain, Sir Richard Pole, and his wife. Margaret Pole was the daughter of George, Duke of Clarence, and consequently a princess of the royal blood. It was probably at this time that the friendship between the two women, which was to survive the ravages of fortune over many years, first began to form. Arthur died on 2 April 1502 of 'consumption', which in this context probably means pneumonia rather than tuberculosis, leaving his parents devastated and his bride, as far as we can tell, still a virgin. Catherine did not see the rain-soaked pomp of her husband's funeral at Worcester Cathedral three weeks later. She too was ill, and it was not until the warmer weather came that she could be moved by easy stages to London.[4]

Arthur's death had many consequences beyond the distress of his seventeen-year-old widow. Henry and Elizabeth, now seriously alarmed by the deaths of two sons, decided to try again. Elizabeth conceived, but the child was a girl, and in bearing her on ll February 1503, the queen also died. Meanwhile in Spain the reaction had been one of political alarm rather than personal sympathy. Ferdinand, preoccupied with his war with France, was mainly concerned not to lose the English connection. He was not, however, disposed to reveal this weakness to Henry, and Hernan Duque d'Estrada was despatched to London with stiffly worded instructions to demand the return of that portion of Catherine's dowry which had already been paid (one hundred thousand crowns), her dower rights to one third of the revenues of Wales, Chester and Cornwall, and her immediate repatriation to Spain.[5] This was, of course, a bargaining position, and Estrada knew that perfectly well, but unlike the resident ambassador, Roderigo de Puebla, he was not a professional diplomat and soon became bogged down in the complexities of the case. Henry was equally anxious to maintain the alliance, and equally reluctant to disclose his hand. He demanded the outstanding balance of Catherine's dowry. However, as Estrada gradually moved towards the main point of his instructions, a sordid dispute erupted over the consummation of the late prince's marriage. The protagonists were de Puebla, who had it on the authority of Catherine's confessor that consummation had taken place and that the princess was very possibly with child, and Dona Elvira who swore that her charge was *virgo intacta*, and roundly abused the ambassador for telling his master lies. It is almost certain that de Puebla was misinformed, but since it was he, rather than Estrada, who had to carry out the serious negotiations, his position was accepted as being the safer assumption. In the spring of 1503 Henry made a tentative suggestion that he might even marry the young widow himself, but he accepted Isabella's rebuff with good grace, and on 23 June 1503 signed a new treaty betrothing Catherine to his surviving son, Henry, then aged twelve.

*Catherine of Aragon (1485–1536) as a young girl (portrait by Michael Sittow)*

It was this treaty which was to cause much of the subsequent trouble, because it contained an agreement that, as the parties were related in the first degree of affinity, the signatories bound themselves to obtain the necessary dispensation from Rome. That having been done, the marriage was to take place as soon as Henry had completed his fifteenth year. The king was to receive the outstanding balance of the dowry, and Catherine renounced her widow's jointure in consideration of a similar settlement to be made upon her second marriage. Although this treaty satisfied Ferdinand's priority to maintain his link with England, it left Henry holding much the stronger hand. He was not bound to honour the treaty for two years, and then only upon the payment of a further one hundred thousand crowns. Meanwhile Catherine remained in England, if not as a hostage, at least as the object of the king's bounty, and very much under his control. The princess seems to have accepted this situation with something very much more positive than resignation. England was, so to speak, her 'posting', her place of duty, and she may even have been excited by the prospect of marrying a lad who already bade fair to be twice the man his brother had been.[6] So she settled down to wait, at Durham House in the Strand, the residence which had been allocated to her. Henry allowed her £100 a month, and appointed one of his own surveyors to oversee the management of it. For about eighteen months Catherine's household marked time, reasonably comfortably, although the expatriate community of about fifty was not without its squabbles and tensions. The negotiations in Rome followed their ponderous course, and finally at the end of November 1504, Julius II issued a dispensation from the first degree of affinity to enable Catherine and the young Henry to marry. In other words, it was officially accepted by the Pope that Arthur and Catherine had enjoyed sexual intercourse. However, Henry's fifteenth birthday would not fall until 28 June 1506, so there was still some time to wait, and much could happen before the treaty had to be put into effect.

The first thing that happened was that on 26 November 1504, within a few days of the issuing of the dispensation, Isabella died and the political situation within Spain was transformed. Castile passed by inheritance, and by the late queen's explicit instructions, to her daughter Juana. Should Juana and her husband, Philip, succeed in making good their claim, Ferdinand's authority would be confined to Aragon, and his international standing would be significantly reduced. Moreover, as Philip and Juana had two sons, and Maria of Portugal a daughter, there was little prospect of Catherine suddenly becoming queen of Castile. There was also a sharp deterioration in Anglo–Spanish relations when the Council of Castile refused to ratify Isabella's last commercial treaty with England, and several hundred English merchants were expelled from Seville, and their cargoes confiscated.[7] Even if he had wanted to, Ferdinand could have done nothing to alter this situation, and Henry began to suspect that the balance of Catherine's dowry would never be paid. On 27 June 1505, the eve of his fourteenth birthday, the young Henry entered a formal protest against his betrothal, as having been contracted during his minority and without his consent. The king was now free to fish in other waters. In the circumstances his action was prudent and justifiable. Its corollary, however, was neither. In the summer of 1505 he stopped Catherine's allowance, knowing full well that her father was in no position to make it good. Perhaps he intended to force her to return to Spain. If so he underestimated her tenacity and sense of purpose. Nor did Ferdinand want his daughter back. He was not giving up Castile without a fight, and Catherine was a complication he could do without. Moreover, the English marriage treaty was now more important to him, rather than less. So Catherine remained at her post, with virtually no money, and very little hope.

The detailed politics of the next three years do not need to concern us, but Henry shifted his main focus of attention from Spain to the Low Countries. There were three possible marriage links to strengthen such an alliance. The king himself could wed Philip's twice-widowed sister, Margaret; the Prince of Wales could take his daughter, Eleanor, who was of a suitable age; and Henry's younger daughter, Mary, could be matched with Philip's six-year-old son, Charles. Ironically, one of the chief negotiators on Philip's behalf was Don Juan Manuel. An erstwhile servant of Ferdinand's, he was now wholly committed to ending Aragonese rule in Castile, and to the establishment of Philip and Juana. The irony lay in the fact that it was his sister, Dona Elvira, who presided over Catherine's dwindling establishment with such an iron hand. Together, brother and sister conspired to involve the princess in setting up a meeting between Henry and Philip which would be aimed directly at forcing Ferdinand out of Castile. The plot was detected in the nick of time by Ferdinand's ambassador, de Puebla, and after an awesome demonstration of Trastamara wrath by the twenty-year-old Catherine, Dona Elvira was dismissed and Henry drew back from the meeting. These were extremely difficult days for the princess. Released from tutelage to Dona Elvira, she grew up rapidly, but without the protection of her chaperone and virtually without resources she was unable to resist the king's pressure to give up her separate establishment, and to live at court with an even more reduced retinue. Moreover, her defeat of the machinations of the Manuels had been only temporary. Early in 1506, more by accident than design, Philip came to England. A treaty of alliance was signed, and the way was opened for the marriage settlements which had already been mooted. Catherine, in spite of the brief pleasure of seeing her favourite sister for the first time in many years, was in despair. Her father's interests and her own hopes of marriage to the Prince of Wales now both seemed to be completely destroyed.

It was Ferdinand who rescued her from this aimless survival, not by sending the desperately needed money but by giving her a job to do. De Puebla was an honest man who did his best, but Catherine did not trust him, and he was totally lacking in charisma.[8] Without withdrawing him, the king of Aragon formally accredited his daughter as an additional ambassador. This threw Catherine into the deep end of the political pool, broke down her isolation, and led to a dramatic improvement in her knowledge of the English language and English affairs. It did not cure her chronic poverty, nor her dependence upon casual hand-outs from both Henry and Ferdinand, but it enabled her to work for her own future, because Henry made it abundantly clear to her that her chances of marrying his son depended upon the state of Anglo-Spanish relations, not the other way round. After the despair of early 1506, events ceased to conspire against her. During the summer of that year, as Philip progressed through Castile, it appeared that Ferdinand was willing to give up the struggle, but by October Juana's husband was dead and the queen herself, temporarily at least unhinged. This may have been a great private grief to Catherine, but it took Castile off the agenda for the time being. Henry continued to angle for a Habsburg alliance after Philip's death, but this was no longer incompatible with friendship for Ferdinand, and the latter, secure in the Regency of Castile by the end of 1507, was even prepared to find the balance of his daughter's dowry. Unfortunately this hopeful situation was inadvertently sabotaged by the princess herself. Unable to overcome her aversion to de Puebla, she pressed her father hard to send a more worthy envoy, and at the beginning of 1508 he yielded to her importunity. On 22 February Don Gutierre Gomez de Fuensalida presented his credentials in London, and swiftly began to alienate everyone with whom he had to deal. Having ruined every negotiation by his self-righteous intransigence, he was eventually expelled from the court, and Spanish influence collapsed. Part of the trouble was caused by his ill-concealed indignation over Catherine's treatment. This filled his letters to Ferdinand and was promptly relayed back to England by Henry's envoy, John Stile. Even Catherine, who had originally welcomed him as a gentleman and a champion, eventually realized that he was doing far more harm than good. When he finally endeavoured to forbid her to attend the betrothal ceremony between Princess Mary and her nephew, Charles (the only one of the Habsburg marriage negotiations to come to anything), she broke with him, choosing not to offend Henry without good cause. 'Your ambassador', she wrote to her father 'is a traitor. Recall him and punish him as he deserves.'[9]

By then, however, the damage had been done. The hoped-for resumption of her own marriage negotiation had disappeared again below the diplomatic horizon. On the other hand, there were compensations. The young Henry was not yet married elsewhere, and Catherine had not only developed a new confidence in her own judgement, she had also learned to put her trust in God. Always deeply pious, she had relied after her husband's death chiefly upon confessors provided by Dona Elvira, and after the latter's departure under a cloud in 1505, had suffered grievously from a lack of spiritual guidance and consolation. Then, early in 1507, she found an Observant Franciscan called Fray Diego Fernandez. Fray Diego was a Castilian who had lived for some years in England, and he spoke the language fluently. He quickly established himself as her most confidential friend and advisor, and encouraged her wholeheartedly in her determination to persist with her mission in England. It seems to have been to Fray Diego's support that she owed her total conviction that God would reward her constancy in His own good time. One of Fuensalida's worst mistakes was to clash with Fray Diego. The ambassador was persuaded, probably at the instigation of Catherine's homesick and demoralized servants, that she should withdraw to Flanders, where proper financial provision could be made for her. It was Fray Diego who uncovered this conspiracy, and prompted the princess to write the fierce denunciation alluded to. Nevertheless, by the end of 1508 no objective observer would have considered the confessor's position to be tenable. Henry's attitude to Ferdinand had never been more hostile, and as his health deteriorated early in 1509 the parties which were lining up to influence his heir were the French and the Habsburgs. The former were looking to consolidate their influence by marrying the future king to Marguerite d'Alençon, while the latter clung to the existing candidature of Eleanor, the sister of the young Archduke Charles. Fuensalida, still glumly and ineffectually at his post as the old king's life waned, could see no grounds for optimism, either in the existing distribution of forces, or in what he could learn of the heir to the throne.

The Spaniard, however, was too far from the centre of events for his opinion to carry much weight. According to him the young Henry had been forced by his father's paranoid fears to lead the life of a virtual recluse. It is true that few details of his education are known, and that he was not entrusted with any public responsibility during his father's lifetime. On the other hand, his later accomplishments make clear that his education was both thorough and enlightened, and we know that the king subjected his raw athleticism to the finest tuition in both tennis and jousting, both sports in which he was later to excel.[10] Henry VIII, in fact, was the man that his father had made him, both for good and ill. The most obvious thing about him was that he was a magnificent physical specimen. Extremely tall and well built, he had the dashing good looks of his maternal grandfather, although with a ruddier colouring. Catherine, now approaching twenty-five, would have known him well by sight, although they can have had few opportunities for conversation. By the same token, he would have been sufficiently familiar with her small stature and delicate auburn beauty, although whether they had been in any way attracted to each other over the previous five years is unknown. Considering his youth, and complete lack of experience, Henry was remarkably quick to establish his own imprint on the government. Within a few days his father's valued but unpopular servants, Sir Richard Empson and Edmund Dudley, were in the Tower, and the king had chosen a wife. Writing years later, and with the benefit of hindsight, the chronicler Edward Hall wrote,

> . . . the kyng was moved by some of his counsail that it should be honorable and profitable to his realme to take to wife the lady Katherine, late wife to Prince Arthur his brother disseased, least she havyng so great a dowrie, might mary out of the realme, which would be unprofitable to him: by reason of which mocion, the kyng being young, and not understandyng the lawe of God, espoused the saied lady Katherine, the third daie of June. . . .[11]

Such an explanation is quite unsubstantiated by contemporary evidence. Henry himself declared that he was acting in response to his father's dying wish, but this seems to have been no more than a pious fraud. The new king might wish to appear a dutiful son in this, as in other matters, but the simple fact seems to have been that he pleased himself.

Three years earlier he had referred to Catherine as 'my most dear and well-beloved consort, the princess my wife', but a lot of water had passed under the bridge since then, and there is no evidence to suggest that he felt himself to be bound by that earlier agreement. Perhaps, like Edward IV, he was determined to demonstrate his independence, or perhaps he was taking his advice in a quarter which has never been detected. Whatever the truth, Fuensalida had no prior warning. On 27 April, five days after the old king's death, he was assured by two members of the council that his successor was completely uncommitted.[12] He was then suddenly summoned to the council again, to be told of the king's extremely positive feelings towards the princess, and assured that the little matter of her dowry (or rather the balance of it) was a trivial matter which he was expected to clear up at once. An obstacle which had held up negotiations for months, if not years, was simply brushed aside in a matter of minutes. The councillors seem to have been as astonished as the ambassador by what they found themselves saying. Archbishop Warham's qualms about the validity of the six-year-old dispensation which had removed the bar of consanguinity, were treated in the same way as the dowry – *nihil obstat*. If there were serious objections (and that is not clear) Henry simply bulldozed them aside, and on ll June 1509 he married Catherine in the Franciscan church at Greenwich. His bride was five years older than himself, and had suffered much ill health from the frustrations and privations of the last few years, but she remained extremely handsome, and was to prove herself remarkably tough, both in body and mind. Quite suddenly, Catherine had achieved the objective for which she had waited, hoped, and prayed since Arthur's death in 1502. Inevitably she attributed her dramatic change of fortune to the direct intervention of God, who turns the hearts of princes in accordance with His pleasure. Henry might allude to treaty obligations, and the need to curb the overweening power of France, but his wife believed, and was to believe until her death, that he had responded to the will of God.

At the outset of his reign, Henry was full of joy and life. 'Our king is not after gold or gems or precious metals, but virtue, glory, immortality . . .' wrote the enthusiastic Lord Mountjoy, and ambassadors competed with each other to sing his praises. His coronation, which he shared with his queen, was celebrated in the fashion of the time with a magnificent tournament, featuring the 'Knights of Pallas' and the 'Knights of Diana', symbolizing both the chivalric values and the classical aspirations of the court. On this occasion the king himself did not joust in his lady's honour, but his devotion was made manifest in the trappings of the lists,

> . . . and in every losenge, either a Rose or a Pomegranate, or a Sheffe of Arrowes, or els H. and K. gilded with fine gold, with certain Arches or Turrettes gilded to support thesame castle . . .[13]

In the midst of the celebrations, Catherine wrote dutifully to her father, who must have been as taken aback as anyone by the rapid turn of events in England, '. . . these kingdoms . . . are in great peace, and entertain much love to the king, my lord, and to me. Our time is spent in continual festival. . . .' She was not given to outbursts of enthusiasm, but her happiness and satisfaction shine through the correspondence of these early months. Her part was not always an easy one to play. Henry frequently behaved like the overgrown schoolboy he was, bursting in on her in elaborate disguises at all sorts of unseasonable hours, and expecting her to be perpetually charmed and surprised. If she ever felt irritation at such pranks, she never showed it, and her indulgence was more than that of tact and good

The Coronation of Henry VIII and Catherine of Aragon *(woodcut from Stephen Hawes'* A Joyfull Medytacyon . . ., c. *1510)*

breeding. In spite of the strange circumstance in which it had come about, the marriage of Henry and Catherine was a warm and loving relationship.

Both in public and in private they were a well-matched couple. Their intellectual tastes and educational backgrounds were similar; both loved finery and display, rode well, and hunted with enthusiasm. Catherine was serene where her husband was exuberant, and her piety was probably both deeper and more heartfelt than his. His anxiety to please her was ostentatious and occasionally childish, but her desire to please him was no less, and she not only took great care with her physical appearance, but was also meticulously deferential. It is hard to estimate her influence on affairs of state. She remained very much her father's ambassador, and could be represented as the architect of Henry's early foreign policy, except that there is good evidence to believe that the king needed no influencing in the direction of war with France. More subtly, however, the queen became a trusted councillor. Henry did not have the training in state affairs which would have enabled him to be at ease with experienced statesmen of his father's generation, such as William Warham or Sir Henry Marney. Wisely, he retained their services, probably not knowing what else to do, but until the rise of Thomas Wolsey in 1512 there was no councillor of his own choosing in whom he had complete trust.

*Heads of Henry VIII and Catherine of Aragon (details of chapel window at the palace of New Hall/watercolours by Daniel Chandler)*

Catherine filled that gap. She may not have known much about English affairs, but she was highly intelligent and a shrewd judge of men. Moreover, she had a gift for friendship, and quietly repaired some of the relationships with major aristocratic families which Henry VII had either accidentally or deliberately allowed to decay. Her friendship with Margaret Pole is a good example, but by no means the only one. It was also her unique responsibility to build up the self-confidence which Henry, for all his magnificence, appears to have lacked.

A royal prince, and particularly one so generously endowed with physical energy, could reasonably be expected to have indulged in a certain amount of sexual experimentation by the time that he reached Henry's age. However, there is no evidence that this was true of the young Tudor, and it may have been this circumstance to which Fuensalida had alluded when he described Henry as having been kept before his accession 'like a young girl'. Catherine, if we accept that her first marriage had been unconsummated, was equally inexperienced despite her advantage in years. Fortunately they seem to have pleased each other very well. Like Elizabeth of York before her, the queen conceived with commendable promptness, an excellent omen, demonstrating the fertility of both

*Henry is escorted to the tournament in honour of the birth of Henry, Prince of Wales, 1511,*
*(from the Westminster Tournament Roll)*

partners. There, however, the similarity ended. On 31 January 1510 Catherine
was delivered of a stillborn girl, many weeks premature. With the benefit of
hindsight this looks like a portent of disaster, but it did not appear nearly so
sinister at the time. It was a setback which neither of them took too seriously, and
within a few weeks the queen was pregnant again. In the meantime she had
played a major part in negotiating that new treaty between her husband and her
father for which Ferdinand's newly accredited ambassador, Don Luis Caroz, was
able to claim the chief credit.[14] War with France did not immediately follow
because Ferdinand was prepared to bide his time, and Henry, in spite of his
impatience, had sufficient sense not to act unilaterally. By the end of the year the
authority they were supposed to be supporting, the Pope, had already moved
against a recalcitrant Louis XII but still Ferdinand waited, and on New Year's
Day 1511 his daughter presented him with a grandson. Rejoicing in England
exploded like a firework display. The child was christened Henry, and his proud
father immediately took him to Walsingham to give suitable thanks for the
greatest benefit which God could bestow upon a king. As soon as the queen was
churched, the court moved to Westminster, where a mighty tournament was

*Henry jousts before Catherine of Aragon in celebration of the birth of a son, 1511 (from the Westminster Tournament Roll)*

staged, not only to celebrate the birth of an heir, but also to demonstrate that loving accord between Henry and Catherine which promised a bountiful harvest for the future. The king jousted magnificently, under the name of *Coeur Loyale*, blazoned his devotion to the world, and laid his trophies at her feet.

Just over seven weeks later, the fireworks turned to ashes, and the latest Henry Tudor died in his magnificent nursery at Richmond. This time there was both grief and anxiety. Catherine resorted to prayer; Henry to rather extravagant self-questioning and self-pity. What had he done to offend God? As far as we can tell there were no recriminations. The customary wisdom of the time always blamed the absence or deformity of children upon the female partner, but infant mortality could only be seen as a punishment for sin. The question was, what sin? The king recovered from this blow more quickly than the queen. He was younger, and he had the onset of war to keep him occupied. He may also have taken refuge in other diversions, for it was at this time that the first ripple of discord was reported. The story is circumstantial, and comes from Don Luis Caroz, who was not particularly close to the royal couple. It concerns Anne Hastings and Elizabeth Ratcliffe, the two married sisters of the Duke of Buckingham. Elizabeth was a member of the queen's privy chamber, and allegedly told her brother that Anne was being solicited by William Compton, a close companion of Henry's, on the king's behalf. Buckingham was rash enough, or angry enough, to remonstrate with Henry and to withdraw from the court, which was always a risky thing to do. The king in turn insisted that his wife should dismiss Elizabeth from her household, and she complied after a furious quarrel. Garrett Mattingly was probably right when he conjectured that this plausible tale had been fed to Caroz by a former attendant of Catherine's, Francesca de Carceres, and it has no corroboration from other sources; but even if untrue, it has a certain significance.[15] The king's marriage was no longer an idyll, and it was to be over two years before Catherine again became pregnant. If Henry was amusing himself with other women he was unusually discreet about it, and begot no recorded bastards. In public he continued to be conspicuously attentive to his queen, and she remained the model of a dutiful wife, but their continued childlessness was beginning to cast a shadow over their relationship.

Catherine was also, in a sense, a hostage to diplomatic fortune as she had been ten years before. In May 1511 Henry sent a force of a thousand archers under Lord Darcy to assist Ferdinand in an attack on the Moors. The expedition was a fiasco, mainly because when it arrived the king of Aragon declared that it was not needed, and sent it home. Henry would probably have been a good deal more indignant if he had not been in the process of signing the Holy League when his discredited force returned. This agreement, which gave him his opportunity for war against France, took the form of an alliance with Ferdinand and the Pope. So Henry curbed his annoyance, and began immediately to prepare a second and much larger expedition to the south, which was intended to be part of a joint Anglo-Spanish attack upon Acquitaine. However, in 1512 the fiasco of the previous year was repeated upon a larger scale, and for similar reasons. Ferdinand provided none of the support which had been promised, and simply used his allies as a cover for his own seizure of Navarre. The Marquis of Dorset and his troops were left at Fuentarrabia without supplies, or transport, or any agreed plan of campaign, and after several weeks the army became mutinous. Yielding to pressure, the officers hired ships and returned to England, to Henry's bitter chagrin. Not only had Ferdinand sabotaged the campaign, he had also been presented with a perfect pretext to complain that his allies had abandoned him.

> The king of Arragon was sore discontent with their departyng for thei spent much money and substaunce in his country, and saied openly, that if thei had taried he would have invaded Guyan, and the Englishmen were glad that thei were departed out of such a countrey, where thei had litle health, lesse pleasure and much losse of tyme: but by their liyng there, the Kyng of Arragon stale the realme of Naver, and the Englishemen left as muche money there, as he sent into England with his daughter.[16]

Learning nothing from his father-in-law's duplicity, Henry continued with his preparations for the following campaigning season, humiliated rather than angered by what had occurred. As it happened, his effort in northern France in 1513 was a good deal more successful, resulting in the capture of Thérouanne and Tournai, and a somewhat meaningless victory at the Battle of the Spurs, but none of this owed anything to his alliance with Ferdinand. Meanwhile Catherine had been given her husband's ultimate gesture of confidence, being named as Regent during his absence in France.

The victory which the Earl of Surrey won on her behalf against the Scots was far more devastating and significant than anything which Henry achieved. He sent her his trophies with a boyish enthusiasm, and received in return the bloodstained coat in which James IV had fallen at Flodden. These successes were to be merely the preamble for the triumph which was to follow in 1514, but before that season had even begun Henry had changed his mind and entered into negotiations for peace. There seem to have been two reasons for this development, and neither of them was propitious for Catherine. The first was that Ferdinand had made a separate peace without honouring any of the obligations which he had undertaken towards the alliance, thus exposing his self-righteous rhetoric of 1512 for the sham that it was. The second was the rise to power of Thomas Wolsey. Wolsey had been superbly effective in organizing the campaign of 1513, but for reasons of his own he was anxious to steer the king in the direction of peace.[17] Henry was finally disillusioned with his father-in-law, and the more angry for having been made a fool of in 1512. This combination of circumstances caused rumours to circulate that he would repudiate Catherine and marry a French princess. There was probably no truth in the reports, but the long-standing betrothal between Ferdinand's grandson, Charles, and Henry's younger sister, Mary, a relationship which Catherine had done her best to promote, was broken off and Mary was married instead to Louis XII of France. For whatever reason, the queen's voice was no longer dominant in the king's counsels. Catherine was wise enough to know how to beat a strategic retreat, and her marriage does not seem to have suffered. At some point early in 1513 she

*Detail from a painting at Hampton Court showing the city of Thérouanne and part of the city of Tournai (left) in the background, with the Battle of the Spurs in the foreground*

*The Battle of the Spurs, 1513*

seems to have conceived again, because although there are no contemporary references to her condition, on 8 October the imperial agent, James Banisius, reported that she had been delivered of a son. If this was true the child was almost certainly dead, and many weeks premature. The fact that there was no fuss or lamentation must cast some doubt upon the reliability of Banisius' sources. In September 1514, however, the queen was undoubtedly pregnant, and in January of the following year was delivered of a stillborn son 'of eight months'.[18]

This time there was grief and lamentation. Catherine was now thirty, her beauty was beginning to fade, and her piety was becoming obsessive. Exactly how Henry reacted we do not know. There are no references to the exchange of consolation which had followed the death of Prince Henry in 1511, but nor is there any sign of overt estrangement. The queen certainly understood, and may even have sympathized with, her husband's anger with her father. She certainly gave Don Luis Caroz the sharp side of her tongue on more than one occasion, and he complained that she was forgetting Spain in order to gain the love of the English. If so, it was a lesson which she had been slow to learn. It was at about this time also that Henry began to dally with an attractive young lady called Elizabeth Blount. After six years of marriage, Catherine's position was beginning to look increasingly beleaguered. Nevertheless, the year which had begun in despair ended in hope. The death of Louis XII had brought an end to the brief Anglo-French *rapprochement*. Mary was home again, albeit clandestinely married to the Duke of Suffolk, and the new king, Francis I, was doing his best to outshine Henry as a Renaissance Prince, which was a sure way to guarantee a renewal of hostilities. There had been a reconciliation between Henry and Ferdinand, and, far more important, Catherine was again pregnant. On 18 February 1516 in the palace at Greenwich, she was delivered of a healthy child. The rejoicings were genuine but muted, for the child was a girl, who was christened Mary with all the pomp of which the court was capable.[19] At long last the queen had proved her ability to bear a healthy child. Henry talked blithely of the sons following 'by the Grace of God', and there was a somewhat unrealistic air of optimism about the court. It was as though this success had cancelled the past, and people began to speak as though Catherine was a young bride, with many years of childbearing before her. She knew better. Her time was now short, and although there is no suggestion that Henry's pastimes kept him from her bed, it was early in 1518 before she conceived again, and, as it was to prove, for the last time.

By then there had been other changes in the queen's circumstances. Her confessor, Fray Diego, had committed one indiscretion too many, and had returned to Spain. The last of her Spanish ladies-in-waiting, Maria de Salinas, had left her service to become Lady Willoughby, and most important, her father had died on 23 January 1516. All these events loosened her ties to the home country which she had not seen for nearly twenty years. Her nephew, Charles, who succeeded to the Crowns of Spain, was hardly a fellow countryman, having been born and raised in the Low Countries. Catherine's role as an ambassador, which had occupied much of her time and attention during the first five years of her marriage, had now come to an end. Instead she had become a sort of domestic bursar, fussing over her husband's clean linen, and embroidering his shirts with her own hands. She still dressed magnificently, and presented a seemly figure in public, but the flattering asides which had accompanied every reference to her in diplomatic reports were a thing of the past. 'Old and deformed' commented Francis I when he was particularly concerned to rile his royal brother; 'rather ugly than otherwise' observed a more objective Venetian. She had also lost what little taste she had ever had for Henry's boisterous amusements. Occasionally she hunted, and even more occasionally danced, but increasingly her time was taken up with works of piety, with her domestic responsibilities, and with her daughter. She began to wear under her royal robes the harsh habit of a Franciscan Tertiary, and references to her pilgrimages, her alms giving and her constant devotions multiply in contemporary reports. Nevertheless, for the time being her political role remained central. Throughout the summer of 1518 Thomas Wolsey, now cardinal and lord chancellor, strove to bring about a European peace upon the basis of an Anglo-French treaty. At the end of July a papal legate, Cardinal Campeggio, arrived in London to assist the process by inviting Henry and his fellow Christian princes to bury their differences in a crusade against the infidel. On 2 October the grand plan was revealed: a general non-aggression pact, involving over twenty powers, great and small. There was little to object to in so bland a formula, which involved almost nothing in the way of specific commitments. Most of the intended participants adhered to the so-called Treaty of London during the following months. A rapid, but very short-lived increase in English prestige was the only tangible result.[20]

The specific Anglo-French agreement which was signed on 4 October, although not much more durable, had far more important immediate consequences. Its core was the betrothal of the two-year-old Princess Mary to the Dauphin François, an

*Illumination from a bible for Henry VIII and Catherine of Aragon,* c. *1509 or recently dated to* c. *1530 (anon. Flemish artist)*

infant even younger than herself. Before agreeing to this clause the French negotiators had insisted upon the young princess being recognized as her father's heir. In spite of the Salic law, the French had no objection to acquiring realms by matrimonial conquest, as they were to demonstrate in the case of Scotland thirty years later. Bearing in mind the extreme youth of the parties, perhaps the English negotiators did not take that distant threat too seriously, but the acute Venetian Marian Giustinian believed that the treaty would never have been signed in that form if the queen of England had not been pregnant at the time.[21] On 5 October Mary was solemnly betrothed in her mother's chamber at Greenwich, in what must have been a very distasteful ceremony to Catherine, and just over a month later, on 9 November, the queen was delivered of a daughter. We do not even know whether the child was born alive. If it was it cannot have survived long, as there is no reference to baptism. The reaction was one of disappointment bordering on dismay. The country passionately desired a prince, wrote Giustinian, and although Henry ratified his treaty with France on 15 December, the anxiety which everyone hoped that Catherine could have dispelled remained and deepened. Tournai, the conquest of 1513, had been surrendered, not for a gain but for a potential danger.

Of course nobody knew at Christmas 1518 that the queen's childbearing days were over. She was only thirty-three, but repeated pregnancies, and the strain of repeated still births and miscarriages had undermined both her spirits and her health. Nobody (least of all Henry himself) blamed the king for this frustrating dynastic situation. It was Catherine who had failed in her primary duty, a duty which both her mother and her elder sister had discharged successfully. As if to emphasize the point, at some unknown date in 1519, Elizabeth Blount, who had been Henry's mistress for about two years, gave birth to a healthy son, who was immediately acknowledged and named Henry Fitzroy. Cardinal Wolsey was godfather at his christening. For Catherine, 1519 was a bleak year. Like other queens before and after her, she was compelled to turn a blind eye to the unavoidable evidence of her husband's infidelity, and to maintain a convincing show of amity in public. In February the Emperor Maximilian died, and after a protracted campaign her nephew, Charles, was elected in his place. This was a positive result, but it soon became apparent that the new emperor regarded her husband's relations with the French with suspicion and disfavour. Henry went out of his way to be affable to Francis and his envoys, responded enthusiastically to anxious enquiries from the French court about Mary's state of health, and set up a personal meeting with the French king for the summer of 1520. With no further evidence of pregnancy, and with Wolsey ever more firmly entrenched in the king's favour, the queen became increasingly marginalized. Her response, which was probably not consciously political, was to increase her charitable activities and her patronage of scholars.

Like every other royal consort, Catherine had been given a jointure on her marriage: lands to an annual value of about £3,000 which could give her considerable freedom of action. It is difficult to be sure how much of this income was dispensed by her almoner, or by the stewards of her various manors, in the form of poor relief, but it was sufficient to give her the reputation of a lady bountiful. It was to be part of the legend which grew up around her during her subsequent misfortunes, that hundreds of poor families had been sustained by her generosity, and it was alleged somewhat sourly that the commons of England loved their queen because she fed them.[22] The truth was probably less dramatic, but there is evidence that some of her receivers did hold reserves which were specifically allocated to charitable purposes. There is no sign that she had, or attempted to persuade Henry to have, any view of poor relief which went beyond the distribution of cash, food, or clothing for immediate necessity. Such activity was to her a work of corporeal mercy, not a social policy. It was expected of her, both as queen and as a good Christian woman. In the same way she was expected to intercede for offenders, and to hear the petitions of widows and orphans. Just as the Virgin Mary was seen as the most effectual intercessor with her Divine Son on behalf of penitent sinners, so an earthly queen had a special part to play in tempering royal justice with mercy. It was a woman's nature and a woman's role. Consequently, although it is reasonably well established that Catherine did intercede successfully for the condemned Londoners after the Evil May Day riots of 1517, it is equally certain that this was a piece of role-play for which she was cast by the king and Wolsey. Perhaps she did have a pitiful nature, but it should not be deduced from that occasion, which was set up for public consumption and later exploited by those for whom the discarded queen was a saint and martyr. Thomas Churchyard's ballad encapsulates the legend,

*Juan Luis Vives, one of the scholars who received patronage from Catherine of Aragon*

For which, kind queen, with joyful heart
She heard their mothers' thanks and praise . . .
And lived beloved all her days.[23]

Catherine's devotion to learning may not have been any more genuine than her
devotion to good works, but it was less subject to pious exaggeration. The tutors
engaged by her mother had instilled good Ciceronian Latin, and she wrote her
native Castilian with elegance and precision. Erasmus, whose views were never
entirely free from self-interest, declared 'the queen loved good literature, which
she has studied with success since childhood'. He was correspondingly distressed
when she criticized his Greek New Testament of 1516 on the grounds that he was
pretending to be wiser than St Jerome. It appears that her interest in the new
learning developed slowly, and was never allowed to challenge her religious
orthodoxy. Lord Mountjoy, himself a patron of scholars, became her chamberlain
in 1512, and she later engaged her distinguished countryman Juan Luis Vives as a
tutor for Princess Mary. Vives came to England in 1523, and in the same year
Catherine commissioned him to write *De Institutione Foeminae Christianae*. This
work was not written specifically for Mary's instruction, but rather because of the
queen's general interest in the subject.[24] Vives was not the only scholar patronized
by Catherine, but he was probably the closest to her in sentiment and purpose.
She seems to have been well read and intelligent rather than learned in the
academic sense, and would probably have considered profound scholarship
unsuitable both to her sex and to her station in life. Her role was to encourage and
support rather than emulate her protégés, and Thomas Linacre, John Colet,
Richard Pace and Richard Whitford all benefitted to some extent from the
hospitality of her household. She encouraged Henry in his rather dilettante
intellectualism, and was wise enough to flatter his self-esteem in that direction.
Probably the only art of peace in which her husband excelled her was music, but
at least in the early days of their marriage they seem to have managed to discuss
many issues in a manner which surprised their courtiers and sent a ripple of
admiration through the commonwealth of letters. Such golden opinions availed
Catherine little when the political storms struck after 1525. Only John Fisher was
to defend her cause with learning and resolution, and he probably owed least to
her friendship, having been an established scholar and ascetic long before she was
in any position to offer her patronage.

By 1520 Catherine was a substantial figure in her own right. As she became less
an ornament and a foil to Henry, so the distinctiveness of her own personality
gradually emerged. At the Field of Cloth of Gold she was far less conspicuous than
Wolsey, discharging her duty with a minimum of fuss and enthusiasm. If Henry
wanted friendship with France she was in no position to oppose him, but she had
no desire to promote what might turn out to be a warlike alliance against her
nephew the emperor. In fact, as Francis suspected, Henry was playing a double
game, and it may have been for that reason that the Princess Mary, whom the
French were so anxious to see, remained behind in England.[25] That decision would
certainly have pleased the queen, even if she had played no part in making it.
Charles had visited England very briefly just before the Field of Cloth of Gold, and

*John Colet (1467?–1519), Dean of St Paul's, 1504–19, and refounder of St Paul's School*

had met Catherine for the first time at Canterbury. If it was any part of the queen's intention to regain some of the political ground which she had lost to Wolsey, this interview provided the opportunity. The emperor probably knew perfectly well that his aunt had been working on his behalf behind the scenes, but may well have been sceptical of her influence. However, during the three days which he spent with Henry he should have been reassured. The talks resembled a family gathering, and to many parts of them not even the most intimate councillors were admitted. To Catherine it must have seemed like the honeymoon days of a decade before, a comeback for which the distasteful antics of the meeting with Francis were a price well worth paying. Henry, however, was far less biddable than he had been when Ferdinand made a fool of him. Wolsey was struggling to preserve the peace which he had so ostentatiously created in the Treaty of London, and the queen was nudging him discreetly towards an imperial alliance, but he was the architect of his own policy during these years. Early in 1521, while solemnly assuring Francis that their friendship was perfect and intact, he began to angle for a Habsburg marriage for his daughter. His timing was shrewd because in May the king of France took advantage of his rival's preoccupation with the revolt of the *communeros* to invade and overrun Spanish Navarre. Full-scale hostilities were clearly imminent, and England's price on the diplomatic market was significantly enhanced. At first Henry offered his arbitration, but on 29 July he formally

*Thomas Linacre (1460?–1524), drawn by an unknown artist. A physician and classical scholar, he became Latin tutor to Princess Mary in 1523*

commissioned Wolsey to negotiate a new agreement, and on 14 September the Treaty of Bruges was signed.[26]

Mary, now aged five, was betrothed to the twenty-one-year-old emperor, to be married as soon as she achieved the canonical minimum of twelve. If she was still Henry's heir when that time came, her dowry was to be £80,000, otherwise £120,000. Gratifying as this was to Henry, and no doubt to Catherine, it could not be taken too seriously. Would Charles really be prepared to waste seven years of his prime waiting for a child-bride to grow up? Henry realized that such a treaty '. . . will not prevent the Emperor from marrying any woman of lawful age before our daughter comes to mature years, as he will only be bound to take her if he is then at liberty'.[27] In fact the betrothal was more symbol than substance. The substance of the treaty lay in an agreement to join the emperor in arms if the French had not ceased hostilities by November 1521, although England would not be bound to a full-scale campaign until May 1523. Knowing Wolsey's aversion to war, and not entirely trusting his ally, Charles returned to England in May 1522 and stayed for over a month. His visit was a huge success. He knew exactly how to flatter Henry's vanity, and by the time that he left on 6 July he had secured a ratification of the Treaty of Bruges, and a renewed commitment to a joint campaign in the following year. He had also met his intended bride. On 2 June when he arrived at Greenwich,

The Embarkation of Henry VIII at Dover *(unknown artist, c. 1545). The fleet sets sail for France, 1520. The five principal vessels can be seen in the foreground, with Dover Castle on the left*

*The Field of Cloth of Gold, showing the meeting between Henry VIII and Francis I*

*Double portrait of Henry VIII (right) and Charles V, probably from Charles's visit to England in 1522 (unknown artist). On the table before them is a document, presumably a treaty*

> . . . at the halle doore the Quene and Princes and all the Ladies received and welcomed hym . . . and the Emperor had gret ioye to se the Quene his Aunte, and in especiall his young cosyn germain the Lady Mary.[28]

Later in the evening they danced, and he treated the child with a solemn courtesy which impressed all observers, and which she was to remember for many years. Like her mother, Catherine had no particular aversion to war if she felt that it was justified, and she confided to one of her nephew's representatives that she regarded the king of France as worse than the Turk who was at that moment menacing Hungary and Venice. In this respect, at least, the daughter of Isabella was a great disappointment to Erasmus, but she was a suitable mate for a warlike king.

Whether that marriage was anything more than a formality by 1523 may, however, be doubted. Elizabeth Blount had been succeeded in the king's bed by Mary Boleyn, the elder daughter of Sir Thomas Boleyn and Elizabeth Howard, daughter to the Duke of Norfolk. Mary was married in 1520 to William Carey, a gentleman of the privy chamber. Whether this was a marriage of convenience, arranged by the king to conceal an existing affair, or whether she only became his mistress after her marriage, is not clear. Their relationship was over by 1525, and produced no acknowledged children. It was later alleged that Henry Carey, who was born towards the end of that year, was actually the king's son, but that is almost certainly untrue. Mary bore her husband two children in 1525 and 1527, which suggests that she did not begin co-habiting with him until late in 1524. It also suggests that the king's fertility was a rather hit-and-miss affair. Either his normally fertile mistress failed to conceive while sharing his bed, or else she suffered as the queen had done from a miscarriage or still birth. Whichever is the case, it has significance for the whole saga of his married life. William Carey received generous royal grants every year from 1522 to 1525, which is also suggestive. Years later, when Henry was endeavouring to clear his way to a marriage with Anne Boleyn, Catherine's supporters accused him of having 'had to do' both with her sister and her mother, to which the king could only reply somewhat lamely 'never with the mother'. The aspersion on Elizabeth Boleyn's honour probably arose, as Eric Ives suggests, from a confusion with Elizabeth Blount.[29] After 1525 the king must either have resorted to casual liaisons which have gone unrecorded, or commenced a prolonged period of abstinence. By that time he had given up hope of Catherine having any more children, and had almost certainly ceased to have sexual relations with her.

Politically, also, these years were somewhat barren and frustrating. Almost before the ink was dry on the Anglo-Imperial treaty, Wolsey was endeavouring to use Mary as a bait to undermine Scotland's traditional relationship with France. James V was a boy of nine, a much more suitable age than the emperor. Unfortunately, although it was quite reasonable to suppose that the latter would not wait, until he made that decision for himself the princess could not be regarded as available. It would have been so much simpler if Henry had had more than one daughter, let alone a son. Moreover, even the rumour of a Scottish match was sufficient to raise aristocratic hackles in England. The prospect of being ruled by a Habsburg was bad enough, but to be ruled by a Stuart . . . ! The one thing that this episode demonstrated beyond all doubt was the fact that Henry's anxiety about his lack of a male heir was fully shared by his subjects. The war was almost equally unproductive. In spite of a lot of brave talk, most of the summer of 1523 passed without any serious military effort. Only when the Duke of Bourbon quarreled with Francis over a personal matter and offered his services to the emperor, did there appear to be a prospect of serious action. Suddenly, in August, plans were thrown together for a three-pronged attack upon Paris, and in September the Duke of Suffolk landed in Picardy with about ten thousand men. Considering the speed with which it was prepared, this expeditionary force was remarkably efficient, but in the end it achieved nothing. This was not Suffolk's fault, or Wolsey's, but a combination of bad weather and lack of support. Bourbon's campaign simply fizzled out, while the emperor's promised force was both too little and too late. Incensed with his ally, Henry responded positively to a fresh initiative from his sister in Scotland, and by the autumn of 1524 it looked as though he was prepared to make a separate peace with France and drop the Habsburg marriage treaty. Charles became increasingly suspicious of his intentions, and at one point believed that a Scottish marriage had been agreed. However, in February 1525 the whole situation was transformed by the shattering imperial victory at Pavia, which left the king of France a prisoner and the whole of northern Italy at the emperor's mercy.

Henry, who had been ruled by Wolsey's prevarication since the failure of Suffolk's expedition, was now fired with enthusiasm. There was talk of a massive invasion, even of the partitioning of France. Unfortunately campaigns required money, and since Wolsey had bungled his negotiations with parliament in 1523, that was in short supply. The emperor, moreover, was as disillusioned with the English as they were with him, and used Henry's failure to make any kind of effort in 1524 an excuse to negotiate for the hand of the Infanta Isabella of Portugal. On 7 June, when his negotiation was almost complete, he confronted Henry with an ultimatum. He would raise an army for the invasion of France provided that the king would pay for it, and would marry his daughter provided she was handed over at once with a full dowry. Both demands were equally unrealistic, and he knew that perfectly well. Henry was as poor as he was, and Cardinal Wolsey's attempt to remedy that situation by means of a Benevolence hopefully known as the Amicable Grant was a complete fiasco.

> When this matter was opened through Englande [wrote Edward Hall], how the great men took it was marvell, the poore curssed, ye riche repugned, the light wittes railed, but in conclusion, all people curssed the Cardinal and his coadherents as subversors of the Lawes and libertie of Englande. For thei saied, if men should geve their goodes by a Commission, the were it worse then the taxes of Fraunce, and so England should be bond and not free. . . .[30]

Henry was forced to retreat as gracefully as he could, and his confidence in his minister was severely, if temporarily, shaken. The king had been humiliated both at home and abroad, and the only thing to do was to cut his losses. On 30 August he concluded the Treaty of the More with France. The Habsburg alliance was dead, and Mary was again a disposable asset. This, however, was a limited advantage because neither the French nor the Scots were eager to seek her hand, and questions began to be asked about her status.

At first these questions were innocuous enough, but in the circumstances they were unanswerable. Would Mary inherit the kingdom, and if she did, what would be the position of her husband? As early as November 1524 one observer in Rome conjectured shrewdly 'it does not seem very probable that the daughter of the king of England will bring that kingdom with her as dower. . . .'[31] The xenophobia of the English was notorious, and although Henry had carefully stressed the fact that Mary was his heir when he was using her as bait, he refrained from implying that she would continue in that position. By 1525 the situation was becoming urgent and the king had to consider his options. If he reaffirmed that Mary was his heir – and she was, after all, his only legitimate child – then it would be sensible to secure her marriage at the earliest moment in order to give her the best possible chance of producing a son who might reach maturity during his own lifetime, and possibly under his own control. However, the princess was only nine, and showing no sign of physical precocity, rather the reverse. Such a course must therefore mean a delay of at least five years, followed by the usual genetic gamble. Even if all went well another eighteen years would be required to remove the threat of an alien regency. If Mary remained the heir, the chances were that she would inherit the realm, and that her husband would at best be regent for her son. At worst he would be king, and England would lose both its Tudor monarchy and its independence. In order to avoid this, Henry had two choices, both of them fraught with extreme difficulties. The first was to legitimate Henry Fitzroy. This would have been technically possible with papal cooperation, but would have been hazardous because such dispensations could always be challenged. To have declared him the heir by statute without canonical legitimation was not considered to be feasible at this time, although it would be done for the benefit of both Mary and Elizabeth in 1544. The alternative was to repudiate his wife of sixteen years and marry again. This too was feasible with papal help, and the more so since there had always been some doubt about the dispensation which had validated it in the first place. Such a course, however, was beset with both political and emotional difficulties, and it is not surprising that Henry hesitated in doubt and perplexity for some time.

On 18 June 1525 the six-year-old Fitzroy was created Duke of Richmond and Somerset, and shortly after despatched to the north of England with the honorific title of lieutenant, a council and a large household. Catherine, who was clearly not in Henry's confidence over this move, was mortified. Seeing this as a threat to her daughter's position, she was uncharacteristically and unwisely outspoken. In fact Richmond's elevation may have had more to do with Wolsey's schemes to consolidate his position than with any plan for the succession, but the queen was not the only person who believed that they could read between the lines. However, a few weeks later Mary was similarly despatched to Ludlow to act as the nominal head of the council in the Marches of Wales. This appeared to signal her elevation to the title of Princess of Wales, which would have been an unequivocal recognition of her status as heir. Thereafter she was often referred to by that style, but it was never formally conferred. As with Fitzroy, her household and council were largely the creation of the cardinal. Henry also seems to have been concerned to signal his daughter's temporary withdrawal from the marriage market, and he certainly wished to reduce her mother's influence. So the real conclusion which should be drawn from these moves is not that Henry was thinking aloud about the succession, but that the cardinal had secured a major tactical victory over the queen. In 1523 Catherine's influence appeared to have recovered with the renewal of the imperial alliance. Two years later, her position had collapsed. This was not entirely Wolsey's doing, although he benefited from it. In April 1525 Charles had withdrawn his ambassador, Louis de Praet, with whom the queen had enjoyed a reasonable rapport, and replaced him with a Spanish soldier named Penalosa. The handover was botched, and Penalosa had no idea of the role which Catherine had previously played. He consequently made no contact with her at all, and when his mission resulted in a rupture of relations, there was nothing which she could do to reduce the impact of his message. Nevertheless, in spite of these disappointments and uncertainties, the year ended on a quiet note. The queen's health, which had given cause for anxiety earlier, and intermittently over the past three years, improved. At forty-one she was past the menopause, and resigned to her dynastic failure. Henry rejoined her at Richmond in October, after his summer travels, and their relationship seemed to have recovered something of its old closeness. Mary wrote, carefully and dutifully, and Catherine replied with anxious little admonitions, 'For it shall be a great comfort to me to see you keep your latin, and fair writing and all . . .', and with commendations to her old friend Margaret Pole, now Countess of Salisbury and her daughter's lady governess.[32] If Henry was considering resolving the succession by re-marrying, he was giving no sign of it at the end of 1525.

At that point Anne Boleyn was a cloud no bigger than a man's hand. The Boleyns were a court family. Her father, Sir Thomas, had been an Esquire of the Body to Henry VII, and had been sufficiently in favour to marry into the Howard family at some point before 1500. In 1512 he had been given his first diplomatic assignment, to the court of the Archduchess Margaret, Regent of the Netherlands. There he made himself sufficiently agreeable for Margaret to agree to take his younger daughter as one of her eighteen *filles d'honneur*, and Anne had consequently been despatched to Brussels in 1513 at the age of about twelve.[33] The Regent was favourably impressed. 'I find her so bright and pleasant for her young age', she wrote to Sir Thomas, 'that I am more beholden to you for sending her to me than you are to me.' The arrangement was short-lived, not because of any change of heart on either side, but because of the international situation. In 1514 Henry made peace with France, and relations with Spain and the Low Countries cooled. The king also needed girls of suitable birth and expertise in the French language to accompany his sister to her nuptials in Paris. So Anne was recalled, with regret all round, and found herself at the ripe age of thirteen drafted into service as an interpreter. It appears that she did not cross to France in Mary's train, and Eric Ives's deduction that she probably joined the French court direct from the Low Countries may well be correct.[34] If so, when she arrived she found her sister already installed because Mary Boleyn, probably the elder by about two years, had accompanied the new queen from England. Within a few months, however, Mary Tudor was a widow, and Henry sent his trusted friend the Duke of Suffolk to bring her home. An extraordinary sequence of events then followed. Charles Brandon was an attractive man with a complex, not to say unscrupulous, matrimonial history. His name had recently been linked with no less a person than Margaret of Austria, and in 1514 he was contracted to marry his eight-year-old ward, Elizabeth, Lady Lisle.[35] *La Reine Blanche*, however, had other ideas. It is alleged that she had only agreed to marry Louis on the condition that she could have her own choice the next time round, but it is hard to imagine the king agreeing to so open-ended a condition, and the story is probably a romantic fabrication. Mary decided without consulting anyone (least of all Brandon himself it would seem) that the duke would be her second husband. As a recent historian has put it, 'Before he knew what was happening, he woke up in Mary's bed. . . .' The couple were secretly married, and returned to England to face the worst six months of Brandon's life.

Mary Boleyn returned with the new Duchess of Suffolk, but did not remain in

*Miniature of Henry VIII (attributed to Lucas Horenbout, c. 1525–7). It gives the king's age as thirty-five*

her service. Sir Thomas was too astute to have taken such a risk, and Mary seems to have been placed in the queen's household. Anne remained in France. It is not known who suggested the arrangement, but she was quickly taken into the service of the new queen, Claude. Anglo-French relations continued to be amicable at the beginning of Francis' reign, so there was no reason why she should not have stayed, but it must have required some outstanding quality to have persuaded Claude to find a place in her chamber for a fourteen-year-old English girl, who did not even have the benefit of being particularly well connected. She was certainly bright and intelligent, but was too young to have acquired the sophisticated gloss which was normally required at the French court. Perhaps Claude, who was only sixteen herself, found her an agreeable companion, or perhaps the coming and going of English courtiers, messengers and diplomats persuaded the queen that she needed someone who could speak the language. Whatever the reason behind it, the arrangement obviously worked well, because Anne remained in Claude's service until 1521, when the Anglo-Imperial Treaty of Bruges, and the accompanying deterioration in relations between France and England led to her recall. Claude, in spite of her frail physique, endured almost annual pregnancies during this period, and Anne must have learned a great deal about confinements and about the care of the ailing and fragile. Later, when she was notorious throughout Europe, Lancelot de Carles remembered that it had been in France that she had learned her musical

*Margaret Pole, Countess of Salisbury, c. 1530. A devout Catholic, she was a long-term friend of Catherine of Aragon and governess to the Princess Mary; she ranged herself with her charge and the queen over the divorce*

skills, and her extraordinary gracefulness and poise in dancing.[36] The French court at that time, even more than its English counterpart, was a centre of literary and artistic patronage, and Claude herself had excellent taste in miniature painting and in illumination. As one of the queen's ladies Anne would not have received any further formal education, but there is every reason to suppose that she picked up the interests of a sparkling Renaissance court, and refined her own natural gifts of intellect. She also encountered, although how intimately is not known, Francis's sister, Marguerite, Duchess d'Alençon. Marguerite was a leading patron of the Christian humanists, and was later to be suspected of heresy. Anne's later interest in religious reform may well have sprung from that connection. She attended the celebrations at the Field of Cloth of Gold in Claude's service, and may well have proved her value on that occasion. However, by this time she was nineteen, and there do not seem to have been any negotiations for her to marry in France, so we should probably conclude that her father always intended to recall her, and that she would have left the queen's household fairly soon, even if there had been no change in the international climate.[37]

In fact her name was already being linked with that of James Butler in 1520 in a characteristic bit of matrimonial trading designed to settle a dispute over the inheritance to the Irish Earldom of Ormonde. Thomas Butler, the previous Earl, had died in 1515, leaving a dispute between his heir male, Sir Piers Butler, and the heirs general, Sir James St Leger and Sir Thomas Boleyn. In 1520 Anne's uncle and Sir Thomas' brother-in-law, the Earl of Surrey, was Lieutenant of Ireland, with instructions from the king to settle the dispute in Boleyn's favour. Surrey, however, found Sir Piers firmly entrenched and with the local community very much on his side, while the king's interest was intermittent and his own resources inadequate. He therefore proposed a marriage between Sir Piers' son, James, and Sir Thomas' daughter as a more or less amicable compromise. James was conveniently located in Wolsey's household at the time, and the cardinal undertook to 'perfect' the match. It did not take place for a variety of reasons connected with the tangles of Irish politics, and only in 1529 did Sir Thomas Boleyn eventually secure that title to Ormonde. Meanwhile an unmarried and distinctly eligible Anne Boleyn was unleashed on the English court at the beginning of 1522. Her first public appearance was in a pageant connected with a tournament held on Shrove Tuesday, the assault on the *Château Verte*, in which Anne appeared as the allegorical character of Perseverance. Her sister, Mary, featured in the same pageant as Kindness, and the Duchess of Suffolk (long since restored to favour) as Beauty.[38] Unlike the king's sister, Anne was not a great beauty, less pretty, it was later agreed, than either her sister or Elizabeth Blount. However, she was extraordinarily attractive, and stood out in any company. She was tall, and had a fine head of dark hair, but the reason for her attractiveness lay partly in her French-trained accomplishments, and partly in a kind of animal magnetism which was extremely hard to define, but which could perhaps be most simply described as sex appeal.

Rather surprisingly, after the failure of the Butler marriage to materialize, Sir Thomas did not immediately embark upon other negotiations on his daughter's behalf. This was not because she had caught the king's eye. At this stage it was Mary who was sharing the royal bed. Most likely, being a strong-minded young woman, she made it clear that she had no intention of being rushed. No doubt she was also enjoying herself a good deal. The game of courtly love, an invention of the troubadours of Languedoc some four hundred years earlier, and revived by the Burgundian chivalry so much favoured by the Tudors, offered great scope to a young woman of wit. Catherine had never really had the opportunity to play it. She had only known the English court as queen, apart from occasional appearances on sufferance, and although Henry himself lavished attention on her, it was not permitted for anyone else to do the same. Her ladies, however, particularly the unmarried ones, were expected to participate with enthusiasm. The court was always short of women, and boredom was a constant enemy, so this relatively harmless pastime was very popular, and the queen's ladies were always besieged by gallants.[39] Normally the exchange of compliments and tokens, the arch dialogue and clandestine assignations meant very little, particularly as the male players outnumbered the female by five or six to one. Anne, who had been given a place in Catherine's chamber on her return from France, was an exceptionally skilled player, and more than usually in demand. This could have unfortunate consequences. According to Wolsey's gentleman usher, George Cavendish, she inadvertently ensnared the unfortunate Henry Percy into a genuine infatuation. Percy, who was the son and heir to the Earl of Northumberland, was living in

Wolsey's household at the time (between 1522 and 1524), and was rather a gauche young man. He was also contracted to marry Mary Talbot, the daughter of the Earl of Shrewsbury. The affair caused something of a scandal, and the removal of the unfortunate young man in disgrace.[40]

Anne herself seems to have suffered nothing worse than a dressing down from her father, but by 1525 she must have been a source of some anxiety to him. She was now twenty-four and a most accomplished courtier, sitting in the middle of the most prestigious marriage market in England, and yet no marriage was in prospect. A few more scrapes like her flirtation with Henry Percy and she might well lose her place in the service of a queen who had always been rather strait-laced, and was now becoming distinctly dowdy as well. It was at this point, sometime during the winter of 1525/6, that she began to play the game of courtly love with the king himself. There was nothing particularly remarkable about this. Henry had been an assiduous gallant for years, but apart from his dutiful attentions to his wife, he had never advertised his real relationships in such a manner. Nothing is known about their early exchanges, which is a reasonable indication that no one at the time thought them to be in any way noteworthy. However, at the shrovetime tournament in 1526 the king appeared bearing the device of,

> . . . a mannes hate in a presse, with flaems about it, and in letters were writte, *Declare ie nose*, in Englishe Declare I dare not. . . .[41]

This was a far cry from *Coeur Loyale*, but in itself it meant little. Only when Henry made allusion, a year or more later, to the duration of his love, does it appear to have been significant. Imperceptibly during the early months of 1526 a conventional game of courtly love became a serious affair, and this time the partner was not a naïve young nobleman but the king himself. If Anne had intended such a development, then she was playing very dangerously, but it seems quite likely that she was taken completely by surprise. She knew her own attractiveness, but by comparison with Francis, the husband of her former mistress, Henry did not have a particularly roving eye, and his court was a model of propriety by comparison with that of France. Anne knew how to look after herself in normal circumstances, but by the summer of 1526 she knew that she had hooked a very dangerous fish.

The Tudors always wanted their own way, with sex as with everything else. Henry had married Catherine because he wanted her, without regard to the politics of the situation. Mary had insisted upon having Charles Brandon, although she knew perfectly well that he was committing high treason in having intercourse with her without the king's consent. Margaret, after the death of her first husband, James IV, at the Battle of Flodden in 1513, had married Archibald, Earl of Angus, without consulting her brother, or anyone else, in all probability. Politically it had not been a sensible move, and had exposed both her and her son to danger. Later she abandoned him, to Henry's somewhat hypocritical rage. Consequently when the king decided he wanted Anne Boleyn, the only question related to how he was going to achieve it, and no one expected the answer which was eventually to emerge.

# TWO

# The King's 'Great Matter': Catherine and Anne, 1525–33

Courtly love was an ambivalent pastime. Often the participants themselves do not seem to have known how serious they were, and the spectators no doubt relished the possibilities. When we find a professional poet like John Skelton writing the passionate verses which convention demanded, but which many gallants lacked the skill to produce for themselves, we are entitled to deduce mere role-play. However, when the sonnets in question are the work of a gentleman who was also one of the finest poets of the century, it is much less easy to be certain. Sir Thomas Wyatt undoubtedly addressed love songs to Anne Boleyn in this courtly context, and on that basis a story was later fabricated to demonstrate that she had a sexual relationship with him before the king began to pay her serious attention. If this occurred at all, it must have been in the latter part of 1526, but the genuine evidence for such an episode is non-existent. Wyatt's early poems which appear to allude to her are either of doubtful authenticity, or very obscure in their wording. The genuine sonnet which contains the lines,

> Yet may I by no means my wearied mind
> Draw from the deer, but as she fleeth afore
> Fainting I follow. I leave off therefore,
> Sithens in a net I seek to hold the wind.

and concludes with the famous words,

> There is written her fair neck round about:
> *Noli me tangere*, for Caesar's I am
> And wild for to hold, though I seem tame.[1]

was written much later, and may have been a response to the news of her death. Moreover, all the surviving poems in this vein contain unambiguous and 'politically correct' references to the fact that the adored mistress is unattainable – and unattained. The story that Wyatt warned his royal master that he was becoming interested in a lady of easy virtue may therefore be dismissed. Whether Wyatt and the king were playing the same game with Anne at the same time must remain uncertain. It is a possibility, and there may even have been some friction, but the only evidence

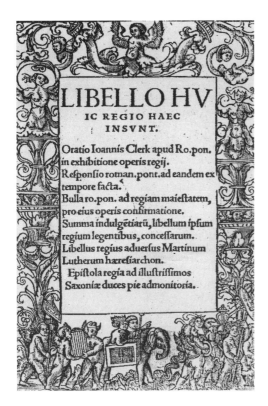

*Title page of the* Assertio Septem Sacramentorum, *Henry's book attacking the ideas of Luther, 1521*

was communicated many years later by Anne Zouche, a former attendant, and related to Wyatt's theft of a trinket, a routine incident in the game of courtly love.

At this stage Henry's attraction to Anne Boleyn had probably got more to do with a longish period of sexual abstinence than with any decision about his marriage, but it is hard to be sure because the two things were happening at the same time. Anne's enemies later represented them as cause and effect, but that is certainly unfair. The king had been brooding intermittently for about ten years on the subject of children, and particularly sons. Since the birth of Henry Fitzroy in 1519 he had become increasingly convinced that his union with Catherine had attracted some kind of Divine disfavour. He knew, of course, that there had been an impediment, but that had been properly dispensed, and in 1521 he had written a book against the German heretic Martin Luther, which had contained generous recognition of the fullness of papal power. However the *Assertio Septem Sacramentorum* had been very much an occasional piece, written in the hope of securing a papal title, and did not necessarily represent the fullness of the king's convictions. Criticism of the papacy was widespread in the early 1520s, and was not confined to heretics. Some of Henry's favourite humanists were distinctly unflattering about the court of Rome in its present condition. The much-admired Erasmus had even published, in 1513, a particularly biting satire entitled *Julius exclusus e coelis* against that very pope who had granted the dispensation. The king, moreover, had a good conceit of himself as a theologian, and knew his bible well, following the modern educational fashion. It is not, therefore, surprising that he became increasingly convinced that he had incurred the curse of childlessness decreed in the book of Leviticus (20:21) against the man who takes his brother's widow to wife, nor that he had grave doubts about the efficacy of the papal dispensation.

There were, as he must have realized, two major objections to this view of his situation. One was the so-called 'levirate', decreed in the book of Deuteronomy, which required a man to take his brother's widow if the first union had been childless. The second was the fact that his marriage to Catherine had not been childless. They had a healthy, if somewhat undersized, daughter. The first was swept aside on the specious ground that Deuteronomy was ambiguous, and the second was met by a hebraist named Robert Wakefield, who produced a translation of Leviticus to challenge the Vulgate version. This conveniently claimed that the original Hebrew said not 'they shall be without children' but 'they shall be without sons'.[2] By 1527 Henry was committed with the whole strength of his obstinate nature to the conviction that he had broken the law of God in marrying Catherine, and that the Pope was powerless to dispense with such an impediment. It was a disastrous conviction for a number of reasons. In the first place it led to a head-on conflict with the queen, who was equally convinced that her marriage had been specifically made in heaven, and believed that her husband's qualms, if not hypocritical, were certainly blasphemous. In the second place it involved telling the Pope that his predecessor had acted *ultra vires*, and eventually lecturing the Curia on biblical exegesis. Finally it prompted the rejection of other, lower-key arguments on canonical technicalities which might have had a much better chance of success. In fact the whole story of the king's 'great matter' is the story of a self-opinionated man destroying his own chances of success by mistaken tactics and unnecessary provocations. By 1530 Henry seemed to be incapable of taking sensible advice, or of seeing the realities of the political situation which confronted him.

At what point Anne became a serious factor in this situation is not clear. By September 1527 he was seriously considering re-marriage, but whether this had been preceded by an attempt at seduction remains unclear. The traditional story is that Henry offered Anne the chance to follow her sister into his bed, and that she refused, insisting on marriage, thus forcing the king into his search for an annulment.[3] However, it seems certain that the king had decided that his marriage was invalid by the end of 1526 at the latest, and there is no reliable evidence of his proposition, if he ever made it. In the spring of 1527 several unconnected events began to form a pattern. Since the Treaty of the More, Wolsey had been anxious to strengthen ties with France, and the proposal of a French husband for Princess Mary was revived. Francis himself, a widower since 1524, was seriously considered, and that alone would be a sufficient indication that Catherine's political influence was in total eclipse.[4] However, by February 1527 the more suitable suggestion of his second son, Henri duc d'Orléans had come to the fore. This was alleged to be a match which the Pope greatly favoured in his efforts to break the imperial stranglehold on northern Italy, and Henry was anxious to ingratiate himself in Rome. The French were keen to settle, and wished to insist

*Anne Boleyn (1507–36) (artist and date unknown). This image, authenticated by the B-shaped pendant, is the standard portrait of Anne, of which several examples survive*

on having custody of the princess straight away. That, however, Wolsey would not allow, and the envoys, having seen Mary in April, concurred. She would, they agreed, not be ready for a marriage bed for at least three years. Meanwhile, they wished to be reassured that she was still Henry's heir. This was a routine bargaining point, and does not mean that they had received any intimation of a change in the king's position, but in the circumstances it was an embarrassing enquiry. Wolsey was reassuring, but vague, and an open-ended agreement was signed on 18 April. Before it could be ratified, bad news arrived from Italy. Early in May an imperial army had mutinied and run amok, sacking the city of Rome, and confining the Pope as a prisoner in the Castel San Angelo. There is no reason to suppose that the emperor was a party to this atrocity, but it greatly strengthened his position and made it impossible for Clement VII to make the slightest move without his permission. By an ironic coincidence, at exactly the same time, Wolsey, by a collusive action, summoned Henry to answer for the sin of having co-habited for eighteen years with his brother's widow.

Catherine was not informed of this move, nor did she find out about it. This was not because the king was trying to obtain an annulment by stealth – that would not have been possible in law – but because he needed to obtain some confidential opinions on the strength of his case before risking a public declaration. If he expected enthusiastic endorsement, then he was disappointed. Both the canon lawyers and the senior bishops who were consulted were divided.[5] All agreed that such a union was incestuous, but upon the status of the Levitical prohibition, and the sufficiency of the papal dispensation, there was no consensus. A number of sessions were held between 17 and 31 May, but on 1 June the news arrived from Rome, and the secret court was hastily abandoned. For the time being there was no prospect of a verdict against Catherine being ratified in Rome. To Wolsey, however, the situation presented a golden opportunity. With Clement temporarily *hors de combat* he could summon a group of cardinals to Avignon, declare an interim government for the Church, and get a number of pieces of urgent business settled, including the annulment of the king of England's marriage. Such a scheme could possibly have succeeded if Henry's intentions had been kept secret. However, perhaps because he was ashamed of his own dissimulation, or because he was simply impatient, on 22 June he confronted Catherine with the news that they had never been truly married. He could hardly have made a worse mistake. At this stage the queen probably had no suspicions about Anne Boleyn, and indeed there may have been nothing very much to suspect, so that a frank discussion of the succession problem, and an appeal for her cooperation, might have produced a very different response. As it was, there was first an emotional scene of passionate intensity, and then a steely determination to fight the threatened annulment every inch of the way. The king's indiscretion also cut the ground from under his chancellor's feet. Before Wolsey could even convene the cardinals whom he hoped would endorse his plan, the emperor had been alerted to what was afoot. One of Catherine's few remaining Spanish servants, a man named Felipez, had been despatched to Charles at Valladolid, and had reached him before the end of July.[6] Henry knew of Felipez's mission, and had given orders that he was to be intercepted, but the

*Cardinal Thomas Wolsey (1475?–1530)*
*(artist and date unknown)*

Spaniard had eluded his pursuers, travelling swiftly by sea. The emperor reacted with unwonted swiftness, and seems to have been genuinely shocked by the threat to his family honour. He immediately pledged his full support to Catherine, wrote to Henry begging him to desist from his intention, and to the Pope insisting that he deny Wolsey any facility to hear the case.

By the autumn of 1527 there was no chance that Henry or Wolsey would be able to smuggle a decision through, and no chance that Clement would be able to oblige the king of England, as he might have been willing to do under more normal circumstances. Wolsey was already in France, and half-way to his planned meeting when the news of these untoward developments reached him. No sooner had his back been turned on England than his influence seemed to have been superseded. The king was much in company with the Dukes of Norfolk and Suffolk, he was told, and with Thomas Boleyn, Lord Rochford. Rochford was Anne's father, and his familiarity with Henry signalled a major advance in his daughter's prospects. The Boleyns were not at this stage hostile to Wolsey, because he appeared to offer the best chance of getting the king's existing marriage annulled, but they were not necessarily willing to serve his purposes. Whether the cardinal had any firm intention of trying to find a French bride for his master is not clear, although it would have been a rational move from his point of view. What is clear is that Wolsey had no understanding of the king's real intentions. By October Henry had decided that he would marry Anne, and that he would withhold that information from his minister. He sent his secretary, William Knight, direct to Rome with a very strange request. The Pope was to be asked to provide a bull allowing Henry to marry any woman, including one to whom he was related in the first degree of affinity, even if that affinity was illicit, provided that his first marriage had been properly annulled.[7] The purpose of this subterfuge seems to have been no more than to enable him to carry out his intended purpose immediately Wolsey's main mission had been successful. On its own it could have accomplished nothing. Perhaps Henry, or those around him, suspected that the cardinal would drag his feet if he knew the king's true mind. The suspicion was less than fair to Wolsey's loyalty and efficiency, but it marks a critical step in the breakdown of the confidential relationship between king and minister. Had the cardinal's main mission succeeded, he might well have recovered that ground, but it did not. The other cardinals were uncooperative, and the emperor was adamant. There would be no interim government for the Church, no opportunity for Wolsey to usurp the papal function, however briefly, and consequently no annulment. He returned to England at the end of September 1527 to face a bleak future.

Having made her own position abundantly clear, and having alerted her nephew to the nature of her troubles, Catherine's policy then became one of masterly inactivity. However distressing Henry's attitude may have been, she was in possession of the high ground, and justifiably confident that she could not be moved. Her insistence on continuing in public as though nothing had happened rubbed salt in the wounds of the king's frustration, but he accepted it and they continued to live together, more or less, as man and wife. For the time being Anne also remained patient. Secure in her knowledge of Henry's intentions, she realized that it would take time to bring her purpose to effect, and that there was nothing to be gained from trying to force the issue. Personal relations between the two women remained correct, if not amicable, because nothing had been said in public about the king's feelings for mistress Boleyn, and their behaviour had been reasonably discreet. It is even possible that in the winter of 1527/8 Catherine had no idea of the identity of her rival, or was even certain that such a rival existed. Meanwhile, Wolsey made another attempt to exploit the changing international situation. After his release from captivity in 1526, Francis almost at once repudiated the treaty which he had been compelled to sign, and renewed his war against the emperor, in spite of the fact that his two sons remained as hostages in Madrid. The League of Cognac was welcomed by England, although Henry did not initially become a member. Its explicit objective was to force Charles to moderate the terms of the Treaty of Madrid, and release the two French princes. In such circumstances a captive pope was a liability rather than an asset, and in an attempt to draw some, at least, of the league's teeth, Charles allowed Clement to withdraw to Orvieto in December 1527. For a few short weeks the Pope was sufficiently at liberty, and sufficiently resentful of his situation, to have been willing to exact a petty revenge. Had Wolsey known of this in time, a renewed request, accompanied by a substantial financial inducement, might have received a sympathetic hearing.[8] However, he did not know, and Clement soon decided that resentment was an unprofitable attitude, and that he should 'live and die a good Imperialist'.

Consequently when Henry's emissary arrived, the Pope was prepared to give the king of England a dispensation to marry whomever he liked when he became free, but not to grant him the annulment which he sought. Nothing had changed, and in January 1528 Wolsey adhered to the League of Cognac. The formal declaration of war was made against the emperor on 28 January.

This was largely bluff, and no hostilities followed, but the Pope was persuaded to make what looked like a concession. He was prepared to grant powers to Wolsey and one other cardinal to hear the king's case in England. Meanwhile, Henry was endeavouring to cope with a domestic situation of increasing difficulty. Anne remained at court, and her behaviour continued to be discreet, but the strain was beginning to tell on both of them. The only gainer in the first half of 1528 was Wolsey. His apparent success in obtaining the special legatine commission was optimistically misinterpreted, and his relationship with Anne became positively cordial. When he wrote in July to congratulate her on her recovery from the sweating sickness, she replied,

> . . . all the days of my life I am most bound of all creatures, next the king's grace, to love and serve your grace: of the which I beseech you never to doubt that ever I shall vary from this thought as long as any breath is in my body.[9]

The sweat had temporarily disrupted the royal romance, because no devotion could persuade Henry to run the risk of infection, and he had ungallantly fled in the early part of June, travelling incessantly until the danger was over in the early part of August. Wolsey welcomed the improvement in his relationship with the king which was signalled by Anne's cordiality, but did not deceive himself about the nature of his achievement. Throughout the spring his agents struggled to get his commission converted into a decretal commission, which would have rendered his and his colleague's decision final and not subject to appeal. They failed, and Wolsey therefore knew that the eagerly anticipated arrival of his fellow commissioner, Lorenzo Campeggio, did not necessarily spell the beginning of the end of Henry's frustrations. In September, with rather pointless rectitude, the king sent Anne down to live with her mother at Hever Castle, and on 8 November he unburdened his conscience to a specially convened meeting of councillors, courtiers and City Fathers of London:

> But when we remember our mortalitie and that we must die, then we thinke that all our doynges in our life tyme are clerely defaced & worthy of no memorie if we leve you in trouble at the tyme of our death. For if our true heyre be not knowen at the time of our death, se what mischiefe & trouble shall suceede to you and your children. . . . And although it hath pleased almighty God to send us a fayre doughter of a noble woman and me begotten to our great comfort & joy, yet it hath been told us by divers great clerkes that neither she is our lawfull doughter nor her mother our lawfull wife. . . .[10]

There is no reason to doubt his sincerity, but even the loyal Edward Hall could not disguise the fact that his scruple was ill-received,

To see what countenaunce was made amongest the hearers of this Oracion it
was a strange sight, for some sighed and said nothyng, others were sory to heare
the kyng so troubled in his conscience. Other that favored the queene much
sorowed that this matter was now opened. . . .[11]

Campeggio had already reached London, and had met the king on 24 October. He
had found him furiously impatient, and utterly convinced of the justice of his
cause.

In spite of this conviction, Henry's mood was unstable. He seems to have been
totally disconcerted by the unsympathetic reception which his oration of
8 November had received, and while endeavouring to bully Campeggio, he was also
desperately seeking support and reassurance. This he received, most obviously and
inevitably, from Anne herself. He may even have made a renewed attempt to
persuade her to become his mistress. If he did, it was totally without success. All he
was told, in no uncertain terms, was to get on with the business of securing his
annulment. Not surprisingly, she also insisted on returning to court, and was back
by 9 December when the French ambassador, du Bellay, noted that she was grandly
accommodated, and close to the king's own quarters. When the court moved to
Greenwich for Christmas, Anne was similarly given rooms in the palace.
Catherine's reaction to this *ménage à trois* was muted but unmistakable. When
Henry knighted Campeggio's son during the festivities '. . . the queen showed to
them no manner of countenance, and made no joy of nothing, her mind was so
troubled'.[12] She had every reason to be troubled, because by this time it was obvious
to all that she had completely lost her influence over her husband to a much
younger and more attractive woman. She might succeed in preventing him from
marrying her, and take comfort from the sympathy and support which she was
receiving from the English people, but that was a poor and negative consolation for
having lost the love and respect of the man with whom she had lived for nearly
twenty years, and who had treated her with so much deference and affection.

Anne had little or no support outside her own family, but by January 1529 she
had revealed that she had the kind of power which comes by exercising a
dominant influence over the king in a personal monarchy. In the summer of 1528
she intervened decisively, if not very positively, in the appointment of a new
Abbess of Wilton and, perhaps unintentionally, caused Wolsey a bloody nose. It
was later alleged that she was used as a catspaw by members of the council who
were resentful of the cardinal's prolonged dominance.

They knew right well [wrote George Cavendish], that it was very difficult for
them to do anything directly of themselves, wherefore they perceiving the great
affection that the king bare lovingly unto Mistress Anne Boleyn, fantasying in
their heads that she should be for them a sufficient and an apt instrument to
bring their malicious purpose to pass; with whom they often consulted in this
manner. . . .[13]

However, this is almost certainly mistaken. Anne had no incentive to undermine
Wolsey's position with the king as long as he seemed to be the most likely person

to secure the annulment of Henry's marriage. Once he had demonstrated his inability to deliver that prize, the king's indignation scarcely needed stimulation. The handful of gentlemen for whom Anne had been able to perform political services, Thomas Wyatt, Sir Thomas Cheney, and her brother-in-law William Carey scarcely constituted a political party, despite the fact that they were all members of the privy chamber. The idea that she was masterminding a powerful anti-Wolsey coalition, including the Dukes of Norfolk and Suffolk, seems to have originated in the fertile mind of Inigo de Mendoza, the imperial ambassador, although Cavendish also believed it many years later. In fact very little is known about Anne's direct political activity before the summer of 1529. Deductions and inferences can be made from the rise of men like Sir Francis Bryan in the king's favour, but there was no such thing as a 'Boleyn faction' before Wolsey's fall, and if he had survived the crisis of 1529/30, there is no reason to suppose that they would not have worked together in amity.

At the beginning of 1529 the key man was (or appeared to be) Lorenzo Campeggio. As soon as his powers were disclosed, they were discovered to be inadequate, but further promises were extracted from the Pope, and the king continued to be resolutely optimistic. Wolsey, on the other hand, had no illusions. The best that he could hope to do was to convince Campeggio of the absolute necessity to grant Henry's suit, so that they could together apply the heavy pressure which would be essential to budge Clement from his imperialist stance. However, both of them knew that the king's case in canon law was not a strong one. Wolsey would have preferred Henry to plead that Julius' dispensation was inadequate, on the grounds that it had removed the impediment of consanguinity, but not that of public honesty (in other words it had been issued on the assumption that Catherine's first marriage had been consummated, whereas in fact it had not). The fact that consanguinity was a greater impediment than public honesty would not have mattered. The invalidity would have been purely technical, but that would have been sufficient to have enabled Clement to find in Henry's favour, without making any judgement on the real merits of the case. The king, however, would not allow this argument to be used. Perhaps he could not bear to admit that Catherine had been right all along about her first marriage, and he had been wrong; or perhaps he was so obsessed with his own conviction about the 'Levitical curse' that he simply refused to plead on any other ground. Campeggio, realizing that the king was immovable, and not amenable to any rational argument, concentrated upon Catherine. His secret instructions were to delay the issue as long as possible, and not in any circumstances to find in the king's favour. On the other hand, he was becoming convinced of the political dangers created by Henry's intransigence. Only if the queen could be persuaded to yield could a clash between irresistible force and immovable matter be avoided.

The legate's solution was simple and plausible. If Catherine could be persuaded to take the veil, there would be a good enough canonical argument to allow her husband to re-marry. The matter was not beyond dispute, but there was a very respectable body of opinion which maintained that if either partner to a marriage entered religion, then the union was dissolved.[14] Such a solution would have had the great merit of accepting Catherine's view of her own marriage, and

*Seal of Cardinal Campeggio who was sent by Pope Clement VII as legate to preside with Wolsey over the ecclesiastical court at Blackfriars*

of leaving Mary's legitimacy intact, while giving Henry the freedom which he so desperately wanted. Unfortunately for Campeggio, his plan appealed greatly to the king; so greatly that he insisted with intemperate violence that Catherine should accept it at once. If there had ever been any chance that she would do so, Henry's outburst killed it. Her total and adamant refusal, while perfectly understandable in human terms, casts an interesting light upon her motivation. She knew, as well as Henry did, that she would never bear him another child. She also knew, although she may not have sympathized with, his burning desire for a son. She was a deeply pious woman, and the religious life had appealed to her in the past. There would have been no question of dishonour, and no need to defend her daughter's rights. Her decision was therefore based rather upon pride, and upon the public face of events, than upon the moral substance of her case. Since her husband had already in a sense, publicly repudiated her and clearly intended to take another woman, such a withdrawal would have been interpreted as surrender, as a tacit concession that he had justice, or at least force, upon his side. Consequently she would be moved by neither threats nor entreaties, and there was no alternative to a trial of the case *in foro publico*, by legatine court. Wolsey and Campeggio therefore summoned the king and queen to appear before them at Blackfriars on 18 June 1529.

By that time, Catherine felt herself to be beleaguered and friendless, but in fact

The Resentment of Queen Catherine *(engraving from a painting by William Hamilton).*
*The queen is visited by Cardinals Wolsey and Campeggio but adamantly refuses to submit to*
*their entreaties*

her position was much stronger than that of the king. With Henry's permission
she had appointed a council to present her defence to the court, and its members
included William Warham, the Archbishop of Canterbury, John Fisher, the
formidable Bishop of Rochester, Luis Vives, and George Athequa, her Spanish
confessor, who also held the see of Llandaff. More important, Henry's case was in
a state of collapse. A brief, supplementary to Julius's bull of 1503, and bearing the
same date, had turned up in Spain.[15] Catherine had a copy, which she was keeping
to herself, but it was fairly obvious from information which had leaked out, that it
would entirely undermine the cardinals' decretal commission, which only

referred to the bull. The king had made frantic attempts to circumvent this difficulty by renewed diplomatic efforts in Rome, and when they failed canvassed a number of alternative ways in which the Pope might allow him to resolve his main problem. It was even suggested at one point that both Henry and Catherine should agree to retire from the world, on the secret understanding that the Pope would then absolve him from his vows! Clement declined to be a party to such trickery, but it is not recorded whether he managed to keep a straight face. To make matters worse the Franco-Imperial war was coming to an end, and the Pope and the emperor were becoming steadily closer allies. Henry could find no leverage anywhere. In April Catherine had secretly petitioned Clement to revoke the case to Rome, and by the time that the court convened, the emperor had seconded her appeal with a formal request of his own. In spite of her distress, the queen not only had the better legal advice and the better case, but all the political odds were stacked in her favour.

In England the pressure for a swift decision was unrelenting, and in Rome the pressure for revocation became even more remorseless. Both Clement and Campeggio became frantic with anxiety and indecision, and for several weeks the right hand hardly knew what the left hand was doing. In the first session at Blackfriars the queen unexpectedly appeared in person, but only to make a protest against the court and formally notify her appeal to Rome. At the second session, on 21 June, both Henry and Catherine addressed the court; he to explain the compelling nature of his scruples, and she to plead with him, surely for the benefit of the world at large, not to dishonour her or disown their daughter. She then withdrew, declaring that she did not recognize the legate's jurisdiction. She was declared contumacious and the case proceeded without her, but that was the only success which the king enjoyed – if it can be called a success. John Fisher continued to argue the queen's case in her absence with a powerful and abrasive display of learning which left him a marked man, but he did not halt the steady procession of evidence and witnesses, many of them supporting Henry for reasons more or less creditable. For a few days a false optimism prevailed in the king's camp which was, of course, ignorant of Campeggio's true instructions. However, by 27 July the case was bogged down in a quagmire of technicalities, which may have arisen spontaneously, or may have been injected by the crafty and increasingly desperate legate. Wolsey professed himself baffled, and wrote urgently and secretly to Clement, begging him to allow the case to come to a speedy conclusion, and not for any consideration to allow it to be revoked to Rome.[16] By the time that his letter arrived it was already too late. On 13 July the Pope had yielded to imperial pressure, annulled the legatine commission, and summoned Henry to appear before the Rota.

Fortunately this news did not reach England for some time. The situation was bad enough without such a débâcle, because on 31 July Campeggio announced that the court would follow the Roman calendar, and adjourn for the vacation, which meant until October. Henry was furious, and sent the Dukes of Norfolk and Suffolk to demand that the court continue and reach a decision. When this request was refused, Suffolk, who was almost as angry as the king at the rebuff, uttered the prophetic words '. . . by the mass, now I see that the old said saw is true, that there was never legate nor cardinal that did good in England'. It may well have been Henry's own incompetence which had brought about this humiliating reversal, but he had good reason to be angry about the dishonest subterfuges to which the papacy and its agents had resorted. Catherine may well have been popular in England, but the king's nobles, even those who did not much approve of what he was doing, shared his indignation in August 1529. Henry's periodic personal interventions had undoubtedly hampered his cause, but the man who received the chief blame for failure was inevitably Wolsey. He was the man whose status in the Church and influence in the Curia was supposed to steer the annulment through the rocky waters of papal politics, and all he had achieved had been a farcical shouting match at Blackfriars. The king was disillusioned, and Anne Boleyn, dismissing the legate as a broken reed, became frankly hostile for the first time. How long Wolsey might have survived the combined assault of the Boleyns and his other aristocratic enemies had Blackfriars been his only failure, we shall never know. Despite his fury, Henry did not immediately give up in Rome. There seemed to be no alternative to persistence, however slender the chance, and the cardinal might still turn out to be a key man. However, he had been so concerned about the legatine court that he had taken his eye off the diplomatic scene, and had only realized when it was almost too late that an important Franco-Imperial treaty was about to be signed. He managed to rush envoys across to Cambrai, but not in time to make any impact on the settlement. The treaty was signed on 3 August, with only notional English participation.[17] Not only was Henry humiliated for the second time in a few days by being so sidelined, but Wolsey compounded his error by quarrelling with the French ambassador, and seeking to blame Francis for his exclusion from the negotiations. Given the nature of his problem with the emperor, the one person Henry could not afford to fall out with was the king of France. By the beginning of September, Wolsey was teetering on the brink, and Anne was exercising all her influence to force him over the edge.

There are many stories surrounding his actual fall at the beginning of October, but the most dramatic, telling how Anne persuaded the king to refuse him audience while she charmed her lover away to hunting and picnics, seem to be no more than romantic fabrications. In fact the cardinal had a number of intimate conversations with the king during September, and many observers thought that he had successfully appeased the royal anger. But Henry's distrust had been thoroughly aroused, and his decision to remove his long-time servant was not occasioned solely, or even mainly, by the feminine wiles of Anne Boleyn. Nevertheless, when Wolsey was charged with praemunire on 9 October, and dismissed as chancellor a week later, his fall was interpreted as a triumph for Anne and her supporters. Whether Catherine, who had predicted this outcome, derived any satisfaction from the accuracy of her prediction we do not know. She certainly had no cause to lament the fall of Wolsey, but the triumph of the Boleyn faction at court left her more than ever dependent upon the protection of her Habsburg kindred, and that was a position which had serious disadvantages. Her victory over the king had been decisive, but purely negative. She could remain his wife in the eyes of the law and the Church, but she could not compel him to treat

*Wosley (seated) surrenders the Great Seal of England – the emblem of the lord chancellorship – to his enemies, the Dukes of Norfolk and Suffolk (from the biography of Wolsey written by his servant George Cavendish)*

her as such, and nothing could restore the relationship which had once existed between them. Whether Henry lacked courage, or had a peculiarly scrupulous regard for outward forms we do not know, but he took no further action against Catherine for about two years. She remained queen, with her household and her dignity undiminished, but in a political limbo, with no active role in public life. On 8 December Thomas Boleyn was created Earl of Wiltshire, and his allies, George Hastings and Robert Radcliffe, Earls of Huntingdon and Sussex respectively. A grand celebration followed, over which Anne presided at the king's side. By the end of the year a new regime had been created, with the Duke of Norfolk as president of the council and, as du Bellay wrote '. . . above everyone Mademoiselle Anne'. Her ascendancy was sufficient to wrest the crown matrimonial from her rival.

Henry, having brought this predicament upon himself, was assailed from both sides. When he dined with the queen, as he did from time to time, or had any conversation with her at all, he was upbraided for his neglect, and informed that it was only his wilful obstinacy which was preventing him from accepting his defeat with a good grace. On the other hand, when he sought solace with Anne he was quite likely to be greeted with the kind of storm which occurred early in November.

> Did I not tell you that when you disputed with the queen she was sure to have the upper hand? I see that some fine morning you will succumb to her reasoning, and that you will cast me off. I have been waiting long and might in the meantime have contracted some advantageous marriage. . . . But alas! Farewell to my time and youth spent to no purpose at all.[18]

It may well have been that the king found such highspirited performances a part of Anne's attractiveness, but he does not emerge with much credit from the ambassadorial reports which are the main source of information about these exchanges. He spent a magnificent but somewhat joyless Christmas at Greenwich with Catherine, and then retired for a prolonged stay with Anne at York Place, while the queen remained at Richmond. More than Henry's manhood was now at stake, however. Small hints begin to appear that he was becoming willing to question the whole basis upon which the Pope could tell him what he might, or might not do. Relays of envoys continued to plead and threaten and cajole in Rome, but the king of England was also the Lord's anointed, and could be directly answerable to God. Threats to appeal to a general council, or to withdraw England from the papal jurisdiction altogether, were made but were not taken seriously in the Curia. Eustace Chapuys, the emperor's new ambassador, thought they were mere bluff, and most observers shared his opinion. Wolsey had known better. His panic-stricken forecasts of a complete breakdown of relations were based upon a much sounder knowledge of the king's psychology than most people possessed. That same conscience which had between 1520 and 1525 moved slowly to the unshakeable conviction that his marriage was unlawful, was now beginning to move towards a similar conviction that the Pope had no lawful jurisdiction over the issue. Anne Boleyn was not the cause of this seismic tremor in the royal conscience, any more than she had been of the previous one, but she was the occasion of both.

Anne did not eventually destroy Wolsey; he destroyed himself. Alienated from the king, he began an obscure and extremely risky attempt at a *rapprochement* with Catherine and her friends. When this was detected, possibly following French information, it did not need Anne's histrionics to persuade Henry to act against his former servant. The cardinal's arrest was ordered, and it was on his way to answer the resulting charges that he died on 29 November 1530. An unchallenged ascendency at court did not, however, enable the Boleyns to resolve the king's matrimonial crisis. In spite of restless, and sometimes rather directionless dipomacy, all Henry managed to achieve was a postponement of the sentence against him in Rome which everyone recognized to be inevitable. Meanwhile an uneasy *ménage à trois* was maintained, and the obvious lack of momentum, combined with Anne's increasing unpopularity, caused voices of doubt to be raised, even among the king's supporters. Courtiers began to talk secretly of seeking to persuade their master to change his mind, and there was growing alarm about the consequences of a prolonged estrangement from the emperor.[19] This atmosphere of doubt was assiduously fostered by Charles's subtle and extremely skilful ambassador, Eustace Chapuys, who rapidly became the most effective opponent of the Boleyn ascendancy, and one whom Anne, for all her influence over Henry, could do nothing to shift. What she could do, however, was begin to move the king away from his pointless determination to seek the resolution of his troubles in Rome. It was almost certainly she who introduced him to William Tyndale's *The Obedience of the Christian Man*, with its clear message about the full autonomy of royal authority, and encouraged his enthusiasm for the theological views of Thomas Cranmer.[20] At some point during 1530 Henry received the *consulta* known as the *collectanea satis copiosa* which drew his attention to a variety of arguments, both theoretical and historical, which could be used to emancipate himself, wholly or partly, from the jurisdiction of the papacy. This was a line of attack which the queen's friends had not anticipated, and against which their impregnable position in canon law offered no defence at all.

With the benefit of hindsight, later Protestant chroniclers of these events represented Anne as a champion of the reformation.

> . . . al must acknowledge this Princely Lady was elect of God a most eminent agent and actor in the most dangerous and difficult part therof. . .[21]

according to George Wyatt. Her later patronage of reforming preachers and writers can easily be substantiated, but whether this resulted from conviction or from the logic of her situation is less clear. In 1530 she had every incentive to outflank Catherine's position if possible, especially since in March Clement expressly forbade Henry to enter into any other marriage while the queen's appeal was under consideration. In June a step was taken in that direction when Anne's supporters managed to raise a petition, ostensibly from the whole nobility of England, begging the Pope to grant the king's wish in the interest of the commonwealth of England. Should this not be granted, the petition went on to warn, although England's plight would be most miserable '. . . it will not be wholly desperate, since it is possible to find relief some other way'.[22] For the time being Henry was not prepared to go beyond threats of this kind, but if he did not soon act more resolutely it was likely that his own support would wither away. It was probably awareness of this, rather than any specific event, which provoked the next crisis in the summer of 1531. A series of significant moves had taken place in the early months of the year, when the king had charged the whole body of Convocation with praemunire, and forced the clergy to accept his own authority over them 'in so far as the law of Christ allows'. This provoked renewed activity in Rome, and strong indications that the revocation of Henry's case to the Rota, which had been decreed in July 1529, was about to be implemented, and that the king would shortly be summoned to appear.

On 31 May a final attempt was made to persuade Catherine to give way. A delegation of some thirty councillors and peers waited upon her at Greenwich, pleading on behalf of the king and the realm. They were wasting their time and breath. She simply reaffirmed her status as Henry's lawful wife, and her intention to abide by the decision of the papal court.[23] It is hard to believe that either the king or his envoys expected any other response, but it provided the necessary pretext for the break up of the *ménage à trois*. Henry left the court, taking Anne with him, and leaving Catherine at Windsor. After a brief return, on 14 July, he departed again for Woodstock, leaving explicit orders that the queen was to remain where she was. Ignoring the practical realities of the situation, and standing, as she always did, strictly on her legal rights, Catherine complained vigorously at such treatment. The king exploded with wrath, declaring that he would receive no further messages, and never see her again. Directly or indirectly, Anne had now managed to despatch her rival from the royal presence, and put an end to those rumours of reconciliation with which the queen's friends had nourished themselves. But she had not, apparently, altered the legal situation at all. Neither Chapuys nor the Venetian Mario Savorgnano believed that anything had changed. There would be no annulment, not only because the Pope would refuse it, but also because '. . . the peers of the realm, both spiritual and temporal, and the people are opposed to it'.[24] Anne's victory had cleared away some, at least, of the ambiguities. Throughout the autumn of 1531 Catherine kept her own court, and became increasingly, although perhaps unwittingly, a focus for political opposition, not only to the Boleyns but also to the king.

Henry's kingship had now come to the test. Either he must make good his threats to ignore the Pope, and outface the domestic opposition, or he must back down as he had over the Amicable Grant in 1525, and find a scapegoat to cover his embarrassment. Chapuys's optimism was not shared by all the emperor's advisers. As early as November 1530 Roderigo Nino had warned his master that it was possible that the king of England would seek a *de facto* solution from his own bishops. It was even feared that in his desperation Henry would have his wife murdered. Such suspicions, however, merely demonstrate that even well-informed observers had little idea of the direction in which the king's mind was moving. By the end of 1531 he was becoming convinced that the Pope had arrogated more authority to himself than either history or scripture could justify. It was typical of Henry's psychology that, when he wanted something sufficiently, he could convince himself that he was morally and legally justified in taking it. In this case, however, he did not underestimate the difficulties presented by a combination of general opposition and the lack of any clear idea of how to proceed. William Tyndale, for all his good ideas, was a heretic and the king prided himself upon his devotion to the faith. It was probably Henry's new councillor, Thomas Cromwell, a shrewd self-educated lawyer recruited from Wolsey's household, who finally spotted a path through this thicket. Taking advantage of the anti-clerical sentiment which had been stimulated in the House of Commons by grievances over probate and mortuary fees, and by a sudden upsurge in the persecution of heresy, on 18 March 1532 he introduced into the House a petition entitled 'A Supplication against the Ordinaries'.

The meat of this petition lay in an appeal to the king as 'the only sovereign lord, protector and defender' of both the clergy and the laity to legislate in parliament for the establishment of his 'jurisdiction and prerogative royal',[25] and the resolution of the issues outstanding between the temporality and the spirituality. The cleverness of this wording lay in the fact that it took the surrender of Convocation in the previous year at its face value. The king believed that he had been accepted as 'head of the Church', whatever that might mean, while the clergy believed that their saving clause 'in so far as the law of Christ allows' meant that they had conceded nothing. Consequently, when Convocation was invited to comment upon the Supplication in April, it was actually being pressed to declare its hand. Not perceiving the danger, it entrusted the task of replying to Stephen Gardiner, the Bishop of Winchester, who produced a thumping defence of ecclesiastical independence, denying that the king had any right to legislate in parliament for the spirituality. 'We your most humble subjects may not submit the execution of our charges and duty, certainly prescribed by

God, to your highness's assent.'[26] Henry, perceiving that the formula of 1531 had been meaningless, and that he had allowed himself to be duped, reacted with fury. Moreover, because of the way in which the petition had been worded, on this issue the king had the majority of influential laymen on his side. Threatened with renewed praemunire proceedings, and with statutory attacks upon the property of the Church, Convocation surrendered and agreed to submit all future canons to the king's approval. The lord chancellor, Sir Thomas More, already in disgrace for his covert encouragement of opposition in the House of Lords, surrendered the Great Seal the next day, and Gardiner was left to salvage his endangered career by changing sides with as good a countenance as he could muster.

This surrender, as More had been the first to recognize, was the critical turning point. Whatever Convocation may have thought that it meant in 1531, in 1532 it had abandoned its independence. With Thomas Audley's appointment as chancellor, and the emergence of Cromwell as Henry's key adviser, the way was clear for the stalemate over the king's 'great matter' to be broken. Moreover, Henry had now displayed the critical resolution, and those who waited upon the wind began to rally to the Boleyn faction, in many cases almost audibly swallowing their distaste. By July talk of a second marriage was beginning to emerge into the open, but it did not immediately take place. Again the reason seems to have been hesitation over how best to proceed, given the probable obstructiveness of most of the senior ecclesiastical establishment. In this connection the death of the aged William Warham, Archbishop of Canterbury, in August 1532, made life a great deal easier. A successor was not named at once, but the opportunity now existed to appoint a more compliant primate. Henry's relationship with Anne also lost its quasi-clandestine nature. She was constantly in the king's company, and a suitable role had to be found for her in his long-planned meeting with Francis I, which was scheduled to take place during the autumn. This was not easy, because neither the French queen nor Francis' sister, Marguerite of Angoulême, was prepared to meet her as an equal, and Francis' not entirely serious suggestion that he should be accompanied by his mistress was equally unacceptable to Henry. In the event, although she was elevated to the peerage in her own right as Marchioness of Pembroke on 1 September – an almost unique mark of special favour[27] – Anne played no part in the formal proceedings. She did help to entertain the French king when he visited Calais, but that was an informal goodwill gesture, and did not compromise Francis in the eyes of the Pope, with whom he was anxious to cement an alliance.[28]

In spite of this rebuff, Anne's visit to Calais marked another step in her advance, because Henry ensured that just about every peer who was fit to travel accompanied them, and thus became associated with the new order. He may not have bothered with their ladies, because it was eventually agreed that the 'summit' proper would be men only, but he may also have been warned that many would refuse on principle, including his own sister, the Duchess of Suffolk. The trip may also have been significant in another way, because it was probably during the ten days which they spent together lodged in the Calais exchequer that Anne finally surrendered to the king's long-frustrated passion. In the circumstances which then applied, it would have been as good a way as any of forcing him to name the day. Meanwhile, Catherine remained queen. In spite of her political eclipse her estate remained undiminished, and although Chapuys constantly lamented the callousness with which she was treated, that did not extend to any physical hardship, or any loss of liberty. The only place where she was not free to go was into the king's presence. Nevertheless, she felt the dishonour of her situation keenly, and was deprived of the company of her daughter, Mary, now sixteen, which was certainly an emotional hardship. Even communication was in theory forbidden, as Henry tried to detach the girl from her fierce devotion to her mother, but in fact they corresponded regularly through trusted servants, and the king made no great effort to stop it. Although publicly isolated, Catherine cannot have been unaware of the amount of personal support which she still enjoyed, and the invaluable Chapuys provided a constant lifeline to her nephew, the emperor, whom she badgered ceaselessly to put diplomatic pressure on her errant husband.

Catherine either would not, or could not, recognize how the changes which were taking place affected her own situation. When Henry requested her jewels she refused to surrender them, partly on the grounds that the king himself had ordered her to send him no more gifts – a bitter echo of an unhappy exchange which had taken place the previous Christmas – and partly because she would not contemplate them adorning 'the scandal of Christendom'. Understandable as it was, this uncompromising attitude was politically irrelevant, and merely served to increase her own pain. No further deterioration in her relations with either Henry or Anne was possible, but the emperor began to find her an embarrassment. Unwavering in his public support, he would not risk an open rupture with England for her sake, and began to receive her reproaches with noticeable impatience. Even the Pope had not yet declared unequivocally in her favour, and it began to seem that, when he did so, Henry would act in a manner which would have been unthinkable five years earlier, and simply dismiss the verdict as *ultra vires*. The emperor was right in thinking that this new found confidence depended in part upon the understanding which Henry had now reached with Francis, an understanding which extended to a defensive alliance should Charles attack England upon any pretext whatsoever, even the enforcement of a papal decree.[29] However, he was wrong to see it entirely in that light, being confused by his own priorities. Henry was also confident that he had found the right relationship with God, and in discharging his conscience over his marriage he had also found the proper way in which to discharge his responsibility for the spiritual well-being of his subjects. Whatever may have been the case at the beginning of the 'great matter', by the time it was resolved, the issue between Catherine and Anne, and even the need for a male heir, had become part of the larger issue of the authority of the Crown of England.

By the middle of November 1532 Henry and Anne were co-habiting on a regular basis and before the end of December she was discovered to be pregnant. Having gone to such lengths to secure an heir, the king now had to move rapidly to ensure its legitimacy. Towards the end of January 1533 they were married in a secret ceremony with only the legal minimum of witnesses, and the formal dissolution of Henry's first marriage became not only imperative but urgent. Earlier in the same month Thomas Cranmer had been recalled from a diplomatic mission to the emperor to become Archbishop of Canterbury. Cranmer had been a theological adviser to the king for some three years, and was intermittently in the service of Anne's father, who since December 1529 had been Earl of Wiltshire. He was genuinely committed to Henry's cause, and although his opinions were very convenient, both for the king and for himself, there is no reason to doubt their honesty.[30] In spite of the steps which he had already taken, and the further steps which he was proposing to take, Henry duly submitted Cranmer's name to the papal consistory for approval on 21 February. Perhaps he will still hoping that diplomatic pressure would move Clement, or perhaps he was merely hoping to confuse conservative opponents at home. For whatever reason, he followed the traditional procedures. More surprisingly, particularly in view of the warnings which he had received, the Pope raised no objection, and the new archbishop was duly confirmed. A month later he was consecrated, and received the pallium, making at the same time a formal but secret caveat against his oath of obedience. The stage was now set for the last act of the 'great matter'. On 5 April Convocation declared (with a few angry dissidents) that the king's first marriage had contravened the law of God, and that no pope could dispense the resulting impediment. On 7 April parliament was prorogued, and the royal assent given to the Act in Restraint of Appeals, which formally and for the first time severed the jurisdictional links between England and Rome, and made the English clergy the final arbiters of all spiritual issues within the realm. On 10 May Cranmer convened at Dunstable the court which was to give the *quietus* to Catherine's status as queen. She, of course, did not recognize the archbishop's jurisdiction, and the proceedings, in spite of Cranmer's careful appearance of thorough investigation, were a mere formality. On 23 May he solemnly pronounced the marriage between Henry and Catherine null and void, and that between Henry and Anne lawful. Seven days later, on Whit Sunday, Anne was crowned and anointed queen, and the workmen were busy stripping Catherine's arms from the walls of the royal palaces, and even from the royal barge.

# THREE

# The Brief Reign of Queen Anne, 1533–6

Henry did his best to make Anne's coronation a joyful occasion, but it was uphill work. Although the consummation achieved in May 1533 appeared to be a great political victory (as indeed it was) it left a sour taste in the mouth. Several of the king's closest friends had been opposed to his wishes, and accepted the *fait accompli* only very grudgingly, notably his brother-in-law, Charles Brandon. This was one reason why they were all so assiduously marshalled to do the new queen honour over the four days of celebrations from 29 May to 1 June; whatever reservations either citizens or peers may have had about the king and his proceedings, they were not in evidence during that time. In fact the ceremony was a masterpiece of political showmanship. The lavish display, the huge turn-out of peers and dignitaries, the thousands of Londoners lining the route, even the prompt publication of the proceedings in the form of a tract entitled *The noble tryumphaunt coronacyon of quene Anne*,[1] all indicate a shrewd political mind, and a keen eye for detail. Anyone witnessing these events could be excused for believing that Henry had overwhelming support for the hazardous policies which Anne represented, and the more people who believed that, the truer it became. The fact that Henry subjected his wife to such an ordeal, in spite of his concern for their unborn child, is sufficient indication of the importance which he attached to these appearances, and he was right. Nor did Chapuys's contempt for 'the concubine' particularly impress the emperor, who had to decide what reaction to make in the face of such flamboyant defiance of the Catholic Church. Indeed, the king's boldness in seizing the initiative paid excellent dividends. There was actually a papal nuncio, Andrea del Borgho, resident at the English court while these dramatic events were unfolding, and he was armed with a brief ordering Henry to cease co-habiting with Anne, and return to his lawful wife. Neither Clement nor del Borgho, however, wished to precipitate a crisis, and the brief remained unused.

The emperor's advisers were divided. Chapuys urged action, and on 6 May Martin Perez had also written, advising his master to consult with the English lords, and make war upon Henry with their assistance.[2] Charles, however, doubted whether the English had the will to resist their sovereign over such an issue, and on 31 May he received a *consulta* from his council, pointing out that the emperor's concern over his aunt's honour was a private matter, which did not affect his public and political responsibilities. 'It must also be considered', the council continued,

*Title page of* The noble tryumphaunt
coronacyon of quene Anne, *1533*

. . . that although the king has married the said Anna Bulans he has not proceeded against the queen by force or violence, and has committed no act against the emperor which [he] could allege to be an infraction of the treaty of Cambrai. . . .[3]

Constantly watchful against the French, with whom Henry had already become suspiciously friendly, Charles had no desire to drive them closer together, nor to expend precious resources upon knight errantry. All this was exasperating to Catherine and her friends, already stressed by delays and equivocations. On the other hand, it is not clear what they expected the emperor to do. The Pope should pronounce sentence clearly and immediately, threatening the king with spiritual sanctions, but the only effective course for Charles would have been to resort to force, and that the queen had expressly refused to countenance. Nor would she seek refuge abroad, even by returning to Spain. In the event he confined himself to making disapproving noises, and allowing Chapuys to continue with his self-appointed task of fomenting discontent among Anne's numerous enemies.

So far, Henry had won, but it was not a very secure victory. His opponents were divided and unsure of their ground beyond the purely negative tactic of urging the king to change his mind. Catherine was a cause, not a leader, and

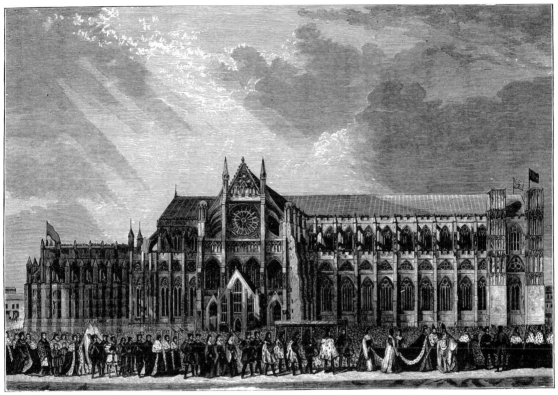

*The coronation procession of Anne Boleyn makes its way to Westminster Abbey (from a drawing by David Roberts in the Tyrrell Collection)*

there was no noble, or group of nobles, with sufficient political confidence to assume that role. Traditional complaints about evil counsel carried no weight when the policy was so obviously the king's own, and a challenge to Henry's incumbency was a last resort which no one had considered. The civil wars of the previous century had grown large in Tudor mythology, and in any case there was no plausible alternative. On the other hand, should a respected leader emerge who had sufficient skill to seize the moral high ground, and persuade the parliament to withdraw its cooperation, then the king would have been in such serious difficulties that he might have been forced to retreat. Hence the continued propaganda offensive, the determined rustication of Sir Thomas More, and the the renewed pressure upon the queen herself. The annulment of Catherine's marriage technically reduced her to the status of Dowager Princess of Wales, and such was proclaimed to be her title. She, inevitably, refused to accept any such designation, and dismissed from her presence anyone who had the temerity to use it. In July a delegation of peers, reluctantly led by her own steward, Lord Mountjoy, visited Ampthill, and required her, upon her allegiance, to accept the king's decision. She refused, declaring that her conscience took priority over all earthly allegiance.[4] The councillors threatened her with prosecution for high treason, but Henry had no wish to proceed to extremes. Studiously refusing to be provoked by her intransigence, he reduced her household to the level appropriate to a princess dowager, and allocated as her residence a former palace of the bishops of Lincoln at Buckden in Huntingdonshire. Chapuys was predictably outraged, and referred to Buckden as though it was a tumbledown shack in the fens. In fact it was a remote but commodious and spacious house in good repair. Living there was something between internal exile and house arrest. She was not allowed to leave without the king's permission, and Cromwell's agents kept a keen watch upon her household, but she was by no means deprived of appropriate service. Some eight or ten ladies were retained, of her own choosing, plus several Spanish servants including chaplains and physicians, with a modest chamber and household staff. The whole establishment cost Henry some £3,000 a year.[5] When Chapuys later described the queen and her ladies preparing their food over a fire in the privy chamber, he was no doubt describing what he had actually seen, but the reason was Catherine's increasingly paranoid fear of poison, not, as he implied, punitive sanctions imposed by a vindictive monarch.

Apart from Catherine, and her daughter, Mary, who shared all her high principled obstinacy, there were few who were prepared to take the risk of refusing royal honours to a duly crowned and anointed queen. A French observer later wrote,

> . . . the English sought, unceasingly to honour their new princess. Not, I believe because they wanted to, but in order to comply with the wishes of their king . . .[6]

and Anne probably had few illusions about the true state of her popularity. However, it really did not matter. As long as she retained the king's favour, clients would continue to wait at her chamber door, and aristocratic enemies would keep a respectful guard upon their tongues, as they had in the days of the equally unpopular Thomas Wolsey. Even the penalties of high treason did not always curb plebeian agitators or alehouse gossips, but they could be safely left to the king's ever vigilant secretary. However, Wolsey's fate also served as a warning of what could happen if Henry became disillusioned and the critics gained his ear. Having at last gratified the king, Anne's security in the summer of 1533 lay in the child which she was carrying, and in any future children which she might conceive. Henry confined his normal progress to the Home Counties out of consideration for her condition, and the court waited in high suspense for the laying-in which was due in September. Anne arrived at Greenwich to begin her customary seclusion on 26 August, indicating an expected birth towards the end of the following month. However, on 7 September she was delivered of a daughter. Whether the child was slightly premature, or the royal couple had deliberately delayed the *accouchement* in order to misrepresent the date of conception, is not known. The important thing was that the child was a girl instead of the desperately needed boy. The celebrations were low key, and

*Buckden Palace, Huntingdonshire (engraving by Buck, 1730). This became Catherine's home after the divorce*

Chapuys could hardly repress a snigger. However, this was not like the disappointment of Catherine's last miscarriage in 1518. Anne had conceived promptly, she had an easy labour, and had plenty of time to try again. Moreover, the child was healthy and perfectly formed, so it could hardly be argued that God had passed judgement against the king's second marriage, even if the fulness of his blessing was for the moment withheld. The disappointment did no recorded damage to Henry's relationship with his new queen, and the christening, which took place at the church of the Observant Friars on 10 September, was used with the same political skill as the coronation.[7]

The friary itself had been a centre of very public and vocal opposition to the divorce, and had been purged for that reason. Many of Catherine's friends were also pressed into a service which they would gladly have avoided, but dared not refuse. The Marquis of Exeter carried the taper, the marchioness was godmother, and Mary's chamberlain, Lord Hussey, helped to bear the canopy. In a ceremony dominated by the Boleyns and the Howards, with Thomas Cranmer as godfather, they were fully compromised. If anyone had hoped that the advent of Elizabeth would weaken the Boleyn ascendancy, they were swiftly and grievously disillusioned. Only time would show that the issue of an heir would continue to leave Anne vulnerable to counter-attack, and the future of the programme which she represented uncertain. For the moment her chariot continued to roll forward. She already enjoyed an independent income of £1,000 a year from the Pembroke lands, plus some other and lesser estates, and early in 1534 parliament transferred to her the queen's jointure, previously held by Catherine. With one or two further gifts from the king, this brought her revenue to over £5,000 per annum, more than that of the Earl of Shrewsbury, who was reckoned to be the richest of Henry's peers.[8] Catherine, in her retreat at Buckden, may have dreaded the onset of winter and resented her diminished state, but she continued to win small victories. When the king foolishly demanded her own christening robe for his new daughter, she sent his messengers packing. If Cromwell had any intention of ensnaring her with the dangerous prophecies of Elizabeth Barton, he failed completely, and in December she successfully withstood a determined attempt by the Duke of Suffolk to move her to Somersham in Cambridgeshire on the king's orders. Her diminished household consistently refused to address her as anything but queen, and although a few were arrested and imprisoned, no attempt was made to disband them.[9] In a sense Catherine was rapidly becoming irrelevant, and there was no point in stirring up further sympathy for her plight when she could perfectly well be ignored.

Politically, Mary had become far more important than her mother. Officially she was the Lady Mary, the king's natural daughter, but she had all her mother's obstinacy, not to say self-righteousness, and would no more accept that designation than Catherine would submit to being called Princess Dowager. On 1 October 1533 a generous household was created for her new status, consisting of 162 persons headed by her old governess, the Countess of Salisbury. This was hardly less than that which had attended her as princess, but it soon became apparent that the implementation of this plan would depend upon her own compliance. She was visited at Newhall by a group of commissioners headed by the Earl of Oxford, who informed her that the king was distressed to learn,

> . . . that she, forgetting her filial duty and obedience, attempts . . . arrogantly to usurp the title of Princess, pretending to be heir apparent, and encourage [others] to do the like. . . .[10]

They warned her that if she did not desist from her pretensions she would incur 'the king's high displeasure and punishment in law'. Confusing the succession when the official heir was another girl only a few weeks old was a far more serious matter than refusing to accept compulsory redundancy from the king's bed. Mary not only rejected this ultimatum, but in a letter of 2 October, proceeded to lecture her father on the error of his ways. Not even the most complaisant monarch could have ignored such defiance from such a quarter, and Chapuys, warmly as he approved her stand of principle, was genuinely and justifiably alarmed by the risks she was taking. In early November the plans for a new household were abandoned, and about a fortnight later her existing establishment at New Hall was disbanded. Amid theatrical scenes from Mary herself and the Countess of Salisbury, the former was despatched to Hatfield with a small group of personal attendants to join the new household which had been created for the infant Elizabeth. In theory this was to be a joint household for the king's two daughters, but of course the legitimate princess would take precedence in everything, and in effect Mary, like her mother, was under house arrest.

What part, if any, Queen Anne played in these painful developments is not clear. Chapuys blamed the whole situation upon her malice, but that is certainly untrue. Henry did not need his wife's prompting to realize that he must act resolutely. However defiant she might be, Catherine would never lead a rebellion against him, or allow herself to be used for that purpose, but Mary was young, and possibly suggestible. 'It is impossible to describe the love these people [the English] have for the Princess,' Chapuys reported on 16 October, and went on to advise the emperor that he should take immediate steps to exploit so favourable a situation.[11] Charles had no more intention of responding than he had earlier, but Anne knew the drift of Chapuys's arguments well enough, and if she did urge the king to harsh measures against Mary, it would have been no more than a prudent defence of her own and her daughter's interests. The best defence of all, however, would be to bear a son, and by February 1534 the queen was pregnant again. Henry was confident, and in April ordered his goldsmith to make an elaborate silver cradle for the expected prince, but then in July disaster struck. While the court was on its summer progress in July, Anne miscarried. The whole episode is obscure, because it seems to have been deliberately concealed. Even the miscarriage is a deduction from the fact that no preparations had been made for laying-in. The foetus must have been almost fully developed after about eight months of pregnancy, but we do not know whether it was male or female. This tragedy seems to have marked the end of Henry's prolonged honeymoon with his second queen. Memories of Catherine's misfortunes came flooding back, and the king seems to have been torn between his instinctive need to blame Anne and genuine doubts about his own sexuality. Surely he could not have offended God a second time?

We do not know how Catherine received this news, but she would have been more than human if it had not afforded her a certain satisfaction. Chapuys was highly gratified to think that God was making his displeasure at the king's behaviour so manifest, and immediately began to spread reports that Henry was having an affair with 'another very beautiful maid of honour'. The identity of this lady is elusive, and it seems likely that the king's interest in her was purely superficial – no more than a conventional 'amour' in the courtly love tradition. Although the ambassador's evidence is suspect there are other reasons for believing that the king's eye wandered during these months, and that Anne was displeased. That did not mean that the affair was serious in itself, but it was an unwelcome surprise to the queen, who had monopolized all such attentions since 1527. Catherine had occasionally been annoyed by Henry's flirtations, but they had never challenged her position. When he decided to end their marriage, it was not because he preferred another woman. Anne's position was different. She had won the king by her charm and sexual panache, and could lose him the same way. Nor would there be any shortage of willing hands to push her if she started to topple. So instead of treating these adolescent pranks with a lofty disdain she became shrewish and threw tantrums. In fact she only knew one way to hold the king's attention. It had worked through five hard and frustrating years of courtship, but it was the way of a mistress rather than a wife. Part of the trouble was that their relationship was one of genuine passion, prone to furious quarrels and emotional reconciliations, and that was not how a queen was supposed to behave. Henry was in many respects a very conventional

*The Old Palace, Hatfield (from the* Illustrated London News, *1846). This was the joint residence of Princesses Mary and Elizabeth*

man, and in making his own transition from lover to husband he had failed to appreciate her difficulty. It would be an exaggeration to say that their relationship began to cool in the autumn of 1534, but it certainly became more erratic. In spite of her resounding triumph in 1533, Anne could never relax and although he was ultimately responsible for this edginess, Henry eventually began to find it tiresome.

Had she borne a son, the whole story might well have been different. The king himself would have been more relaxed, and he might have been able to concentrate on begetting more children instead of playing the platonic gallant with the ladies of the court. Anne, however, could not pretend to be a fool or a nonentity, and the self-effacement customary in a royal consort did not suit her style at all. She remained what she had been before 1533, an astute and determined politician. In many ways her sharpness of perception and readiness of wit made her more suitable for the council chamber than for the boudoir. At first Henry had enjoyed fencing with her, and had listened to her advice, but unlike Catherine she had never learned when to keep quiet. If she disagreed with the king, or believed him to be acting foolishly, she told him so. Like their lovers' quarrels, these episodes became a part of their lifestyle, and often seem to have done no harm, but Anne, rather like Wolsey, was entirely dependent upon the favour of the king, and she was skating on thin ice by the end of 1534. One constant source of tension was Henry's eldest daughter, whose behaviour during the two and a half years which she spent in the household of her half-sister made her an affliction to herself and to everyone with whom she had to deal.[12] As she refused to have dealings with anyone who did not style her 'princess', even routine communication became well-nigh impossible. She also developed her mother's paranoid fear of poison, which placed an immense strain on Lady Shelton, the lady governess, who was responsible for her safety. Exasperated as he was by her attitude, Henry never lost his affection for Mary, and therein lay the danger which she represented to Anne. In March 1534, when the household was making a routine move, Mary refused to budge, alleging some infringement of her status. The infuriated Lady Shelton had her dumped bodily into a litter and carted off, which provoked anguished protests from Mary herself, and from Chapuys. Similarly in September 1534, when the Bishop of Tarbes paid a formal visit to Elizabeth on behalf of Francis I, Mary had to be physically restrained from forcing herself upon the ambassador, on the ground that she was the only princess in the house, and his business should have been with her.[13] Every such episode could be represented as the brutal repression of an honest conscience, and the queen was usually held responsible. This was partly because Lady Shelton was her aunt, partly because hostility could be presumed, and partly because it was politically convenient.

Anne became the equivalent of that useful medieval scapegoat, the evil counsellor. In spite of Chapuys, the emperor needed to maintain a civil relationship with Henry for his own purposes. He therefore chose to believe that Anne was bullying Mary (and Catherine) behind her husband's back. In a similar way Mary deceived herself into believing that it was not really her father who was subjecting her to such remorseless pressure, but the wicked woman who had acquired such an ascendancy over him. In fact the situation was much more complicated, and Anne wavered between somewhat hysterical outbursts against Mary and rather clumsy attempts to conciliate her. The latter were rebuffed, predictably but with quite unnecessary brutality. Early in 1534, when the queen was on a visit to Elizabeth, she offered a deal. If Mary would acknowledge her status, she would use her good offices to affect a reconciliation with the king. The response was that Mary recognized no queen but her mother; however, if the king's mistress was willing to intercede for her, she would be properly grateful.[14] To have absorbed such a studied insult with equanimity would have required either spinelessness or complete security, and Anne had neither. She could not even rely upon the act of succession which formally bastardized Mary and settled the succession upon her own children. The omnicompetence of statute was new and untried, and it was perfectly possible to argue that Mary, having been born '*in bona fide parentum*' remained legitimate in law even if the marriage of her parents was subsequently found to have been defective.[15] This was why it was so important for Anne to try to win her young enemy over, because sanctions, unless they extended to execution, could not resolve the issue definitively. Only if Mary could be persuaded to concede her claim, or if Anne could bear a son, would these doubts be laid to rest. In these circumstances, it is not surprising that the queen occasionally uttered lurid threats, ranging from an intention to curb Mary's insolence to one of having her put to death if the king should carry out his plan of going over to Calais. All these irresponsible remarks were solemnly chronicled by Chapuys, and need be taken as evidence of nothing except Anne's tense apprehensiveness. She was only slightly over-dramatizing when she declared that she was Mary's death, and Mary was hers.

It did not quite come to that, but for all her influence over Henry, Anne was unable to win this battle. In spite of the rigorous ban on their meeting, Mary and Catherine were in regular correspondence, using trusted servants who never seem to have broken faith. When the former was first placed under restraint towards the end of 1533, her mother wrote to her in the manner of an apostle to a martyr '. . . the time has come that almighty God will prove you, and I am very glad of it, for I trust he does handle you with a good love'.[16] There was an element of masochistic satisfaction about the way in which both these ladies endeavoured to increase the persecution which they were suffering, but there may also have been an element of shrewd calculation. Both knew perfectly well that they enjoyed a great deal of support, both among the populace and among the élite, and that Anne could be swept aside in a moment if she lost the king's favour. The more ill-used they could appear, the more indignant their many supporters would become, and the more opprobrium would be heaped on the queen, since everyone, for good reasons, was anxious to avoid blaming Henry. And so the myth of 'that goggle-eyed whore Nan Bullen', promoting heresies and driving a besotted king to further tyranny and brutality, took root in the popular imagination. As one French observer commented after the executions of the London Carthusians, John Fisher and Sir Thomas More, in 1535, 'The people, horrified to see such unprecedented and brutal atrocities muttered in whispers about these events and often blamed Queen Anne'.[17]

Thomas Cromwell, carefully monitoring this discontent, and countermining every attempt to give it tangible expression, knew well before the end of 1535 that Anne was a liability. Her unpopularity showed no sign of diminishing, and was adversely affecting respect both for the king's authority and for the law. 'I was the author why the laws were made', George Cavendish later made her say, 'For speaking against me to endanger the innocent. . . .' Even the religious reformers, whom she certainly patronized with enthusiasm, found her support a mixed blessing. Two generations later, in praising her promotion of 'true religion', George Wyatt acknowledged this problem:

> I have found ever the bright beames of her cleerenes more and more to shine out in every part . . . even the blacke mistes of malice and darke clouds of foule and hatful railings helpinge much therto, of thos that taught and had their tounges instructed to cover and over shaddow her glory with their most blacke and venemous untruithes, which Hel itself could and did no doubt power out against her, so especialy to cloude the blessed splendor of the Gospel beggininge then againe to shew her golden lustre upon our world. . . .[18]

Moreover, although she might be very useful to them, the reformers were in no position to be a support to her if the going got rough. William Tyndale's ideas on royal authority might appeal to the king, but he had no time for heretics, and every reason to wish to demonstrate his doctrinal orthodoxy, especially when he thought the emperor was looking. In international affairs Anne was, for obvious reasons, committed to a French alliance, and Henry was also inclined in that direction in 1534/5. There was, however, only mutual self-interest in this association, and little genuine goodwill. This made the queen's commitment vulnerable, and when in November 1534 a proposal was made for a general reconciliation which involved a marriage between Mary and the Dauphin, Anne felt betrayed, and made no secret of her feelings. Henry made an attempt to redeem the situation by proposing another union between Elizabeth and Francis' third son, but this was not received with enthusiasm, and by May 1535 Anglo-French relations had become decidedly cool. To this chill the offended queen was contributing very noticeably, but diplomatically there was no future for her in any other direction, and Henry was understandably nervous of isolation.

At the turn of the year 1535/6, Anne's fortunes hung in the balance. Her party continued to be narrowly based, but her father was now lord privy seal, and her brother was a nobleman of the privy chamber. The Archbishop of Canterbury was her firm friend, and so, apparently, was the king's all powerful secretary, Thomas Cromwell, who carried with him such satellites as Thomas Audley, the lord chancellor. The strength of her strategic position was also enhanced by the decline of some of her more obvious and powerful opponents. The Duke of Suffolk was a shadow of his former self. His wife, the king's sister, had died in 1533 and he was under heavy financial pressure. The Duke of Norfolk had long since lost all enthusiasm for his niece, but he was Cromwell's enemy rather than the queen's, and kept a very low profile during these years. Stephen Gardiner, the once powerful Bishop of Winchester, was still struggling to rebuild his career after his monumental gaffe over the petition 'A Supplication against the Ordinaries' in 1532, and was presently in France as ambassador. Among Catherine's more conspicuous friends only the Marquis of Exeter retained his place at court, although she had some strategically placed allies still among the gentlemen of the privy chamber. Catherine herself was in the throes of her last illness, and was to die on 7 January 1536, but she had long since ceased to be a leading player, and her death did nothing to strengthen the queen's position. At the same time Anne was pregnant for the first time since the summer of 1534, and Henry's hopes for a son were rising again. Should she produce a son this time, her position would be unassailable for the foreseeable future. Should she fail, all the questions which had been raised over the previous eighteen months would arise again and demand answers.

One of the problems involved in understanding the dramatic events of early 1536 is that they have been clouded by hindsight. For example, in September 1535, when the king and queen were approaching the end of their summer progress, and were at ease with the world, and with each other, they visited Wulf Hall, near Marlborough. This was the home of Sir John Seymour, one of whose daughters, Jane, was to be Henry's third wife. This circumstance has caused it to be supposed that it was in September 1535 that the king began his

*Sir Thomas More (1478–1535) (Hans Holbein, c. 1527/8). Like Fisher he refused to take any oath which assumed the justice of the king's divorce from Catherine, was committed to the Tower and executed in 1535*

pursuit of Jane Seymour, and that the terminal decline in Anne's influence consequently began at that date. There is, however, no evidence that Jane was present at Wulf Hall during the visit, and plenty of evidence that the king had been aware of her presence around the court for several years.[19] The real reason why the king chose to favour Sir John with a visit was probably the developing career of his eldest son, Edward, who was a Knight of the Body and rising in Henry's esteem. In other words the Seymours were a court family in good standing, who happened to have a suitable house in the path of a royal progress. Early in October the French ambassador reported to Francis that the king's feelings for Anne were cooling because he had found a new love, but such reports had been made before at regular intervals, and usually meant nothing more than a dance with one of the ladies-in-waiting and the sending of a conventional token. Later in October several reports speak of the royal pair as being 'merry' together, and in November she was described by a well-placed observer as having more authority with the king than Thomas Cromwell – which was praise indeed. There is no real reason to suppose that Anne was being seriously challenged for Henry's affections until well into 1536. Even the story that his attentions began to wander when pregnancy made her sexually unavailable is purely circumstantial gossip. Even those who were closest to Henry and Anne did

*Cardinal John Fisher (1469–1535), Bishop of Rochester (drawing by Hans Holbein, c. 1532). Strongly opposed to the king's planned divorce, he supported Catherine throughout the trial at Blackfriars and was fined in 1534 for denying the validity of the royal divorce. The following year he was beheaded for refusing to acknowledge the king as supreme head of the church*

not understand the nature of their relationship, where love and hate are the two sides of the same coin, and where anger, laughter and lust are blended in a bewildering kaleidoscope of behaviour. It was an unconventional relationship and Anne was a very unconventional woman. The trouble was that Henry, who was not by nature at all unconventional, had been swept along, not against his will but against his habit of mind. If those habits of mind reasserted themselves, the relationship could easily come to an end. That, however, is not quite what happened.

The story of Anne Boleyn's fall is even more controversial than that of her rise. When Catherine died there seems to have been a general feeling of relief. Perhaps Mary would be less demonstratively intransigent, now that her mother's inflexible will no longer supported her. Perhaps the emperor would feel less inclined to meddle in English affairs, and would require his ambassador to stop acting as an agitator. Perhaps those who had persisted in recognizing Catherine as queen would now become reconciled to the king's second marriage, and the threat of political instability would recede. Henry's tasteless and insensitive rejoicing has often been commented upon, but was entirely understandable in the circumstances. In spite of Edward Hall's remark that she wore yellow for mourning, Anne's reaction was probably more equivocal.[20] There was now less point in challenging her status, but it was Mary's challenge to Elizabeth which really concerned her, and that had not changed. It may also have crossed her mind that if she should lose the king's unpredictable affections, there would be no danger of his being forced or persuaded to return to his first wife. Nevertheless, with her pregnancy developing satisfactorily, and Henry in a tearing good humour, there seemed to be no tangible grounds for apprehension. Anne even made a further attempt to conciliate Mary at this point, offering herself as a 'second mother' in return for recognition. Perhaps she was trying to exploit the vulnerability of distress, or perhaps she was genuinely sympathetic. In either case she was wasting her time, because Mary was no more amenable than before. Chapuys was genuinely distressed by Catherine's death, and offended by Henry's behaviour, but with Franco-Imperial relations going through another difficult patch, there was no prospect of the emperor leaping to his cousin's defence. Moreover, the king had already told the ambassador in no uncertain terms that the relationship between himself and his daughter was none of Charles's business.[21]

Late in January, however, there were dramatic developments. Anne's pregnancy became difficult, causing her to become depressed and fretful, and on 24 January Henry had a serious riding accident which left him unconscious for two hours. He recovered quickly, but was badly shaken. Five days later, Anne miscarried of a son, and the king gave way to a fit of almost hysterical self-pity. Whether the miscarriage was, as the queen alleged, a result of shock at Henry's accident, or the culmination of the difficulties which she had already suffered, we do not know, but the consequences were extremely serious. This was, after all, Anne's second miscarriage in three pregnancies, and it is not surprising that Henry should have felt that he had been this way before. God was still denying him a son. He had been seduced into this marriage, he declared with the selective amnesia which was typical of him, and clearly God did not approve. The marriage was null and void, and he would take another wife. The trouble with the story of this outburst, and much of the circumstantial detail surrounding it, is that it comes from a suspect source, an account given to Chapuys by the Marquis of Exeter and reported to the emperor. Up to a point it rings true, but the suggestion that these rather wild remarks, uttered in the anguish of the moment, represented a considered policy statement by the king, should be treated as mere wishful thinking. It was also alleged that Henry was seriously interested in Jane Seymour by January 1536, and that Anne blamed her misfortunate partly upon the king's infidelity, with which she reproached him bitterly. There is some independent corroboration for this, not contemporary but apparently preserved in an authentic oral tradition derived from one of Anne's ladies, and set down years after by George Wyatt.

> Being thus a woman full of sorrow, it was reported that the king came to her, and bewailing and complaining unto her the loss of his boy, some words were heard to break out of the inward feeling of her heart's dolours, laying the fault upon unkindness. . . .[22]

Anne had reacted badly before, even to superficial flirtations on her husband's part, and this was a more serious involvement, so the story may well be true.

*Henry VIII at prayer (illumination from the* Liber Niger *of the Order of the Garter, c. 1534)*

It cannot, however, be substantiated that these events at the end of January and early in February led directly to Anne's spectacular fall at the end of April. Many years later the story was spread around by Nicholas Sander, the Catholic polemicist and enemy of Anne's daughter, Elizabeth, that the foetus of which the queen had miscarried was seriously deformed, and that Henry had consequently concluded that he could not be the father.[23] If the premise was correct, then the conclusion might well follow, because deformity in children was recognized at the time as a judgement of God upon both parents. It was also associated with illicit conception, and particularly with incest. Consequently it is very tempting to see the charges eventually brought against Anne in this light. The association of witchcraft with incest and other forms of illicit sex could also explain the remarks which Henry is alleged to have made about his having been unwittingly a victim of the black arts. Unfortunately for this plausible and psychologically attractive thesis, there is no contemporary evidence at all that there was anything wrong with the aborted foetus. It was of about three and a half months development, and therefore must have been closely inspected to ascertain its sex. Also, unlike the events of the summer of 1534, there was no attempt to conceal what had happened. Henry lamented the loss of 'his boy', and railed against God and fortune, but not, apparently, against Anne. It was she who accused him of infidelity, not the other way round.

None of this is quite conclusive, but it requires an extreme ingenuity of argument to explain why a deformity which must have been noticed at the end of January passed unremarked until the end of April, when it suddenly became the unacknowledged cause of a dramatic charge of treasonable adultery.[24] The truth seems to have been that Anne's position was seriously weakened by her miscarriage, but by no means destroyed.

This situation relieved the pressure on Mary, because it was no longer necessary to risk the king's wrath by upholding the Aragon marriage as a means of seeking her rehabilitation. Also it no longer mattered very much whether she recognized Anne as queen or not. So Henry temporarily abandoned his pressure upon her to take the oath of supremacy, and Mary misread the signals to mean that any weakening in Anne's position was automatically a strengthening of her own. New possibilities were also opening up. Henry's relationship with Jane Seymour had passed the point of courtly 'service', and had become an emotional reality. On level ground Jane was no match for Anne, but the ground was no longer quite level. The Boleyns carried the burden of responsibility for the policies of the last two years, which so few liked, but which no one except Fisher and More had really summoned up the courage to oppose. There were consequently quite a few guilty consciences around, which might be assuaged by Anne's displacement. For Henry there was the tempting possibility of a new start. However positively he may have felt about Anne, he knew that she represented a coolness in relations with the emperor, and however strongly he insisted, many of his subjects refused to accept Elizabeth as legitimate. A third marriage, about which there could be no doubt, might enable him to put the whole mess of the 'great matter' behind him. Whether Jane herself grasped any of these possibilites we do not know, but her ambitious brother, Edward, certainly did. Appointed to the privy chamber in March, he used his own favour with the king to stimulate Henry's enthusiasm, and entered into an alliance of convenience with Mary's supporters. Their long-term aims were not entirely compatible, because Edward undoubtedly intended to become the uncle of the heir to the throne, but they shared the immediate aim of displacing the queen, and that was sufficient to be getting on with.

Jane was carefully schooled in the kind of 'stand off' tactics which Anne herself had employed between 1527 and 1532.

> She had no greater treasure in all the world than her honour which she would rather die a thousand times than tarnish. . . .[25] etc.

When Henry was crass enough to send her a substantial present and a letter, she returned both with correct and loyal humility, but with a great show of firmness. Left to herself, Jane might very well have become the king's mistress in the spring of 1536, but that would not have suited Edward, or his new-found friends. The impact of this conspiracy upon the king is hard to assess. Chapuys, who was eager to seize upon any signal, however faint, that 'the concubine's' days were numbered, represents him as 'greatly enamoured' of Jane, and talking seriously of marriage to her. On the other hand there is plenty of evidence, almost through to the end of April, that Boleyn influence was still strong about the court, and the faction's patronage system in full working order. One of the statutes which received the royal assent on 14 April removed the town of Lynn in Norfolk from the jurisdiction of the Bishop of Norwich, and shortly after it was added to the possessions of the Earl of Wiltshire, who also received a favourable re-grant of his lease on the royal honour of Rayleigh in Essex. Even unlikely petitioners such as the Earl of Westmorland were still approaching the queen for favours. If her star was in eclipse, there were plenty of well-placed observers who had not noticed it. Politically, Anne and her supporters were fighting back, but their ability to do so effectively had to depend on the queen's ability to retain, or recover, her husband's affection and respect. Here the evidence for the critical three months from February to April is bafflingly inconclusive, but the most likely picture is that she continued to exercise her fitful magic upon him until his infatuation was suddenly turned to loathing, and he was persuaded to destroy her before he could change his mind.

It had always been possible that this would happen, as long as there was no prince to steady Henry's nerves, but the circumstances which eventually 'bounced' him into an irrevocable decision seem to have been political rather than personal. The emperor was in increasing need of English friendship, and once Catherine was dead was disposed to come to terms with the dominant party at court. By March he seems to have convinced himself that the best way to protect Mary, for whom he felt responsible, was through friendship with Anne rather than hostility. He prevented Paul III from publishing a sentence of deprivation against Henry, and let it be known that he was prepared to bargain recognition of the king's second marriage for a reciprocal recognition of Mary's legitimacy. Given the argument of '*bona fide parentum*', that was not quite as contradictory as might at first appear. It also had the immense advantage from Charles's point of view that it would block off any possibility that Henry might be tempted to repudiate Anne in order to marry in France. Perhaps he did not take Jane Seymour seriously, or perhaps his vision was blurred, as it so often had been in the past, with his own preoccupations. Cromwell, who had always been anxious to improve relations with the emperor, was supportive, and the Boleyns, sensing a new and important ally, responded positively.[26] Routine courtesies, of a kind which had always been conspicuous by their absence in dealings between Anne and Chapuys, began to appear and to be commented upon. The king, however, had his own ideas about what kind of a bargain he was prepared to strike, and any deal which involved even a partial reconciliation with Rome was out of the question. This was not at once apparent, and both Chapuys and Cromwell seem at first to have been baffled by his behaviour. When the emperor's proposals were outlined, Henry became angry, demanded that Charles should apologize for his earlier behaviour over Catherine and Mary, and offered no more than a ratification of existing treaties.

By late April the situation had become exceedingly complex. The king's demand for an apology was probably a bargaining counter which he would have been perfectly willing to abandon in return for a tacit recognition of all that he had done, including his break with the papacy. For that to have taken effect, Anne would have needed to remain in place. Mary's legitimacy could then have been conceded without any diplomatic retreat. At the same time Henry was surreptitiously encouraging Francis I to put his own pressure on the emperor, in the hope that this would make Charles more amenable to English demands. This, however, was a dangerous game to play, because Francis had secured a copy of the papal brief against Henry which Charles had suppressed, and was quite prepared to issue it if the king showed any clear indications that he was moving to the imperial side. Cromwell seems for a while to have been at a loss. His relations with Anne had sharply deteriorated, probably because she believed him to be humouring the king by encouraging his fancy for Jane Seymour. He was therefore getting perilously close to the position which Wolsey had been in. If Anne were to fall, Mary's friends might well be strong enough to secure his removal in revenge for all the support which he had previously given Anne. On the other hand, if she survived she was more likely to be an enemy than a friend in the future. Cromwell, moreover, did not believe that Henry had any chance of securing an imperial alliance on any terms which involved Charles in recognition of his ecclesiastical supremacy, and he was probably right. He also seems to have believed that Anne was encouraging the king to hold out for unrealistic conditions in order to secure her own position, and thought that she was hoping to do that by being polite to Chapuys. He therefore decided, probably around 20 April, to take a major political gamble, and changed sides.[27] For all his usefulness to the king, Cromwell could not control court faction. It was a fact of life which he had to take into account, and he must have judged at this stage that the forces were so equally balanced that his defection would make the vital difference, and again he was right.

It was because of the delicacy of the diplomatic situation, and the volatile nature of Henry's relationship with Anne, that her enemies struck in the way that they did. The king had to be temporarily convinced that she had been guilty of a monstrous and unforgiveable betrayal. The very passion which had made their union so politically potent could then be used to destroy it. Everybody, including Anne, knew that Henry's unstable affections could be alienated, but previously these moods had been of short duration, and rapidly followed by emotional reconciliation. That was why it was so important that the charge against Anne should be a capital one, and should be pressed home as quickly as possible, with every exaggeration of which a fertile mind was capable. Anger, and his own insecurity, could make the king gullible, superstitious and vindictive. At the same time her own formidable personality, and the nature of her sexual chemistry, meant that she could not be deposed and relegated to the sidelines as her predecessor had been. The ruthlessness employed against her was a measure of the extent to which she was feared. For Cromwell, however, the removal of Anne was only half the battle. On its own that would merely expose him to conservative revenge. First he had to come to terms with what has been called 'the Aragonese faction', and with the Seymour party so that a united front could be presented against the Boleyns. After that, however, the secretary's agenda was distinct and secret. By this time he knew something about Henry that the conservatives either could not, or would not, understand. Anne's presence or absence no longer made any difference to the king's commitment to his ecclesiastical supremacy.

EARL OF ESSEX.

*Thomas Cromwell, 1st Earl of Essex (1485?–1540) (after Hans Holbein). His influence over the king was highly instrumental in conveying Anne Boleyn to the Tower in 1536*

Consequently destroying the queen would not mean a reopening of negotiations with the papacy, nor would it necessarily improve relations with the emperor. Cromwell was quite happy for Mary and her friends to deceive themselves. The more they did so, the more vulnerable they would be to his second stroke. The Seymours had no particular conservative commitment, and after Anne's death the unchallenged Jane and her family would form the newly dominant faction with which he would work.

Before Cromwell joined them, the privy chamber conservatives do not seem to have envisaged any move more drastic than persuading Henry to repudiate Anne and become reconciled to Mary, an innocent approach which only demontrates how far they underestimated both the queen and her faction. Between 18 and 25 April, however, the secretary moved rapidly to secure their confidence, probably using Chapuys as a go-between. The plan which he was mainly responsible for implementing must therefore have been improvised within a matter of days, although it is probable that the raw material out of which it was constructed had been lying among the detritus of court gossip since January. How Henry became convinced that he was harbouring an adulterous viper remains uncertain, in spite of the great quantity of forensic scholarship which has recently been lavished upon these events. Anne's miscarriage almost certainly had something to do with it, but cannot have been the decisive factor, because the king was still publicly supporting his wife, and endorsing her position as late as the Tuesday in Easter week. Perhaps Cromwell talked to the midwife who must have examined the foetus closely after the miscarriage, and decided that there was enough in her description to warrant his telling Henry that he had been spared a monstrous birth, and that everyone had been too frightened to tell him so. The story need not have been true, or even plausible, to convince the king if he was in a receptive frame of mind. If such a story was used, and was wholly or largely a fabrication, it could explain both Henry's sudden change of direction, and also the failure of anything more tangible than nods and winks to emerge in the evidence presented at the actual trial.[28] Such an interpretation makes the king look a gullible ass, but it is difficult to avoid that conclusion, whichever version of events is accepted. To the contemporary mind a circumstantial tale of deformity would automatically have suggested adultery or incest, so if Henry did swallow such a yarn, it would not be surprising if he had jumped to the obvious conclusion.

If the king was persuaded in this manner, however, it remains to be decided when the critical conversations took place. On 25 April the king referred to Anne as his 'entirely beloved wife' in a formal despatch written to Richard Pate, his envoy in Rome.[29] The words were routine, but would not have been used if she had already been under suspicion, as the letter was signed by Henry himself. At the same time, it is easier to understand the dramatic events of 30 April if his mind was already poisoned with this, or some similar slander against Anne. It was on that day that the queen had a furious and very public quarrel with Sir Henry Norris, one of the king's oldest and closest friends, in which she accused him of seeking her own hand 'if ought came to the king but good', a charge which horrified Norris, and alarmed and embarrassed all who witnessed it. Henry did not respond at once. In spite of the panic signals which began to fly, Norris remained in attendance for two more days, including several opportunities for private conversations with the king, before he was arrested and sent to the Tower on 2 May. Meanwhile, Mark Smeaton, a court musician of humble origins who seems to have been mooning after Anne for some time, had been arrested and interrogated at Cromwell's house in Stepney.[30] At some point, probably on Monday 1 May, he broke down and confessed to an adultery with the queen which was almost certainly fictitious, and probably a fantasy produced by psychological pressure. Cromwell now had the 'evidence' with which to substantiate the suspicions which, if our reconstruction is accurate, he had been sowing in the king's mind over the previous few days. If Henry had been at all reluctant to believe, he was now convinced, and with the conviction came a paranoid certainty that Norris, and perhaps other men, had been involved in the same conspiracy. This conviction gave Cromwell the opportunity to strike still more decisively against the Boleyn faction. Anne's brother, George, like Norris a trusted member of the privy chamber, who could have continued to be dangerous, was caught in the same net. He had been close to his sister, and in the circumstances it was not difficult to suggest to Henry that an incestuous relationship had existed. Anne and Lord Rochford, like Norris, were arrested on 2 May and taken to the Tower. That same evening the king gave vent to his feelings in an outburst of indignation and self-pity, which showed how far his passion had turned itself inside out. Anne was now a 'cursed and poisoning whore', who had conspired to despatch not only Catherine and Mary, but also Henry's natural son, the Duke of Richmond, and the king himself.[31] Both self-control and a sense of proportion seem to have been completely abandoned, and for the time being Henry would believe any evil that he was told, however far-fetched.

It was now essential for Cromwell to prevent the king from changing his mind. This he could do partly by preventing anyone who was not in his confidence, or the confidence of his privy chamber allies, from securing access. Even Thomas Cranmer was unable to breach this security cordon, and was left to express his sorrow and incredulity in writing. The other method he could use was Jane Seymour, and while Anne was under arrest and awaiting trial, Henry pursued his new love with more enthusiasm than discretion. Chapuys was not the only person to comment how little the king seemed to mind being cuckolded, once the initial shock was over. With Anne and Rochford in prison, and the Earl of Wiltshire broken by the disaster, the Boleyn faction no longer had the weapons with which to fight. However, Cromwell did not trust the stability of the king's mood, and could not relax until the trials and executions were over. Henry's utter conviction of his wife's guilt might carry a great deal of weight with the peers who would have to try her, but it was not in itself enough. Nor would it necessarily secure the conviction of the commoners who were her co-defendants in a different court. Norris, Rochford, and Anne herself all steadfastly denied their guilt. Only the insubstantial Smeaton would confess anything relevant, and as one of Cromwell's allies, Sir Edward Baynton, put it, 'here is much communication that no man will confess anything against her, but all-only Mark of any actual thing. Whereof (in my humble conceit) it should much touch the king's honour if it should no further appear. . . .'[32] He went on to explain dutifully that he was himself convinced that they were all guilty but that it really would be necessary to produce some more evidence. Ironically this was achieved, not by investigation, nor through any formal confession, but from the semi-hysterical chatter in which Anne indulged after her incarceration. That emotional intensity which had always been a source of strength in her relations with the king now betrayed her. While not admitting actual adultery in any shape or form, she began to talk about earlier indiscretions, and this useful information was duly relayed back to Cromwell, with the result that several more men were arrested over the next few days – Sir Francis Weston, Sir Thomas Wyatt, and William Brereton, a groom of the privy chamber.

What emerged was a farrago of gossip and innuendo, much of which was unverifiable at the time, and is doubly so now. The most that can be said for it is that there could not have been so much smoke without fire, but given the super-heated atmosphere of a Renaissance court, even that may not be true. The indictments which were presented in Westminster Hall against Weston, Norris, Brereton and Smeaton on 10 May were sufficiently specific, alleging assignation and particular acts at Whitehall or Hampton Court on particular days. With the exception of Smeaton, they pleaded not guilty to all charges, but Cromwell had made sure that a reliable jury was empanelled, consisting almost entirely of known enemies of the Boleyns. These were not difficult to find, and they were all substantial men, with much to gain or lose by their behaviour in such a conspicuous theatre. The defendents were all found guilty and duly sentenced. The queen herself and Lord Rochford were tried two days later in the Great Hall of the Tower, but in Anne's case the verdict already pronounced against her accomplices made the outcome inevitable. Realizing this, she regained her composure and answered the charges in a manner which even her worst enemies found convincing and impressive. She was charged, not only with a whole list of adulterous assignations going back to the autumn of 1533, but also with poisoning Catherine, plotting to poison Mary, afflicting the king with actual bodily harm, and conspiring his death.[33] To the charges of assignation she could only respond that the encounters referred to had been entirely innocent, both in intention and event. Of course she had met and spoken with the men concerned; they were all courtiers whom she would have had some difficulty in avoiding. 'If any man accuse me,' she declared, 'I can but say "nay" and they can bring no witnesses'.[34] Witnesses could testify to the meetings having taken place, but not to anything of substance which had passed. The poisoning charges she simply denied, and the only evidence against her consisted in the unguarded words of threat which she had occasionally been provoked into uttering.

The charges of conspiracy against the king, in many ways the most serious, are also the most shadowy. Probably the bodily harm referred to was impotence, because in a very strange confrontation with his judges it was Lord Rochford who made sure that the court heard a story about Anne and her ladies allegedly joking at Henry's expense. There was a sinister implication that this had been achieved by witchcraft, and a similar innuendo can perhaps be read into the unnecessarily elaborate descriptions of the manner of her alleged seductions.[35] No specific charge of witchcraft was made, but both the long-standing popular view of Anne and also words uttered by Henry after the trial suggest that he was trying to explain his long infatuation, perhaps to himself in those terms. Witchcraft, even more than conspiracy, is in the eye of the beholder, and in the highly charged atmosphere of a sixteenth-century court, equally impossible to disprove. The queen's answer to these charges, as to the other, was composed, lucid and persuasive. 'She made so wise and discreet answers to all things laid against her, excusing herself with her words so clearly as though she had never been faulty to the same,' as one contemporary chronicler put, almost persuaded against his will. With the king's eye upon them, the peers duly did as they were required, and she was condemned. Paradoxically, in this extremity Anne found a popular support which she had never enjoyed in the days of her prosperity. Even her old enemy Chapuys reported that the people 'marvelled' at the speed and manner of her fall, and 'spoke strangely' of the king's justice. Greatly as he wished for her destruction, not even the imperial ambassador believed that the charges brought against the queen were credible.

In the context of the whole indictment the charge of incest with her brother appears superfluous – a final shovelful of evil-smelling dirt with which to bury her reputation. Yet if it was unnecessary to secure Anne's condemnation, it was the only charge of substance against Rochford, and Rochford could have remained dangerous if he had survived his sister's fall. The charge has no more credibility than the others, but he was a notorious womanizer, and was admitted to the kind of intimacies which commonly existed between siblings. Not a great deal is known about his trial, and the story that his wife testified against him may well be apocryphal. There is some circumstantial evidence that she later accepted his guilt, but that may have been the only way in which she could get a property settlement out of the king. It has also been suggested that her revulsion of feeling was due to the discovery of a homosexual affair in which her husband had been involved, but such an interpretation seems to owe more to twentieth-century susceptibilities than to any tangible evidence about the Boleyns.[36] Like Anne, George pleaded not guilty, and defended himself with an incisive wit which left the indictment in shreds. No defence, however, could be of any avail. Henry had convinced himself that the wife for whom he had taken such risks and endured such obloquy had betrayed him, by incest and by a series of adulterous liaisons, and that conviction had been communicated, via Cromwell, to peers and jurors alike. To the modern analyst it was a purely political verdict. Cromwell, the Seymours and the 'Aragonese' had formed an alliance of convenience to destroy the Boleyns, and 'stone dead hath no fellow'. However, to take such a view is to ignore Henry's emotional chemistry. His outburst of fury and injured

*The Tower of London and Traitors' Gate, c. 1550 (A. van Wyngaerd)*

righteousness when the charges sank in not only signalled the victory of Anne's enemies before any trial had taken place, but also the sudden re-activating of the royal conscience. The only way in which he could purge his own sense of guilt was to convince himself that he had been an innocent victim of fraud and deception. It was not simply that he wanted Jane Seymour; he might well have reacted in the same way even if he had never set eyes on her. What he needed again was a scapegoat, and it was Cromwell's clever manipulation of that fact which assured the success of his plot.

The Duke of Norfolk, presiding as Lord Steward over the trials of the two noble defendants, duly passed sentence, leaving it to the king's pleasure whether Anne should be beheaded or burned alive. In the event, both victims were accorded the merciful (and honourable) death of decapitation. Between sentence and execution, neither admitted guilt. Anne declared herself ready to die because she had unwittingly incurred the king's displeasure, but grieved, as Chapuys reported, for the innocent men who were also to die on her account.[37] Before her death, she swore her innocence upon the eucharist, and there is no reason to doubt the honesty of a profession made under such circumstances. Rochford similarly accepted his fate, but with no indication that he accepted the justice of it. Of the others, only Mark Smeaton said anything which could be interpreted as an admission of specific guilt, just as he had been the only one to confess an offence at his trial. Obviously if Smeaton was guilty, then the queen was also guilty, at least on one count, but there seems to be every reason for believing that she was guilty of nothing, except having too many brains and too much sex appeal. The musician's actual words were, 'Masters I pray you all pray for me, for I have deserved the death,' which could mean almost anything, but he also persisted in the truth of his earlier confession from which, at this stage, he would seem to have had nothing to gain. The truth seems to have been that Anne and Rochford certainly, and the other men probably, had indulged in a great deal of salacious banter, which was the unacceptable face of courtly love. As a result the frontiers between fantasy and reality became blurred, allowing Cromwell's adroit manipulations a degree of plausibility which they ought never to have enjoyed. Most dangerous of all were jokes about the king. If he was impotent, whose daughter was Elizabeth? If such words were uttered, they were not intended seriously, but given Henry's unpredictable sensitivities and Cromwell's sharp ears, they were incredibly foolish.

The queen's condemnation did not lead to any immediate relaxation of tension. Until her head was actually off, Henry must not be allowed any time for reflection or regret. So the verdict continued to be improved by countless rumours, some no doubt spontaneous, but others contrived to neutralize that unexpected reaction of popular incredulity which Chapuys had noticed. John Hussey, Lord Lisle's not particularly gullible agent, was one of many who hardly knew what to believe. All the slanders which had ever been uttered against women, he wrote, were,

Verily nothing in comparison of that which hath been done and committed by Anne the queen; which though I presume be not all thing as it is now

*Thomas Howard, Earl of Surrey and 3rd Duke of Norfolk (1473–1554), bearing the Lord Treasurer's staff (Hans Holbein, 1540–1). He acquiesced in the execution of Anne Boleyn, his niece, 1536*

rumoured, yet that which hath been by her confessed, and others, offenders with her, by her own alluring, procurement and instigation, is so abhominabal and detestable that I am ashamed that any good woman should give ear thereunto . . . .[38]

Strongly influenced by those whose interest lay in keeping up the pressure, the king worked himself up into a fresh fury of self-righteousness, and seems to have taken a positive delight in planning the execution of his supposedly faithless spouse. Anne herself seems to have lost that lucid composure which had so impressed observers at her trial as soon as she was returned to prison. Fantasies of rescue or release alternated with moods of almost hysterical exaltation at the thought of death. She spent much time with her spiritual guides, and in the presence of the consecrated host. On the afternoon of 16 May, the day before Rochford and the other men were to suffer, Cranmer was appointed by Henry to hear Anne's confession. We do not know what transpired, but presumably, whatever else she may have confessed, it was not guilt on any of the charges which had been brought against her. The archbishop, her friend and former client, had expressed incredulity in the first instance, and had been kept away from the scene until his intervention could accomplish nothing. Now he must have known that his doubts were fully justified, but respect for the law and loyalty to the king would have kept him silent. The following afternoon, by virtue of his office, he had to preside over what must have been the most distasteful proceeding of his career – declaring null and void the marriage which he had pronounced lawful just three years earlier. The real ground for this volte-face was that the king would have it so. Death might remove Anne, but Henry's mania for self-justification would only be satisfied by the cleaning of his matrimonial slate, and the bastardizing of his once hopeful daughter. Having convinced himself that he had been ensnared into a false marriage by a deceitful whore, he required the whole episode to be expunged from the records. It is not certain what technical pretext was used, but it had to be something which could be represented as unknown when the previous verdict had been pronounced. Professor Ives has argued plausibly that this was connected with Henry's earlier liaison with Mary Boleyn.[39] The fact of that liaison was well enough known; it had, after all, been covered by Clement's dispensation, but it could perhaps have been argued that it was not understood in 1533 to have been an impediment in Divine law which could not be dispensed. That had only been declared in a statute of 1534. An absolute ban on marriages within this particular degree of consanguinity was also included in the succession act of 1536, which followed Anne's execution and supports this line of argument.

*Thomas Cranmer (1489–1556),*
*Archbishop of Canterbury*
*(portrait by Gerlach Flicke,*
*1546)*

When Anne went to the block on 18 May 1536 she was no longer queen and no longer Marquis of Pembroke. Her honours had been stripped away, along with her reputation. Her speech from the scaffold was low key, and entirely conventional, except in one significant respect. In accepting her death, and praying for the king, she omitted all reference to the justice of the sentence, and was reported to have died 'boldly' rather than penitently or 'well'. The piety of her death, and of her preparation for it, was equally conventional. Despite her long patronage of radical preachers, and well-attested reforming sympathies, she showed no sign during these days of spiritual crisis, of being anything other than strictly orthodox in her beliefs, and especially in her devotion to the mass. Whatever we may think of Anne's activites during her lifetime, and however much she may have been hailed as a heroine of the Reformation during the reign of her daughter, she was not a Protestant at the time of her death. The only unusual circumstance was that she was not accompanied by a priest on the scaffold, but since both Protestants and Catholics normally followed that custom, it seems to have had no significance in this connection. Anne was buried in the chapel of St Peter within the Tower, where both her trial and her execution had taken place. She had risen and fallen for the same reason. A bold, high-spirited and independent woman, she had played politics for high stakes, not as an agent but as a principal. In doing so she had used the weapons with which nature had endowed her: wit, charm, intelligence and sexual magnetism. Her contemporaries, both male and female, were outraged or fascinated by her behaviour, and most women came into the former category, having no taste for an emancipation which they could neither have conceived nor utilized. While the king was fascinated her gamble worked and brought high reward, but when he became outraged she was destroyed. She was not an idealist, and was martyred for no cause. Cruel and unjust as her fate may now appear, she suffered the standard penalty of the time for being a dangerous loser. In that sense her execution was in itself a tribute to her power.

As soon as the news of her death reached the king, he set out to meet Jane Seymour at a house on the Thames where he had conveniently placed her a few days earlier. The following day, 19 May, they were betrothed.

FOUR

# The Heir Provided: Jane Seymour, 1536–7

Catherine and Anne both being dead, Henry was free to marry again, and as he still had no legitimate son, it was certain that he would do so. Observers outside England, particularly those in the papal and imperial courts, assumed that he would do what, from their point of view, was the obvious thing. He would find a bride in one of the other royal families of Europe, and renegotiate his relationship with the Church. The emperor, who was perfectly well aware of the king's attachment to Jane Seymour, nevertheless hoped that he could be persuaded to accept a Portuguese princess, or perhaps his own niece, the recently widowed Duchess of Milan.[1] At the same time, however, both Charles and Francis preferred the thought of Henry marrying another lady of his own court to the prospect of a marriage alliance with the other side. Pope Paul III was so convinced that Anne had been the root of the English problem that he was prepared to forgive the execution of Cardinal Fisher, and set aside the sentence against Henry, in return for a formal submission. At the very least it was expected that the king would submit his quarrel to the arbitration of a general council.[2] None of these things happened. Since 1533 Henry had convinced himself of the moral and legal correctness of the course which he had followed, and seems to have detached it completely from the circumstances of his second marriage. Far from repeating his appeal of that year, when Paul actually summoned a general council to Mantua in the June of 1536, Henry began to show symptoms of acute alarm, and did his very best to sabotage the whole operation. Cardinal Campeggio's hopeful preparations to return to England in the role of negotiator and cardinal protector were aborted, and the English schism continued in full force.

Jane Seymour was not the effective cause of any of this. Neither she nor her family were committed anti-papalists, let alone protestants. Mary's friends at court regarded her as an ally, and showed no inclination to divert the king from his obvious intention of marrying her. As far as they were concerned, Henry's marriage and a return to political and ecclesiastical sanity were two quite separate issues. Jane had been born around 1509, the fifth child, but eldest daughter of her prolific sire. In the early days of his reign the king had joked with Sir John about the latter's celebrated virility, but by 1536 he may well have been more than a little jealous. Such a promising pedigree may, however, have been one of the factors which drew Jane to Henry's attention. She was certainly no great beauty, as all contemporary descriptions and Hans Holbein's portrait agree. 'Of middle stature', said Chapuys, but a modern observer would be tempted to call her plain and dumpy. The fact that she was still unmarried at twenty-seven suggests that there had been no great pressure of suitors, although that may have had more to do with Sir John's inability to find an adequate dowry than with the lady's lack of charm. From Henry's point of view she was balm after the exciting but wearing turbulence of his relationship with Anne. Jane was neither passionate nor demanding. She was reputed to be intelligent, but there is little direct evidence of that. Henry's taste did not normally run to stupid or silly women, and she certainly handled her difficult spouse effectively during their short marriage, so perhaps her reputation was deserved. 'The king hath come out of hell into heaven for the gentleness in this, and the cursedness and unhappiness in the other,' wrote Sir John Russell, not without an eye to political correctness in the latter part of May 1536, but perhaps with some justification.[3]

The quality which Jane most conspicuously possessed, and for which Anne had never been noted, was a calm and self-controlled good sense. Perhaps she was docile by nature, or perhaps she had been schooled in docility. For whatever reason, she was the very opposite of her challenging and dangerous predecessor. Jane represented no ideology, and led no faction. The circumstances of her rise to fortune may have been distasteful, but she was not blamed. That virtue which looks somewhat theatrical to modern eyes was taken very seriously, and generally praised at the time, because there was no comparison with the triumph of Anne over Catherine in 1533. Anne's equally genuine virginity had been treated with incredulous scepticism, because her rival had not only been alive, but adept in presenting herself as an injured and totally innocent party. Jane had handled her brief period as 'the other woman' in February and March 1536 with low-key discretion, and it is difficult to imagine her playing the scarlet woman for years on end, as Anne had been constrained to do. On 18 May 1536, the day before her betrothal to the king and the same day as Anne's execution, Thomas Cranmer issued a dispensation for Henry to marry 'in the third and third degrees of affinity'.[4] The reason for this is obscure. There was a very remote kindred between the king and his new bride, going back six generations to Lionel, Duke of Clarence, the son of Edward III, but they were nothing like as close as second cousins. Perhaps Henry had taken one of Jane's second cousins as an otherwise unrecorded mistress; or perhaps, in view of the fragile state of the canon law in England at that time, he was simply taking no chances. Jane then retreated to Wulf Hall to prepare for her nuptials, which were conducted at Whitehall (with what can only be described as indecent haste) on Tuesday 30 May. Henry was a moral man by his own standards, and he wanted Jane badly; he may even have had no sexual relationship since the beginning of Anne's pregnancy during the previous October, and he had to play this particular game by the rules which Jane prescribed. If there was any criticism it was thoroughly muffled because the new queen was in the happy position of having no enemies, or at least none whom we know about.

In spite of its innocuous nature, the political significance of the king's third marriage was not long in emerging. Mary's friends, and the princess herself, took it for granted that her unconditional rehabilitation was only a matter of time. This did not necessarily mean that they were expecting a reconciliation with the papacy, but most of them probably were. However, they had not read the signals correctly. A few days before the destruction of the Boleyns had been put in hand, Henry had warned Chapuys,

> As to the legitimation of our daughter Mary . . . if she would submit to our Grace, without wrestling against the determination of our laws, we would acknowledge her and use her as our daughter; but we would not be directed or pressed therein. . . .[5]

Elated as he was by the fall of 'the concubine', the ambassador was consequently cautious about the possible consequences. When several of Mary's former servants turned up at Hunsdon, expecting immediate reinstatement, he sensibly advised Elizabeth's governess, Lady Shelton, to receive no one unless the king should explicitly order it. The annulment of the king's second marriage now meant that he had two illegitimate daughters, and as a member of the Boleyn kindred, Anne Shelton's own position was extremely precarious. Mary seems not to have appreciated these uncertainties. Throughout the second half of May she was receiving daily felicitations from aristocratic well-wishers, and Anne Shelton's continued presence does not seem to have struck her as having any particular significance. It was not until 26 May that her father's continued silence persuade her that she should make the first move. On that day she wrote to Thomas Cromwell, asking him to intercede for her, now that the woman who had caused their estrangement was no more.[6] The secretary's reply does not survive, but he apparently advised her that obedience was looked for as a condition of reinstatement. If that was the drift of his letter, its true import was not understood, because four days later she wrote again, asking to see her father, and offering merely 'to be as obedient to the king's Grace as you can reasonably require of me . . .'.[7] Without waiting for a reply, she then wrote direct to the king, acknowledging her offences against him, and humbly begging for his blessing. She also congratulated him upon his marriage, to make it clear that she bore no grudges upon that score. What she did not do was accept either the annulment of her mother's marriage or the king's ecclesiastical supremacy. Indeed the wording of her letter made it clear that these matters were still reserved to her conscience, and that her proferred obedience was 'under God', which was a transparent code for the kind of conditional allegiance which she had professed before.

Henry was less than impressed; indeed he seems to have been very angry, and insisted upon a series of interrogatories being drawn up for Mary which would leave no room for equivocation. Since the Treason Act of 1534 it had been high treason to withhold from the king any of the recognition or obedience to which his titles gave him claim. Knowingly or unknowingly Mary was driving the bark of her conscience straight upon the rocks. Both Cromwell and Chapuys could see what was happening, and tried for different reasons to save Mary from herself. On 6 June Chapuys thought he had succeeded, although in what way is not clear. His optimism must have communicated itself to Mary, because on the 7th she wrote to Cromwell, asking him for some token of that forgiveness which she believed to have been accorded her. On the 10th she followed this up with another letter to her father, asking for his blessing now that grace was to be extended to her. At the

*Jane Seymour (1509?–37) (Hans Holbein)*

same time she begged that he would not press her conscience further than it would bear.[8] Henry had heard all this before, and was unmoved. If she was to be received as his daughter, her obedience must be total and unconditional. On or about 15 June the Duke of Norfolk, the Earl of Sussex and the Bishop of Chichester visited her at Hunsdon, bearing the king's commission. They charged her upon her allegiance to accept both her own illegitimacy and the royal supremacy. In a furious and emotional scene, she refused. The judges advised the king that she had incurred the penalties of high treason, and the council went into emergency session. A first-rate political crisis had developed, which played with suspicious felicity into the hands of the secretary. Cromwell had never had any intention of sharing power with the religious and political conservatives who had been such useful allies against the Boleyns. Now he had them over a barrel. The Marquis of Exeter and Sir William Fitzwilliam were excluded from the council. Sir Anthony Browne and Sir Francis Bryan were arrested and interrogated 'concerning talk had of the estate of the lady Mary'.[9] If the princess remained intransigent and paid the ultimate penalty, they would all be tainted with her treason. If she surrendered, their political teeth would be drawn, and he would be left to work with the relatively innocuous Seymours. The evidence is not clear enough to be certain, but it looks very much as though Cromwell brought matters to a head, manipulating both Mary and Chapuys to bring about a rapid and explicit show-down. He had no particular animus against Mary, and his purposes would be better served by her surrender than by her execution, so he probably did use his best endeavours during the critical week of 15 to 22 June to get her off the hook; but it was surely he who had impaled her upon it in the first place.

The pressure was cruel, because Cromwell succeeded in persuading both Mary and Chapuys that the alternative was surrender or death, and the ambassador also urged her to give way, partly on the grounds that self-sacrifice would achieve nothing, and partly that a surrender made under such extreme coercion could not be binding in conscience.[10] Deprived of her mother's moral stiffening, and with friends such as Lady Hussey going to the Tower every day for defending her, Mary's resistance crumbled. On 22 June she signed the full set of articles submitted to her, and wrote to her father a covering letter of unconditional surrender. When the news of this reached the court, there was a universal sigh of relief. Her friends consoled themselves with the thought that she would now live to fight another day, while her enemies congratulated themselves upon the fact that she was now politically innocuous. No matter what casuistry Chapuys might apply she had sacrificed her integrity, and lost all credibility as a potential leader of opposition to her father's policies. Mary's state of mind in the aftermath of this crisis is hard to reconstruct. Chapuys represented her as totally shattered, and begging him to intercede at Rome to secure for her a special dispensation.[11] On the other hand her surviving letters suggest a relaxed, almost exuberant cheerfulness. She was profuse in her thanks to Cromwell for his unspecified help, which may well have included drafting the extremely 'correct' letter which at last secured her rehabilitation. But her letters to her father, and to Queen Jane also show an almost innocent desire for acceptance and reward. If they were calculated to conceal her true feelings, they were very skilfully composed. Her eventual conduct as queen, after 1553, suggests that Chapuys was right, and that Mary never really forgave herself for the betrayal of her principles. On the other hand nothing which she said or did during the remaining years of her father's life suggests that she was dissembling. She was received back into favour, and her only publicly expressed regret was the failure of repeated negotiations for her marriage. The emperor was puzzled and displeased by her attitude, especially when she later and spontaneously confirmed the genuineness of her conversion. As a loyal daughter, she would be no use to those wishing to put pressure upon Henry, and his interest in her welfare waned very perceptibly.

Jane's role in these dramatic events was positive, but low key and extremely limited. She seems to have liked Mary, which cannot have been an easy thing to do, and sympathized with her predicament. It was probably during this tense period, and while she still had the influence of a honeymoon bride, that she entreated the king to receive his eldest daughter into grace, and was told that she should concentrate upon producing children of her own rather than concerning herself over the welfare of others.[12] If she was so rebuffed it did not disconcert her, and within a few weeks she was able to pick up the threads of the same discourse in more favourable circumstances. The good-natured imperturbability which she seems to have shown at this time was Jane's greatest strength. The 'good repose and tranquillity' of the king and his existing children, she pointed out, was conducive to their own happiness, and consequently to their ability to have more children. A little tranquillity after the storms of the last few years would not, she added, do the realm any harm either. This was a theme which Henry was happy to pick up and amplify when the circumstances were appropriate. On the first occasion that Chapuys spoke with the king in Jane's presence, he suggested that she should be called 'the pacific', to which Henry responded that indeed 'her nature was gentle and inclined to peace', so much so that she dreaded war in case it should take him away from her. At the age of forty-five, Henry had become a lover again, and that was good news for the ever present issue of the succession. On 23 July the eighteen-year-old Duke of Richmond died. Whether or not the king had ever intended to name him in the succession became an academic question, but on 18 July he had given his assent to a statute confirming the nullity of both his first and second marriages, and settling the succession on any child he might have by his third wife. If Jane felt the pressure of this expectation, she never showed the slightest sign of it.

In the autumn of 1536 Henry needed all his new-found domestic peace as political opposition moved out of the court and into the country. At first sight it seems paradoxical that rebellion should only stir when the unpopular and radical Boleyn party had been defeated and destroyed. Jane had been welcomed by the conservatives. Even Reginald Pole, well on his way to becoming the king's arch enemy, had written from Italy to express his firm conviction that Henry would see the light now that the goodness of God had removed the 'cause of all your errors',

> . . . because I understand already that in place of her, of whom descended all disorders . . . God hath given you one full of goodness, to whom I understand your Grace is now married.[13]

*Henry Fitzroy, Duke of Richmond (miniature attributed to Lucas Horenbout, c. 1534–5).*

He had fallen into the same error as Mary, and it was only when the victory which they all thought they had won in May turned out to be illusory that the desperate expedient of armed resistance was resorted to. There were other reasons for the Lincolnshire rising and the Pilgrimage of Grace. Both contained a large measure of spontaneous resentment by the commons, against the religious reforms which were blamed on Cranmer and Cromwell, against the dissolution of the smaller religious houses (decreed by statute during the summer), and against the economic pressures generated by a rising level of population.[14] There were also gentry grievances which had nothing to do with the royal supremacy, over enfeoffment to use, and over the intrusion of courtiers like the Duke of Suffolk into the traditional hierarchies of those relatively remote areas. However, there was no particular reason why such discontents should have suddenly come to a head in September and October 1536, except that the critical problem of leadership had been partly solved by the recruitment of a group of disaffected courtiers. It was this factor which turned what would otherwise have been a series of disconnected and ephemeral riots into a purposeful movement which at one point had thirty thousand men in arms.

The great uprising for which Chapuys had long been looking to sweep the tyrant and schismatic from his throne, had now apparently arrived, but the ambassador had changed his tune, and the emperor was no longer even remotely

*Robert Aske, leader of the York rising, affixing his proclamation to the door of York Minster (engraving by Edward Lier)*

interested. Moreover, those great conservative magnates who had grumbled seditiously into Chapuys's ear about the iniquities of the Boleyns and Thomas Cromwell, had no appetite for a show-down with the king himself. The Earls of Derby and Shrewsbury, and even the Earl of Northumberland, whose family were heavily involved, stood aloof. Henry's treatment of his daughter conclusively demonstrated that, however those policies of which they so much disapproved may have originated, by the summer of 1536 they represented the king's true will and intention. However much the dissidents might protest the contrary, and seek to lay the blame on 'evil councillors' such as Cranmer and Cromwell, the Pilgrimage of Grace was a treasonable rebellion, and the great lords whose grandfathers would not have hesitated to lead out their retinues, instead concentrated on keeping their 'countries' quiet and obedient. Confronted by such a challenge, Henry's tactics were a mixture of deceit and bluster. It is by no means certain that he could have defeated the rebels had they continued their march south, but they could be persuaded to defeat themselves. They knew what they wanted to achieve, but in spite of the strength of their feelings they had no idea of how to achieve it. Lord Darcy might well have anticipated the words of the Earl of Manchester in 1643: 'if we beat the king ninety and nine times, yet is he still the king . . .'. There was no plausible pretender to advance against him, and Mary had just renounced any pretensions to such a role. Short of keeping a peasant army permanently in the field, which was a logistical impossibility, the leaders of the pilgrimage had given themselves no option but to believe Henry's promises. By the time that he had dishonoured them, it was too late to do anything about it.

While these great events were unfolding in the north of England, and some observers thought that Henry's Crown was tottering, Jane and Mary were exchanging small courtesies, and the latter was happily rebuilding the household,

*The Pilgrimage of Grace, 1536*

which she was now allowed to enjoy for the first time since 1533.[15] Eventually she assembled a chamber staff of about twenty-five, including several who had served her in earlier days. Jane was solicitous with encouragement and small gifts, continuing to urge the king in the direction of affection and generosity. On 6 July the royal couple had visited Hunsdon and stayed for two days. This was the first time that Henry had seen his daughter in almost three years, and the reunion seems to have advanced her rehabilitation very satisfactorily. In September the king sent her a gift of £20, and Cromwell sent a riding horse. In October the French ambassador noted that 'Madame Marie' was at court, and was 'first after the Queen'.[16] In spite of their illegitimacy, both Mary and Elizabeth were accorded precedence over their legitimate cousins, Frances and Eleanor Brandon, the daughters of Henry's recently deceased sister, the Duchess of Suffolk. The fact that these attentions were being paid at the same time as the northern rebels were demanding Mary's reinstatement in the order of succession makes it clear that the king had no doubts about the genuineness of her newly affirmed fidelity.

Meanwhile, Jane herself began to assume a major symbolic significance. Henry spoke of her as his first 'true wife', and her chamber was assembled with great care. Being, like Anne, of non-royal parentage, her attendants had not only to be of high rank, but splendidly turned out and strictly disciplined. No breath of scandal could be afforded, and in a court which had its fair share of licentiousness,

*Finished design by Hans Holbein for a gold cup made for Jane Seymour, 1536*

this required constant vigilance. Fortunately Jane, both by nature and by the warning of her predecessor, was strict. One of her ladies was Anne Basset, the step-daughter of Henry's illegitimate kinsman, Arthur, Viscount Lisle; the Lisle letters contain a long and detailed account of how young Anne had to be kitted out for her prestigious new service.[17] French hoods were not considered sufficiently decorous, and low necklines had to be discreetly filled in with 'chests'. Anne was later described as 'a pretty young creature', and it may be that the Countess of Sussex, who was responsible for the day-to-day running of the chamber, spotted a potential problem and had moved promptly to head it off. Jane's own tastes certainly ran to magnificent clothes and jewellery, but not, as far as we can tell, to lavish entertainments. In the first flush of enthusiasm, a fortnight after his wedding, Henry provided a pageant on the Thames and a magnificent joust for the amusement of his new queen, but his own jousting days were over, and he confined himself to appearing disguised as a Turkish sultan. Jane appears to have been dutifully impressed, but the event was not repeated. This was not out of any consideration of economy, because a new queen had to be an expensive asset. Masons and glaziers were busy in a dozen royal palaces taking down or defacing Anne's badges and escutcheons, in order to replace them with those of Jane. The king's painter, Hans Holbein, designed, and the king's goldsmiths made, a number of magnificent pieces of jewellery – an emerald pendant, set with pearls, and a huge gold cup weighing $65\frac{1}{2}$ oz. The latter was lavishly ornamented with the royal monogram of H & I, with Jane's arms, and with her eminently suitable motto 'Bound to serve and obey'. During the summer the queen's jointure was also transferred to her: over a hundred manors in nineteen different counties, five castles and several chases and forests, producing an income at least the equal of that which had been bestowed upon Anne.

A magnificent coronation was also intended. It was being discussed at the end of the summer progress, and various dates were being canvassed, from 29 September to the end of October. Both Catherine and Anne had been crowned, and there were those who believed (without a shred of legal justification) that an uncrowned queen lacked an essential element of her status. Chapuys heard that the ceremony was to be particularly splendid, but in the event it never took place. First there was a minor but worrying outbreak of plague in the London area, which always sent Henry running for cover, and the preparations were suspended. Then for a while the king had weightier matters on his mind as he responded to the challenge from the north. On 21 December Jane's father Sir John Seymour died, and shortly thereafter the winter set in with such severity that the Thames froze over. Christmas was kept with unusual splendour and solemnity at Greenwich, although the royal party had to ride from Westminster because of the state of the river. There was even talk of the queen being crowned at York, as part of a scheme to conciliate the north. Such a gesture might well have been appreciated, and it seems as though, for a few weeks, the king was willing to go at least some way towards meeting the grievances of the pilgrims. Robert Aske, one of the most active leaders, although not the most exalted in rank, was actually a guest at Greenwich over the Christmas period, and serious negotiations took place. However, there was to be no coronation in York either. A further rising in Yorkshire in January, led by

Sir Francis Bigod, although nothing to do with the original pilgrimage, put paid to all thoughts of conciliation, if they had ever really existed.[18]

By the end of February Jane was known to be pregnant, and all talk of a coronation was quietly dropped. Anne's condition had been no bar to her enthronement four years earlier, but there had been a particularly pressing reason for Henry to insist on that display. Jane's position was not controversial, and the king may well have considered that an enforced delay of over six months between the wedding and the coronation made the latter appear somewhat redundant.[19] It might even send out a signal of insecurity, which was the last thing that he wanted to do. As the severe winter turned into the spring of 1537, Henry had every reason to feel well pleased with himself. Bigod's rising had been a minor matter, but it had given him the perfect excuse to withdraw from all negotiations, and initiate a policy of harsh repression in the north. There had in theory been a general pardon in December, but in the new circumstances this could easily be ignored. The Duke of Norfolk, this time with adequate military support, was sent north to carry out 'dreadful execution' upon the disaffected regions. In April and May the trials of selected victims were held, and executions *ad terrorem populi* took place in five counties. The leaders of the pilgrimage, including Darcy, Hussey and Aske, none of whom had been guilty of any offence since December, were brought to London, tried and convicted. Darcy and Hussey were beheaded, and Aske taken back to York, where he suffered the same fate on 28 June. At about the same time *Te Deum* was being sung for the quickening of the queen's child, bonfires were lit all over London, and hogsheads of wine provided to drown all doubts or sympathies with 'the northern men'. Again the fervent prayers for a prince appeared in public worship, and in the private conversations of loyal subjects. The Convocation of the University of Oxford, like true academics, found three reasons for rejoicing at this season: that their Godly Prince had rescued them from the tyranny of the Bishop of Rome, that the 'rascals' raised up by the Devil against him had been routed, and that 'our most excellent lady and mistress Queen Jane . . . is great with child . . .'.[20]

This time there seems to have been no bickering or tension to put the pregnancy at risk. Had Henry learned his lesson, or was Jane really the perfect model of docility and submissiveness – the perfect sixteenth-century woman, as she has been called? Her recorded interventions in matters of state are certainly not numerous, and usually earned her a rebuke. She is reputed to have begged the king in the autumn of 1536 to spare the monasteries whose dissolution was being so ill-received in some quarters at the time. If the story is accurate, Henry warned her by the example of her predecessor not to interfere, a decision which she accepted without demur. On the other hand his reported words referred to her 'often meddling', which suggests that this was not a unique incident, but merely an unusually unfortunate one. Another glimpse of her activities six months later also suggests that she played a positive role. When the emperor sent Diego de Mendoza to England with a special commission to propose marriage negotiations between Mary and his brother-in-law, Dom Luis of Portugal, Mendoza bore special commendations to the queen. In response Jane assured both Mendoza and Chapuys that she would always do her best to advance the affairs of the emperor,

*The coat of arms of Henry VIII and Jane Seymour*

and of the princess.[21] She then went on to assure the latter that she was doing her best to persuade her husband out of his preference for France, and was quite prepared to try again. This may have been a polite fiction, but even so it does not suggest that Jane considered herself to be excluded from political discussions, or even entirely without influence. The big difference between Jane and Anne was not one of intelligence, or even of knowledge, but between a woman who knew when to stop and one who didn't. All the evidence suggests that Jane was not only a committed imperialist but also a staunch religious conservative; not a closet papist, of course, but one who was in sympathy with Stephen Gardiner and the Duke of Norfolk rather than with Thomas Cromwell. Yet her reign coincided with a period when reforming influences were at their height, and when Cromwell and Thomas Cranmer were pressing ahead with their programme against pilgrimage shrines and other traditional practices, with the king's full support. The defeat of the pilgrimage and the surrender of Mary had indicated clearly where the boundaries of Henry's tolerance lay, and the queen had even tested those boundaries herself, so she knew exactly what the rules of the game were – go devoutly to mass, and think as the king thinks. Jane is not known to have patronized divines of any persuasion, but that was more a reflection of her good sense than of her lack of devotion. She might intervene discreetly in politics, but ideological conflict was far too dangerous and stressful.

The Seymours were not, therefore, parties to the main issue which divided the king's councillors and courtiers between 1533 and 1540. With the benefit of hindsight it is hard to believe that they were not supporting the reformers, or at least that Edward and Thomas were, but there is no contemporary evidence to suggest that. Edward was already a knight and a gentleman of the privy chamber before his sister became queen. Thereafter his rise accelerated smoothly. He was raised to the peerage as Viscount Beauchamp on 6 June, and was sworn of the council on 22 May 1537.[22] In support of his new dignity he received a substantial grant of land, mostly in Wiltshire, and became Captain of Jersey. He was later to emerge as a skilful soldier, and the favour which he was to enjoy in the 1540s was to be largely on that account, but the only active service which he had seen at this time had been back in 1522, when he had been little more than a boy. On the other hand, it was not simply his kinship with Jane which earned him promotion. Unlike Sir Thomas Boleyn, Sir John Seymour, although well known to Henry, secured no preferment. Perhaps ill health prevented him from making the most of his daughter's triumph, or perhaps he was an unambitious man who preferred his retirement to the country. If that was the case, then he was followed by his second son, Henry, who never came to court except as a brief visitor, and who lived a long and obscure life on his estate. Thomas, Sir John's third son, was a courtier, but markedly less successful than his older brother. A brilliant but somewhat unstable character, he obtained a place in the privy chamber and the stewardship of Chirk Castle, but lived perpetually in Edward's shadow. The queen's oldest brother was a man of talent in his own right; loyal, sensible and accomplished, he had learned to tread the delicate path of courtly politics and retain the king's favour through numerous shifts of policy and emphasis. His first marriage, to Catherine Fillol, had been annulled on a technicality, and by 1536 he was married to Anne Stanhope. His first son by that marriage was born in February 1536, and his sister was godmother at the christening. Edward Seymour was a more substantial man than George Boleyn and his character was less flawed, but as a family the Seymours were a tractable bunch. Unlike the Boleyns they made no attempt to establish a factional dominance, and in consequence their success was little resented. Had Jane lived to bear the king more children, their uncles might have become a political force much earlier than they did, but as it was they were a danger to no one, least of all themselves.

By the summer of 1537, although Jane's pregnancy was progressing normally, Henry began to show understandable signs of apprehension. On 12 June he cancelled his progress to the north which had been intended to follow up the suppression of dissent, on the grounds that his council had advised him not to go further than sixty miles from where the queen was staying.[23] It has been unkindly suggested that the king was concerned for his own safety in a potentially unfriendly environment, but in the circumstances there was no chance of a violent reception, and his ostensible reason for staying in the south was almost certainly the real one – to reassure Jane with his presence. He may well have remembered that Anne had blamed her disastrous miscarriage in January 1536 on the anxiety which his riding accident had caused her. This time, he would stay where he was and take no risks. This, he was at pains to inform the Duke of Norfolk, who was still carrying out executions in the north, was entirely his own decision. The queen had not pressed him to remain, but rather 'was in every condition of that loving inclination and reverend conformity, that she can in all things well content satisfy and quiet herself with that thing which we shall think expedient and determine . . .'.[24] Throughout the summer the astrologers and the prophets, official and unofficial, were predicting the arrival of a prince, as they had done on numerous previous occasions. They had a 50 per cent chance of being right, and it was obviously what the king wanted to hear. Henry was so convinced that he even had a stall prepared in the Garter Chapel at Windsor for the new Prince of Wales. There seems to have been some uncertainty, even in Jane's mind, about exactly when the happy event was due, and she may well have been confused by the numerous experts, mostly female, by whom she was surrounded. She retreated into the customary seclusion at Hampton Court in late September, which suggests an anticipated birth in late October. But as with Anne Boleyn in 1533, her labour began within a fortnight, on 9 October. After an uneventful pregnancy, the birth was hard and protracted. Two days later the baby had still not appeared. Anxious prayers were offered, and a solemn procession wended its way through the streets of London. Finally, after two days and three nights,

> . . . on saint Edwardes even was borne. . .the noble Impe prince Edward . . . At the birth of this noble prince was great fires made through the whole realme and great Ioye made with thankes gevyng to almightie God whiche hathe sent to noble a prince to succed to the croune of this Realme. . . .[25]

Henry is said to have wept with emotion, as well he might considering what so many people had suffered, including himself, to bring this event to pass. In spite of its difficulty, it was a natural birth. Delivery by caesarian section in the modern sense was impossible in the sixteenth century. There was an operation, which had been known since antiquity, to remove a live child from the womb of a dead or dying mother, but none by which both mother and child could survive. Edward was named, partly for his grandfather, and partly for the date of his birth. He was a perfect and healthy child, and his mother, considering what a hard time she had had, appeared to be in no worse condition than was to be expected. The christening took place at Hampton Court on 15 October, with the traditional splendour reserved to an heir to the throne, which had not been seen in England since the ill-fated baptism of Prince Henry in January 1511. The godfathers were the Archbishop of Canterbury and the Duke of Norfolk, and the godmother Princess Mary. Edward Seymour, Viscount Beauchamp, carried the four-year-old Princess Elizabeth, for whom the day would otherwise have been too tiring. Afterwards the whole company returned to pay their respects to the queen, who was well enough to sit, warmly wrapped, in the antechamber to the chapel. On 18 October the infant prince was proclaimed Prince of Wales, Duke of Cornwall, and Earl of Caernarfon. On the same day, and in symbolic proximity to the main event, his uncle, Viscount Beauchamp, became Earl of Hertford, and received over £600 worth of land in support of his new dignity.[26] The rejoicings continued to thunder around the country for weeks, and incalculable quantities of alcohol were consumed at the expense of those loyal subjects who did not wish any aspersions to be cast upon

*Edward Seymour (1506?–1552),
1st Earl of Hertford and Duke of
Somerset, Jane Seymour's brother*

their devotion. Two thousand guns were fired from the Tower of London, and Hugh Latimer so far forgot himself as to compare the queen's delivery with that of St Elizabeth. 'Thanks to our Lord God, God of England!' he enthused, and many other reformers must have felt the same, because at last the seal of Divine approval had been set upon the king's proceedings. Nobody had the bad taste to mention it at the time, but Henry's deliberate failure to repair his relations with the papacy meant that, in the eyes of Catholic Europe, Edward was no more legitimate than Elizabeth or Henry Fitzroy had been. The king's third marriage, celebrated while the realm was in schism, was no more lawful than the second one had been, celebrated during the life of his first wife. It is understandable that no one in England should have cast this in Henry's teeth in the autumn of 1537 (it would have been a short way to a quick and painful end), but interesting that the idea does not seem to have been canvassed, even among Mary's warmest friends. Mary herself never gave the smallest indication that she regarded her new half-brother as anything less than her father's lawful heir. If there were papists in England by 1537, she does not seem to have been among them.

Meanwhile the queen was not making a good recovery. By 18 October she had developed puerperal fever, and her life was in danger. Her attendants were later blamed for allowing her to eat unsuitable things, and to take cold, but the truth was that contemporary medicine had no effective treatment for her condition. By the afternoon of 23 October septicaemia had developed and she became delirious. The following morning extreme unction was administered, and after lingering through the day, she died late that night. Whether Henry was actually with her at the time, we do not know. He was certainly at Hampton Court, having postponed a hunting trip to Esher when the news of her condition became really alarming. The sorrow was universal and heartfelt,

> . . . and of none in the Realme was it more heavelier taken then of the kynges Maiestie him self, whose death caused the kyng imediately to remove into Westminster wher he mourned and kept him selfe close and secret a great while. . . .[27]

Requiem masses rapidly followed the *Te Deums*, and formal messages of congratulation on the birth of the king's son were accompanied by rapidly composed appendices of condolence. Mary was as devastated as her father by Jane's death, because the friendship between the two women, who were only seven years apart in age, had been warm and close. Jane had not only given Henry the priceless legacy of a son, she had also given him a comfortable relationship of the kind which he had not enjoyed since the early days of his first marriage. Whether this would have endured the test of time we do not know. Perhaps after a while he would have found her meekness and lack of physical beauty as tiresome as he found Anne's passion and political wit. By dying when she did, Jane left an indelible impression of perfection, and, when his own time came, it was beside her that he chose to be buried.

No queen of England had died 'in good estate' since the king's mother, Elizabeth of York, in 1503, so the correct ceremonial required a certain amount of research. First the corpse was 'cered' or purged, and then eviscerated and embalmed. It was then encased in lead and sealed into a wooden coffin, remaining in the presence chamber at Hampton Court until 31 October. Throughout the period a vigil was maintained by ladies and gentlemen of the household, working on a shift system, and twenty-one wax tapers were kept burning. On All Saints' Day, 1 November, the bier on which the coffin rested was carried by torchlight through galleries draped in black cloth, to the chapel which was similarly hung. There for twelve days a new watch was mounted, the clergy of the chapel royal by night and the ladies of the queen's privy chamber by day.[28] Finally, on 12 November the funeral procession set off for Windsor. By tradition the king did not appear, and Mary was chief mourner, riding at the head of the procession on a horse trapped with black velvet. The interment took place in St George's chapel the following day, with great solemnity. The court remained in mourning throughout the Christmas period, which was kept at Greenwich, and it was not until Candlemas – 2 February – that Henry finally cast off his black, and a semblance of normality was restored. Jane's personal jewels were distributed among her ladies and the other members of her family. Mary, who was probably her closest female friend, also received a generous share. Her jointure lands, of course, reverted to the king. For the first time in his reign the king was without a consort, and although there was now a royal nursery, the succession still hung on the thread of one young life. Whatever Henry may have felt about his personal loss, there was soon talk among his councillors of the need for a Duke of York – the traditional title of the king's second son – and consequently plans for a new royal marriage.

Thomas Cromwell had already taken up this theme in his correspondence with ambassadors before Jane was even buried. The council, he declared, had prevailed upon his Majesty 'for the sake of the realm'. Cromwell would hardly have ventured to commit his master in this way if his statement had not been true, but it seems that the minister's enthusiasm was much greater than the king's, at least for the time being. One reason for this was the need for a stable foreign alliance. Twice now Henry had married 'for carnal affection' among his own subjects, foregoing the matrimonial weapon in foreign policy. Should he do so again, it was only too likely that the factionalism of the Boleyn era would return, and Cromwell's own position would come under challenge again. More to the point, there were ominous signs that the emperor and the king of France might be about to resolve their differences, at least for the time being. Should they do so, there would be strong pressure from the Pope for them to combine against England. In the past Francis had shown himself much more sympathetic towards Henry's idiosyncratic ecclesiastical policy than Charles had, and it was to France that Cromwell and his agents first turned. There were two possibilities: the king's own daughter, Margaret, and Marie, the widowed daughter of the Duc de Guise.[29] Marie already had one son, and by the end of December, before he had discarded his mourning, Henry was speculating pleasurably about her charms. His ambassador in France, Sir John Wallop, was enthusiastic, and believed her to be available. Consequently, in February 1538 the king sent Peter Mewtas, a gentleman of his privy chamber, across to France to secure her portrait. By the time Mewtas arrived, Marie was committed to James V of Scotland, a negotiation which had been well advanced before even Henry entered the lists, but which he had characteristically believed he could overturn. Who would want such a beggarly fellow as the king of Scots?

Warming to his task, Henry shrugged off the rebuff and picked up instead a suggestion which had come from his ambassador in Brussels. If the French had the bad taste to bestow their princesses in Scotland, he would teach them a lesson by marrying into the imperial camp. The object of his attention on this occasion was Christina, the sixteen-year-old widowed Duchess of Milan, who was also the emperor's niece. Sir Thomas Wyatt, the English ambassador with the emperor, was instructed to make the suggestion discreetly, as though it was his own idea. Christina was by this time back in the Low Countries, living at the court of the Regent. Mary of Hungary, and another gentleman of the privy chamber, Philip Hoby, were sent over secretly to inspect her. Henry was by this time sufficiently aware of his own limitations not to anticipate a successful sexual relationship with a woman whom he did not find physically attractive. He was not, therefore, sending Hoby as a kind of vicarious voyeur, but in the same spirit that his father had once sent envoys to inspect the young queen Juana of Naples.[30] With Hoby went the king's painter, Hans Holbein the younger, and the drawings which the latter brought back convinced Henry that the young duchess would be more than acceptable. Holbein later worked up these drawings into the splendid portrait

*Christina, Duchess of Milan (the portrait, now in the National Gallery, from Hans Holbein's drawings for Henry VIII, 1538)*

which now hangs in the National Gallery. As the winter turned to spring, the king began to recover his good spirits, and there was much talk of dancing and pageantry. A double marriage was proposed: Henry with Christina, and Mary with (again) Dom Luis of Portugal. By this time the king was hot on the scent, but once serious negotiations began it became clear just how tangled the diplomatic web had become. A marriage alliance with the Habsburgs was not much use in itself. Charles would at least have to undertake to include England in any peace he might make with France, and Henry was also anxious to avoid being abandoned to the tender mercies of a general council of the Church, since the Pope now seemed intent on summoning one.[31] The emperor might possibly agree to the former, but saw no reason why he should undermine his important relations with the Curia in order to get Henry off a hook of his own manufacture. At the same time the status of all the parties involved caused problems. Mary was illegitimate by English law, and had no prospect of inheriting, while Christina and Henry were related within the prohibited degrees of affinity. The kinship was not close, and could easily be dispensed, but by whom? Henry would not bring himself within reach of papal jurisdiction, and the emperor would not accept the authority of the Archbishop of Canterbury.[32]

While these negotiations ground on inconclusively, fresh prospects opened up in France. Francis' main concern may simply have been to deflect Henry from an imperial alliance, but his court was well endowed with eligible young ladies, and their names were duly canvassed: Louise and Renée, the sisters of Marie de Guise, Marie of Vendome and Anne of Lorraine. Philip Hoby chased all over France, with Holbein in tow, to secure likenesses of these alleged beauties, but with only partial success. Henry may have been elated by such a rich menu, but he was not to be deflected from his main purpose, and Francis was faced with the same demands as Charles about inclusion in international treaties and support against the threat of a general council. Nor were the difficulties all of a diplomatic nature. The king's enemies, particularly in Rome, had succeeded in giving him the reputation of a Bluebeard. Christina blenched at the thought of becoming bride number four,

> . . . for her Council suspecteth that her great aunt was poisoned, that the second was put to death and the third lost for lack of keeping her child bed . . .[33]

To have lost one wife might be counted a misfortune, but to have lost three looked like something a good deal worse than carelessness. Henry was also inclined to overplay his hand, because at the end of the day an alliance mattered more to him than it did to either of his sparring partners. When he tried to demand that all the French candidates for his hand should be paraded at Calais for his inspection, Francis taxed him with a lack of chivalry, and declared that French princesses were not brood mares up for sale. Such rebuffs were embarrassing, and eventually harmful to his cause, because as the negotiations became increasingly protracted it began to appear to both Francis and Charles that what the king of England was really doing was seeking to sew discord between them in order to protect his own position, and that the search for a bride was little more than pretence. What gave this impression particularly was the way in which the English negotiators continually probed the question of Christina's rights in Milan, which was a notoriously sensitive territory and of great strategic importance to both sides. To suggest that Milan might come to England as Christina's dowry was to be rather too clever. This was unfortunate from Henry's point of view because it was only partly true. He really did want a wife, and his own clumsiness was undermining the efforts of his ambassadors to no good purpose. In June 1538 Francis and Charles met at Nice and signed a ten-year truce which made no allusion to England whatsoever. The marriage negotiations struggled on, but made no significant progress, and by the end of the year Paul III, sensing a new advantage in the international situation, prepared to promulgate the bull of excommunication which had been prepared against Henry three years earlier,[34] declaring him deposed and his subjects absolved from their allegiance. It looked as though the lack of a wife might soon be the least of Henry's problems.

For his part, the king also began to suspect that he was being trifled with, and the threat which could be clearly perceived after the Truce of Nice prompted him to look to his own defences. Mary was now innocuous, but were her erstwhile supporters equally harmless? Politically the 'Aragonese faction' had been completely defeated in the summer of 1536, and its radical wing had been destroyed in the aftermath of the Pilgrimage of Grace, but could the loyalty of families like the Poles and the Courtenays now be trusted? The Marquis of Exeter and the Countess of Salisbury had once been high in Henry's confidence, and their support for Catherine had been muted and discreet; but there could be no doubt about their opposition to the policies which the king had been pursuing since 1533, and since the fall of the Boleyns they could be under no illusions about who they were opposing. Jane Seymour had offered a prospect of reconciliation, but since her death Thomas Cromwell was stronger than ever, the great religious houses were surrendering under pressure, and radical preachers were becoming increasingly audible. In these circumstances it was not difficult for Cromwell to persuade the king that nobles who were so completely out of sympathy with what he was doing might constitute a papal fifth column. The actions of Reginald Pole, the countess' third son, made such an idea only too plausible. Reginald had been brought up and educated largely at the king's expense, and in 1529/30 had been pressed very hard to support the campaign against Catherine.[35] When he had made it clear that his conscience would not allow him to continue down that road, Henry had, with a reasonable grace, allowed him to withdraw to Italy to continue his studies. There he had been recruited by the reforming party in the Curia, and in 1536 had been created a cardinal. In the same year he had published in Rome a fierce attack on the king of England, entitled *Pro Ecclesiasticae Unitatis Defensione*. Henry had been mortally incensed, not only by the substance of the argument, but also by what he perceived to be the perfidious ingratitude of the author. To make matters worse, at the time of the pilgrimage Pole had been sent north by the Pope to coordinate action against Henry in the hope that the emperor could be persuaded to assist the rebels. That mission had been a waste of time and energy, but it had confirmed in the king's mind the view that Reginald Pole was a traitor.

Not only might the pilgrimage have offered a lever to his foreign enemies, it also served to remind Henry that he was not entirely without challengers at home. The Countess of Salisbury was the daughter of George, Duke of Clarence, and consequently niece to King Edward IV. The Plantagenet royal blood ran in her sons, Henry, Lord Montague, Reginald and Geoffrey. Similarly the mother of Henry Courtenay, Marquis of Exeter, had been Edward IV's daughter, Catherine, and he was thus the king's cousin. The dangers of 1536 reminded Henry that there was still a White Rose, and when the international scene began to look ominous in the summer of 1538, he was alarmed to hear that it was being openly said in Italy that 'If anything should fortune to the king [of England] . . . then Lady Mary, the king's daughter, might marry with the Marquis of Exeter's son, and so they to enjoy the realm'.[36] How important such gossip was, and whether it constituted a serious threat, may well be doubted, but the king was edgy over his failure to complete a satisfactory marriage contract, and Cromwell was always on the alert for potential threats to his own ascendancy. Consequently, in the late summer of 1538 Henry was bounced into action against the Poles and the Courtenays, rather as he had been against the Boleyns. In August Geoffrey, Reginald Pole's younger brother, was arrested and taken to the Tower. There he was terrified into disclosing all sorts of inconsequential conversations which had taken place between his kindred and friends, which a determined advocate could twist to sinister purposes: the old idea that Reginald should marry Mary (which was still theoretically possible as he was only in deacon's orders), vague doubts about the sincerity of Mary's submission, and criticism of the king's ecclesiastical policy. Upon such evidence the marquis, his wife and son, Geoffrey's elder brother, Lord Montague, and Sir Edward Neville were arrested and charged with high treason.

There never was an 'Exeter conspiracy', nor is there any evidence that those accused were refusing to accept Jane Seymour's son as the lawful heir. That was the import of the story from Italy, but it is not known who the anonymous Englishman may have been who originated it, or whether he had any connection with the Courtenays. What did emerge was disaffection in the wider sense: a profound unhappiness with Henry and all his works. If thought was treasonable, then the conspirators were guilty of treason, but not in any other sense that a modern court would recognize. Nevertheless, in November the three men were convicted, and on 9 December they were executed. The marchioness and her young son remained for the time being in prison. In one sense their fate was even less justified than that of Anne Boleyn and Lord Rochford, since they were not competing for power at court, but on the other hand their alienation from the course which the king had chosen for himself made them a dangerously unpredictable element when there was a serious possibility that England might be attacked in the name of Catholic unity. Could Henry have counted on their military support if Reginald had returned in the company of an imperial army, as he was endeavouring to do? It is not surprising that on 9 January 1539 Cromwell should have told Chapuys that 'the Marquis had designed to usurp the kingdom by marrying his son to the princess and destroying the prince . . .'.[37] It was what he needed to believe. Later that month the international situation deteriorated still further. On 12 January in Toledo, Charles and Francis signed a treaty in which each undertook to make no further agreements with England. It appeared that Henry's attempts to escape from isolation had finally run into the sand, and that there would be no bride from either the Habsburg or the Valois camp. Musters were ordered all over England against the expected invasion, and some surviving conservatives such as the Countess of Salisbury and Sir Nicholas Carew were arrested, interrogated and charged with treason. Carew was executed on 3 March, while the countess was convicted and returned to prison. In case anyone should feel that Henry was not justified in his precautions, in February Cardinal Pole addressed a long exhortation to the emperor, in his own name and the Pope's, denouncing the king of England as a conscienceless tyrant, and urging all Christian princes to turn their swords against him, as against the infidel.

# FIVE

# Trial and Error: Anne of Cleves and Catherine Howard, 1540–1

At the beginning of 1539 the storm signals could not have been more clearly set. The Treaty of Toledo was the most visible warning, but it was by no means the only one. Two days after Christmas Reginald Pole, full of the bitterness which he had expressed only a few weeks before, set out from Rome with instructions to persuade both Francis and Charles to withdraw their ambassadors from England and impose a commercial embargo.[1] His unofficial but scarcely concealed agenda was to endeavour to bring about a full-scale invasion by one or both powers. At the same time the Scotsman, David Beaton, was created a cardinal and sent home with the intention of bringing James V into the anti-English alliance. The collapse of his matrimonial prospects was therefore the least of Henry's worries. War panic gripped the country. Musters were held, emergency measures were taken to strengthen the defences of Calais, Guisnes and Berwick, and hasty defence works were improvised all along the south coast.[2] The navy was mobilized, and the departure of all foreign ships embargoed. A hostile army was alleged to be assembling in the Low Countries, and invasion fleets to be gathering at Antwerp and Boulogne. However, the only thing which actually happened was that the French ambassador was withdrawn. It seems that there was also a half-hearted intention to withdraw Chapuys, but it was never implemented. Pole met with a very chilly reception from the emperor, who clearly wished to use his respite from war with France to tackle the urgent Lutheran problem at home rather than to seek problematic adventures in England in the interest of the Pope. Francis pretended to be more sympathetic, but in early March he replaced his ambassador in London, and the following month wrote to Henry disclaiming any hostile intention. As late as May the king was still reviewing his fleet and watching a march past of troops at St James', but by then the danger, if it had ever really existed, had passed. Paradoxically, the main gainer from this crisis was Henry, who in the summer of 1539 had his country behind him in a way which the dissent of 1536–7 had seemed to make impossible.

There were two main reasons for this. First, no matter how unhappy Englishmen might be with some aspects of their king's policy he was still their king, and they would defend him against his foreign enemies. Only unworldly prelates like Fisher and Pole believed that Henry's subjects would set aside their allegiance for doctrinal reasons, let alone to defend the papacy. Secondly, Henry made a calculated gesture of conciliation towards the religious conservatives in passing the Act of Six Articles in May. It is difficult to understand this act except in the context of the international situation, because it ran counter to the whole drift of policy over the previous five years, was very patchily implemented, and was virtually a dead letter five years after it had been passed. Acts of attainder against Pole, his mother, and several exiled companions, were designed to reinforce the same message. The king was no heretic but merely a victim of the Pope's malice, and any Englishman (or woman) who could not grasp that point was a traitor. It may well be that Henry had also understood how disruptive the activities of some of the more radical preachers had become, and wished to curb them.[3] There may have been an element of 'cold feet' about the Act of Six Articles but it did not signal any fundamental or long-term change of direction in religious policy. The tactical nature of these moves becomes clearer when we look at the remainder of the diplomatic context. In January, at the height of the alarms, Henry had sent Christopher Mont to the Duke of Saxony and the Landgrave of Hesse to negotiate an alliance with the Lutheran League of Schmalkalden. Similar approaches were made to Denmark, with a view to forming a common front against the Pope, but the Lutherans were not enthusiastic.[4] They suspected, rightly, that these approaches had more to do with the king's diplomatic isolation than with any genuine enthusiasm for the promotion of the Gospel as they saw it. They pressed Henry to endorse the Augsburg Confession, and he backed off. The negotiations lingered on until May, by which time the Lutheran princes had come to terms with the emperor, and the king dismissed their delegation in England with recriminations. A few days later the Bill of Six Articles was introduced into the House of Commons.

At the same time as this highly conservative piece of religious legislation was proceeding through parliament, the king was demonstrating the robustness of his anti-papalism with a calculated piece of popular propaganda. A mock combat was staged on the Thames between two barges, one representing the king and his council and the other the Pope and his cardinals. After a great deal of huffing and puffing the papal crew was duly emptied into the river to the plaudits of the multitude. Plays and interludes with a similar message were being performed on village greens and in inn courtyards all over the south of England during these months, but the same people who were applauding the downfall of make-believe popes and cardinals were gratified to discover that their king was still a devout defender of the mass and an upholder of many aspects of the ancient faith. Cranmer was disconcerted, and Cromwell discreetly withdrew his support from some of his more notorious protégés, but Henry seems to have been primarily concerned to keep his country united and his options open.

It is in this light that the king's fourth marriage must be viewed. However much he may have been 'enamoured' of Christina of Denmark or Renée of Guise, his pursuit of them had served no useful purpose. By the summer of 1539 Henry knew that he did not need to commit himself to either a Habsburg or a Valois bride in order to secure his position. If the Pope could not exploit the Treaty of Toledo, then he was unlikely to be able to mount any effective counter-attack. Since the king's roving eye had not on this occasion been captured by any beauty nearer home, there was a lot to be said for a 'neutral' foreign match. As early as June 1538 John Hutton, Henry's representative at the court of Mary of Hungary, had raised the possibility of a link with the Duchy of Cleves. The first suggestion was for a match between Mary and the duke's heir, William, but the possibility of the king himself finding a wife in the same quarter was also mooted.[5] In January 1539 the latter project was resurrected, and in the middle of March a specific negotiation began. Cleves was a significant complex of territories, strategically well placed on the lower Rhine. In the early fifteenth century it had absorbed the neighbouring county of Mark, and in 1521 the marriage of Duke John III had amalgamated Cleves-Mark with Julich-Berg to create a state with considerable resources. John and Maria had been married for some ten years before she came into her inheritance, and had three daughters in addition to William. The eldest, Sybilla, had been matched in 1527 with the Lutheran Johann Frederick of Saxony, but John was an Erasmian rather than a Protestant, and Maria was a staunch Catholic. It was their second daughter, Anne, born in 1515, who was now the object of English attention. Thomas Cromwell was the main promoter of the scheme, and with his eye firmly on England's international position, its attractions became greater with every month that passed.

In the summer of 1538 William had been recognized by the estates of Gelderland as their rightful duke, on a claim derived from his mother, but this action incensed the emperor, who refused to accept their decision. Gelderland was not a rich province, but it had access to the sea, and its acquisition by Cleves would have made the duke much too powerful for Charles's comfort. Duke John died in February 1539, but his son was, if anything, keener on the English connection than his father had been. This was not entirely for sensible reasons, because William suffered from ambitious dreams, and saw Henry as an ally against the emperor in the struggle over Gelderland. That was never a realistic prospect, but it suited Cromwell not to allow that to appear. The Duke of Cleves had the immense advantage from the English point of view of being an opponent of the Habsburgs who was not also a committed Protestant. William's position, like that of John, could best be described as 'reformed Catholic'. He was an educated, liberal man, but lacked his father's toughness and grasp of reality. Unfortunately, his sisters had not shared his upbringing. Dominated by her strong-minded and extremely conservative mother, Anne had received no education worthy of the name.[6] She had been brought up to be the bride of some neighbouring German princeling, and the only accomplishment for which she was noted was needlework. Music was not considered a becoming skill in that extremely limited world, and Anne could neither sing nor play any musical instrument. She could dance, but her repertoire was restricted to those traditional German measures which her mother had considered seemly. Those who favoured the marriage made much of her 'shamfastness', her modesty and unimpeachable virtue, trying to make her appear like another Jane Seymour. At the age of twenty-three she has been fairly described as shy, ignorant and humble. She could speak and read only Low German, and if she had any intellectual qualities they had never been allowed to appear.

None of this might have mattered if she had been a striking beauty, but unfortunately the poor girl did not possess that quality either. Cromwell, repeating what he had heard from Christopher Mont, assured Henry that Anne, '. . . excelleth as far the Duchess [Sybilla, her sister] as the golden sun excelleth the silver moon', which sounded reassuring, but actually meant nothing in the absence of a realistic likeness of Sybilla. When Henry sent, as was his custom, envoys to inspect the lady, she appeared so wrapped up that very little could be seen of either her face or body, a situation which was indignantly defended by her guardians on the grounds of her modesty.[7] It looked as though the king of England might have to take his bride on trust, which Henry was determined for sufficient reason not to do. Salvation of a sort could again be found in the talents of Hans Holbein, because it was decided that a portrait was not an affront to modesty, and he was duly admitted. The result was the well-known portrait which survives in the Louvre, and which was described by Nicholas Wotton, who certainly knew what Anne looked like, as 'very lively'. The young woman who stares blankly out of Holbein's canvas is reasonably good looking to modern eyes – more so than Jane Seymour – but totally without animation. If Henry was persuaded to allow the negotiations to be brought to a conclusion on the basis of Holbein's work, as seems to have been the case, then he was more optimistic than perceptive. By September it had been established to the satisfaction of both sides that Anne was free to marry,[8] and the English were undemanding on the matter of a dowry. The treaty was finally signed on 4 October 1539.

By comparison with the high-profile role which he had adopted while in pursuit of Christina and the French princesses in the previous year, Henry had played very little part in these discussions. He professed himself to be satisfied with the arrangements, and prepared to greet his new bride, but with none of the expectancy which had characterized each of his three previous marriages. With the benefit of hindsight it is easy to see this as significant, but it may well not have been. The king knew perfectly well that this was a diplomatic match, and accepted the reasons for which it had been made. It was a success for Thomas Cromwell's foreign policy, and given the assumptions of the time no one could reasonably have been expected to foresee how incapable this hapless German girl would be of responding to any of the expectations which were entertained of her. Anne set off at the end of October, which was not the best time of year for an unseasoned traveller, but there could be no question of waiting until the spring. Rather surprisingly in view of the way in which she was otherwise cosseted, no member of her family accompanied her, even part of the way. The excuse given for this was the whole court was still in mourning for Duke John, but since John had died in the previous February the real reason must have lain elsewhere. The English expected her to sail from Antwerp, or some other port in the Low Countries, but her officers rejected this route on the grounds that a long sea voyage might damage her health. She therefore came overland to Calais, where the governor, Lord Lisle, received her on the morning of 11 December. Whatever else her journey may have been, it had not been hasty. The first impressions were favourable. In spite of language difficulties and the deteriorating weather Anne remained gracious and sweet tempered. Lady Lisle wrote to her daughter at court that the new queen would be a pleasant and easy mistress to serve.[9] She was lavishly welcomed, and appeared to be pleased with everything, including the great ships which Henry had sent across to escort her, although it must be doubted whether she had ever seen an ocean-going ship before. She also asked to be taught some English card games, and instructed in English court etiquette.

Until the middle of December all had gone as well as could be expected, and the courtiers on both sides were speculating happily about how long it would be before a Duke of York appeared. Thereafter, however, fortune began to turn her back. The weather became stormy, delaying Anne's departure for England until 27 December, and the king was constrained to keep a solitary and impatient Christmas at Greenwich. As Anne made her somewhat stately way towards him, Henry began to fantasize. It seems that he built her up in his own mind, not only into a great beauty, but into a true romantic mistress. Fired by desire, he decided to waylay her, as he had done to Catherine in the Robin Hood impersonations of his youth. It was a silly idea for a man of his age and dignity, and it went disastrously wrong. On 31 December Anne and her train reached the bishop's palace at Rochester, and on the following morning her chamber was suddenly invaded by a group of cloaked and anonymous gentlemen who claimed to be bearing a new year's gift from the king. The princess had no idea how to respond. She spoke no English, and may well have feared that she was about to be abducted. Her servants had been given no chance to warn her, even if they knew who the mysterious visitors were, and Henry, who had led the foray in person was devastated with disappointment by her lack of wit and panache. He withdrew, and returned a few moments later in his own persona, with his companions abasing themselves on every side in case the lady should continue in ignorance. By this time it must have dawned on Anne what was going on, and she 'humbled herself very lowly'. They talked a little, as best they could, and the king embraced her, but the damage had been done. 'I like her not' he declared succinctly as he set out to return to Greenwich.[10]

An immediate crisis was avoided, because even Henry realized that he had committed himself, and could not draw back on a whim. The marriage was delayed for a couple of days in case any more or less respectable loophole could be discovered, but it could not, and the Anglo-Cleves alliance was sealed in the Queen's Closet at Greenwich on Twelfth Night, 6 January 1540.[11] In the circumstances, it is not surprising that it was a total failure. The formal splendour of Anne's official reception on Shooter's Hill, the magnificent wedding robes and jewels thinly disguised a bitterly disappointed man and a bewildered young woman who may well have been wondering what on earth she had done wrong to provoke the chill of which she must have been aware. Between that first ill-omened meeting and the wedding itself, the king had not ceased to complain: he was putting his head into a yoke, he was 'not well handled', he was going through with it only to 'satisfy the world', and so on. Nor did the attitude of his subjects help very much. The Germans, so the popular comment ran, were 'a sort of beggarly knaves', and the new queen was a heretic who would lead the king astray. All this must have been extremely alarming to Thomas Cromwell, the architect of the match. He did his best to soothe his master, and must have hoped ardently that this solemn but far from ugly girl could perform well enough in bed to

*Anne of Cleves (1515–57) (attributed to Barthel Bruyn the Elder)*

persuade her tetchy lord to put his chagrin behind him. Instead, the situation went from bad to worse. The wedding night was a fiasco. Anne was not merely a virgin, she had a kind of total innocence which might have baffled a much more ardent lover. Not only did she not know how to respond to a man, she did not even realize that a response was necessary. Her lover needed to be gentle, sympathetic and patient, and Henry was none of these things. He had been intermittently impotent for years, and was deeply unsure of his virility. What Anne herself thought of her wedding night was never recorded, although one of her English ladies expressed the view that at the present rate of progress it would be a long time before they could look for a Duke of York.[12] The queen seems to have been neither humiliated or particularly disconcerted by what had happened, and rejected with horror the suggestion that she might take some advice from a lady of experience.

The king subsequently explained his failure to consummate his marriage in terms of Anne's physical repulsiveness, which he elaborated graphically, but that may well have been a rationalization. It seems that at the time he was polite and reasonably kind, persisting for four nights before giving up with a mixture of bafflement and relief. Inevitably, the failure was not his fault. There was nothing wrong with his sexual reflexes, it was just that she did not excite him: 'I liked her not well before, but now I like her much worse.' He had done his best to do his duty against impossible odds, and reminded Cromwell, fairly enough, that this was the first time he had attempted to marry for policy rather than love. The experience did not suit his constitution. Meanwhile the policy remained valid. Charles and Francis may have had no serious intention of combining to invade England, but they were still showing too many signs of friendship for Henry's comfort. Charles V was actually in Paris on his way from Spain to Germany, and was being lavishly entertained at the French court. The Duke of Cleves may not have been a great power, nor even a particularly congenial ally, but he was well placed to make a nuisance of himself to the emperor, and whatever people in England might believe, he was not a Lutheran. Henry seems to have decided quite soon that Anne would have to go. From his point of view she had no redeeming feature, being as useless at the centre of a lively and cultured Renaissance court as she was in bed. On the other hand he did not want to upset the Duke of Cleves. However cross he may have been with Cromwell for landing him with an unsatisfactory wife, there were no signs in the spring of 1540 that the king and his chief minister were pulling in opposite directions in foreign policy.

For a while the uninformed spectator would hardly have realized that anything was amiss. Anne was not crowned, but neither had Jane been, and the royal couple appeared together in public as was expected. On 4 February they proceeded by barge from Greenwich to Westminster, and a thousand rounds of ordnance were fired from the Tower in greeting. It may have been significant that there was no grand procession through London, but in the absence of a coronation little comment was provoked. Anne's household had, of course, been set up before her arrival, amid the usual scramble of eager place-hunters. It numbered a total of 126, including a number of German ladies, a chaperone to keep them in order, and a German doctor named Cornelius.[13] Henry had insisted,

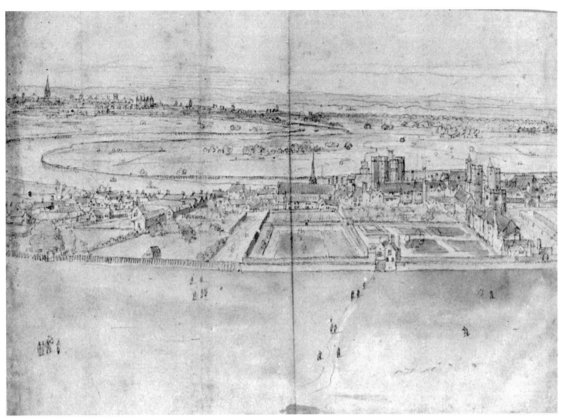

*Greenwich Palace, showing the 'recreational complex' (detail from the drawing by A. van Wyngaerd)*

as he had in the past, that all his wife's female attendants should be 'fair' – ironically in view of the fault that he found with the queen herself – and one of these well-placed damsels was a niece of the Duke of Norfolk named Catherine Howard. For the time being the public life of the court proceeded without disruption, but behind the scenes Cromwell's agents were beginning to look for ways to unravel the king's unsatisfactory marriage. A pre-contract between Anne and a son of the Duke of Lorraine going back to 1527 was resurrected. This had been known about, but the German negotiators had dismissed it as being of no significance, and the English, who had been at that time anxious for a deal, had accepted their assurance. Now they began to find it a serious obstacle, but parliament duly confirmed the queen's dower lands in April, and Cromwell had more urgent problems on his mind than the state of the king's domestic happiness.

The politics of the period from April to June 1540 are extremely hard to disentangle, but the main fact is that Cromwell was under attack from an alliance of religious and political conservatives.[14] This was not the 'Aragonese faction', which had finally been destroyed in 1538, and had nothing to do with Mary, who was now secure in her father's favour, and happy to remain so. The chief protagonists were Stephen Gardiner, the Bishop of Winchester, and the Duke of Norfolk, both long-standing political rivals whom Cromwell had outdistanced in the race for the king's favour between 1532 and 1534. Their opportunity had arisen because the Lord Privy Seal had begun to make mistakes. The Cleves marriage was one of these mistakes. On its own it might not have mattered, because there is every sign that a solution to that problem was on the way before the crisis finally exploded in June. The annulment which was finally pronounced in July would almost certainly have come at the same time if Cromwell had remained in power. The same might be said of the foreign policy which the marriage represented. Instead of picking up the second leg of the matrimonial alliance which had been canvassed – his own marriage to Mary – Duke William veered off in search of a French bride. This was a set-back, but it would not necessarily make him any less useful as an ally, and Henry continued to be anxious to make friends with the emperor's German opponents. Charles's victory over the rebels in Ghent in February 1540 made such a course more, rather than less necessary. More importantly, Cromwell misjudged the situation in Calais, and exposed himself to charges of supporting radical, even sacramentarian, preachers.[15] On 19 May he struck back, having the somewhat ineffectual Lord Lisle arrested on a charge of secret dealings with Cardinal Pole, and a week later committed Bishop Richard Samson of Chichester to the same prison.

At the end of May it appeared that the Lord Privy Seal had again emerged victorious, as he had in 1533 and 1536. He was successfully managing the affairs of what promised to be an extremely busy parliament, and as recently as 18 April had been created Earl of Essex and Lord Great Chamberlain. This time, however, he misjudged the king's political reflexes. Henry had suddenly, and for no very obvious reason, become acutely concerned about the religious disputes which were raging in London, and even in the very public pulpit of Paul's Cross. This was happening because of policies of which he was fully aware, and which had enjoyed his full backing. However, it was typical of the king that he would never accept responsibility for anything which seemed to be going wrong, and someone (probably Gardiner) succeeded in convincing him that Cromwell was responsible for the unseemly quarrels which were disrupting his Church. In a similar fashion he had condemned Wolsey eleven years earlier for exercising a jurisdiction which, at the time in question, he had fully accepted and endorsed. Very suddenly everything which had recently gone wrong, including the Cleves marriage, became Cromwell's fault, and his alone. On 10 June he was arrested, condemned by act of attainder shortly after, and executed on 28 July. Norfolk and his friends had bounced the king into a decision against Cromwell in much the same way that Cromwell had bounced him into a decision against Anne Boleyn. In both cases an irrational weakness in Henry's character had been exploited with devastating results. The unfortunate queen had nothing to do with these dramatic events. Everyone had recognized her as an expendable error, and the fall of the chief minister made no difference to that situation. Her only contribution was the purely negative one of having reawakened Henry's interest in pretty girls.

Suffering from intermittent and unsatisfied lust, and keenly aware of his advancing age and corpulence, the king was in the mood by the summer of 1540 to seize any bait which was offered him with uncritical zeal.

Catherine Howard was nineteen, a younger daughter of Lord Edmund Howard and Joyce Culpepper. Edmund, who was a younger brother of the Duke of Norfolk, sired ten children altogether, and it is not known exactly where Catherine fitted in to this brood. She was brought up in the enormous household of her step-grandmother, the dowager duchess, and seems to have received little or no intellectual training. She is normally represented as a stupid and credulous girl, but in fact there is no means of judging her true level of intelligence. She was given the conventional training of a young aristocrat, and although she had none of Anne Boleyn's exceptional courtly accomplishments, she was sufficiently presentable to be placed by Howard family influence in the household which was set up for Queen Anne late in 1539. Although there was only about five years difference in their ages, there could hardly have been a greater contrast than that between Anna and Catherine. Whereas the former was so innocent that she did not know what was supposed to happen on a wedding night, the latter was an experienced flirt. The 'maids' quarters' in the rambling great Howard mansion at Horsham had been very imperfectly chaperoned, resembling nothing so much as a modern student dormitory. The girls entertained their admirers more or less at will, and Catherine's first affair had come at the age of fourteen with a young music teacher named Henry Mannox.[16] That relationship had probably lasted no more than a year, but her involvement with Francis Dereham was much more serious and prolonged. Unlike Mannox, Dereham had sufficient status and wealth to be a serious candidate for her hand, and it may have been that consideration which prevented the duchess, who knew perfectly well what was going on, from stepping in and putting a stop to it. Catherine and Francis were lovers in the full sense for about two years, from 1537 to 1539. Contraceptive knowledge may have been primitive in the early sixteenth century, but such as it was, Catherine possessed it. In response to a warning, she replied that '. . . a woman might meddle with a man and yet conceive no child unless she would her-self . . .'[17] and whatever method she used, it worked for her.

No authentic likeness of Catherine Howard is known to survive, but she was described as being of very small stature and mediocre beauty. It was probably her youth and vivacity rather than her appearance which first attracted the king's attention, and a powerful sexuality, veiled by the compulsory discretion which must have inhibited any woman in Anne's service. She cannot have been deliberately planted by the ambitious Howard to ensnare their susceptible lord, because when her position was obtained only a few diplomats knew what the Lady of Cleves looked like, and nobody knew how Henry would react to her. However, when the king did begin to show an interest in their fledgling, in March or April 1540, neither the duke nor the dowager duchess were slow to profer their advice on how the situation could be turned to advantage. It is unlikely that Catherine's charms had much to do with Henry's determination to put an end to his fourth marriage, although they may have given him an additional incentive to complete the annulment quickly. Even a young woman of Catherine's complaisance would not have failed to see that she had everything to gain from holding out on her royal admirer. Anne's last public appearance as queen came at the May Day celebrations, but she does not seem to have been given any inclination of the king's intentions until the end of June. Meanwhile she seems to have enjoyed herself in a modest way, learning English, and making an unexpectedly favourable impression upon her husband's subjects. They liked her modesty, and as she became more at ease she obviously developed a certain charm. The fact that Henry no longer made any attempt to sleep with her does not seem to have struck her as being of any significance. It may well have been a relief.

Unravelling the marriage presented a number of problems, but nothing to compare with those which had beset the king's similar quest in 1529. Discreet probing failed to produce conclusive proof of a pre-contract, or rather failed to produce sufficient evidence of exactly what the pre-contract had been. So the main argument was non-consummation, which constituted a perfectly adequate case in canon law. Ill-informed observers who got wind of what was going on were incredulous. 'A likely thing, forsooth' scoffed the London Protestant Richard Hilles in a letter to Henry Bullinger in Zurich.[18] The king might have been flattered by this evidence of his popular reputation, but he would also have been

*Portrait miniature said to be Catherine Howard (d. 1542), c. 1540 (Hans Holbein)*

disconcerted to know that knowledge of his intentions was spread so rapidly, and that the charms of Catherine Howard were generally held to be responsible. Everything hinged upon Anne's reaction when the situation was at length made clear to her. Theoretically she and her brother were Catholics, and he at least could have refused to accept the jurisdiction of an English ecclesiastical court. Anne could have sworn that her marriage had been consummated (having been instructed in what that meant). By custom the courts always accepted a woman's testimony, although in this case it could probably have been overturned if she had been subjected to the indignity of a physical examination. If the queen had decided to fight, her brother could hardly have failed to support her, and although he was no Charles V he could have made life difficult for Henry by countermining his diplomacy.

In the event these potential difficulties evaporated. On 24 June Anne was sent to Richmond ostensibly to avoid a minor outbreak of plague, and there, on the 25th, she was visited by the king's commissioners who informed her that her marriage to Henry was invalid. This information was carefully delivered through an interpreter, and to their immense relief was received with the utmost composure. What Anne's real feelings were at that moment remain a mystery. She may have been terrified by the thought of what had happened to one previously rejected wife, whose fate had been the talk of Europe only four years before. She may have been thankful that a burden of responsibility had been lifted. Although she was in one sense at a serious disadvantage, being a stranger in a foreign country without any proper advice or support, the fact that she was free to respond in her own way was an unmitigated blessing. There was no one on hand to instil into her a defiance which was foreign to her nature. She replied that she was content with whatever the king might decide, and when she wrote her formal letter of submssion, she signed it 'Anna, daughter of Cleves'. From Henry's point of view, this was extremely satisfactory, and although the duke may have been chagrined when the news first reached him, it soon became clear that he had lost nothing. Anne's acquiescence was rewarded with a generous grant of land worth some £3,000 a year – about three-quarters of her jointure. This settlement was made for life, on the condition that she remained in England and became the king's subject.[19] The arrangement suited everyone. Henry was free to remarry, and was not worried by the prospect of a disgruntled ex-wife stirring up trouble for him in the courts of Europe. William retained the friendship of England at exactly the same cost to himself as if Anne had remained queen, and Anne herself settled down to a peaceful and affluent life. She could have as many German servants as she wished, and held precedence over all the other ladies of Henry's court, except for his daughters and his subsequent queens. This last point was not purely academic, because although it was some time before Henry could bring himself to invite her to court, her occasional visits were welcomed by both Catherine and Mary.[20] She retired to Hever Castle, which became her principal residence, and lived comfortably on the fringes of English public life.

As she got older, Anne began to show more spirit and independence. She became friendly with Mary and Elizabeth, but deeply resented Henry's sixth and final marriage. After his death she tried to get the annulment set aside, and to claim the full jointure of a queen dowager, but the council of King Edward VI was unsympathetic. Her German household caused constant small problems which occupied a good deal of her time and energy, and she began to show a strong desire to return to her homeland. The English government, however, insisted on sticking to the original agreement, and it was not in Anne's nature to persist against the odds. She consoled herself by turning her house into a miniature Rhenish court, and by soliciting invitations to Westminster or Greenwich once Mary's accession had restored a measure of seemliness to English religious life. She died at Chelsea Manor after a long illness on 16 July 1557 at the age of forty-two. She had never remarried, although there was nothing in the terms of her settlement which forbade that. Probably she had no desire to do so, because there is no suggestion that suitors had to be officially discouraged. She was buried in Westminster Abbey on 4 August with the full rites which she had requested, and mourned by many who had good cause to be grateful for her generosity. She had been a 'bountiful lady', not only to her own servants but to many of her poorer neighbours, and deserved the modest popularity which she had acquired in the later years of her life.

In the summer of 1540, however, the stream of events nudged her aside. On 9 July Convocation duly found that the king's latest marriage was unlawful, citing not only the alleged pre-contract and the non-consummation, but also that Henry had acted under compulsion. This transparent fiction was a mere embellishment, added by Cromwell's enemies to discourage any possible thoughts of reprieving the fallen minister, who was still in the Tower awaiting the attentions of the executioner. Parliament confirmed the findings of Convocation four days later, and Anne's brief reign, of just over six months, came to an end. Both the French and imperial courts greeted the news with loud expressions of incredulity and disgust, which made the lives of the English ambassadors difficult for a few weeks, but made no difference whatsoever to diplomatic relations. If the Duke of Cleves was not prepared to break with Henry over the issue, there was no cause for anyone else to do so. Meanwhile, parliament had petitioned the king to marry again for the sake of the succession, and had conveniently abolished the impediment of consanguinity as it had affected first cousins, the relationship between Catherine Howard and Anne Boleyn.[21] Although Catherine's expectations had not yet been publicly acknowledged, they were well enough known, as the king had been showering her with gifts since early April. They were married at Oatlands on 28 July, and Henry was so aroused that he had the greatest difficulty in keeping his hands off her, even in public. In one sense she was just what he needed, a vital sexual stimulant to revive his flagging energies and hopefully at last to put the succession beyond doubt. The comments on the king's demonstrative affection were therefore indulgent, even gratified, rather than critical, 'The king's affection was so marvellously set upon that gentlewoman, as it was never known that he had the like to any woman,' wrote Cranmer's secretary, Ralph Morice.[22] Ambassadors commented upon his good humour and much improved health. He hunted with zest, rose early, and showed himself at peace with the world.

Unfortunately this splendid improvement was based in part on self-deception.

*Oatlands Palace, Surrey, where Henry VIII and Catherine Howard were married on 28 July 1540 (pencil drawing by A. van Wyngaerd)*

Henry seems to have genuinely believed that his young bride was the innocent rose which she appeared to be at first sight. How he managed not to notice that she had not come to him as a virgin is something of a mystery. Perhaps enthusiasm made him unobservant. Moreover, however excellent Catherine may have been as a bedfellow, she had distinct limitations as a companion. Her education had been as badly neglected as Anna's, although for different reasons; she was also vain, greedy, and totally lacking in political sense. Because she was a Howard, and her relations were as greedy as she was, her complete ascendancy over Henry in the first months of their marriage created a political time bomb. Her lavish household, costing the king some £4,600 per annum, filled up with her numerous relations and their dependants. Suddenly the memory of Thomas Cromwell seemed a lot less obnoxious, and the blatant Howard ascendancy generated bitter jealousies and resentments. The queen needed protection from the hornets' nest which she was stirring up, because she had no resources of her own with which to do so. This was all the more critical because neither Henry nor Catherine had much stamina. If she had quickly become pregnant as a result of his ardent attentions, all would have been well, but she did not. Perhaps she was barren, and that had protected her from any consequences of her early indiscretions, but more likely the erratic fertility of her aging husband was to blame. For whatever reason, the success for which even disgruntled courtiers would have been prepared to overlook Catherine's shortcomings did not materialize.

Henry's fifth queen was never crowned, for reasons which are now obscure, considering how besotted he was with her.[23] On the other hand she was given a far larger jointure than Jane Seymour had enjoyed, including substantial parts of the estates of the late Earl of Essex, Walter Lord Hungerford, and the abbeys of Reading and Glastonbury. Jewels, rich clothes and public adulation were showered upon her, and her character lacked the stability to cope with this sudden onrush of fortune. At first she was a sufficiently dutiful and submissive wife. She chose (or had chosen for her) the admirable motto *Non autre volonte que la sienne* – No other wish but his – and this seems to have represented fairly the spirit with which she embarked upon her marriage. It did not require any great readjustment for the king to be the centre of her universe; she was a courtier and a member of a courtly family. The exact nature of her feelings for her husband, however, are not easy to undestand. On the one hand she seems to have believed him to be as omnipotent and omniscient as God, knowing what sins his subjects had revealed in the confessional by virtue of his office as supreme head.[24] Bizarre as it sounds, she may even have believed that he knew of, and condoned, her own past without any word from her. She was also genuinely grateful for his generosity. On the other hand love in the romantic sense hardly entered into it. She knew all the right physical responses, but passion and emotional commitment could not be summoned up by an act of will. Consequently it was an unequal relationship in every sense and built on sand in terms of compatibility. Within a few months it began to become apparent that in Henry's case an ardent spirit was outrunning a flagging body. At forty-eight he could no longer dance all night and hunt all day, and the realization began to undermine his newly recovered confidence. He became restless and fretful, and then in March 1541 the chronic ulcer on his leg closed up, and for about a week it was feared that he might die. By then his weight had also increased and his temper, always unpredictable, became savage and morose.

In the throes of this illness he began to recall Thomas Cromwell with somewhat maudlin regret, and to blame his present councillors for having destroyed 'the best servant he ever had'. 'He began', as the French ambassador commented, 'to have a sinister opinion of some of his chief men. . . .' His subjects were equally unsatisfactory, '. . . an unhappy people to govern',[25] he lamented. For about ten or twelve days he refused to see Catherine altogether. This was not because she had in any way offended him, but because he was keenly aware what a gross and unattractive figure he presented. After about a fortnight he recovered, but the careless rapture of the previous summer had gone, never to return. Henry continued to have bursts of youthful energy, but the intervals between them became longer and more depressed. His wife had now to prove her mettle. A suitable toy or pet for his days of happiness, she lacked the resources to be equally pleasing and supportive when the black mood was upon him, and pain or illness clouded his judgement. It may have been to avoid the stress of a situation which was beyond her, or it may simply have been on account of an irresponsible streak in her personality, but at some point during the spring of 1541 Catherine renewed a relationship with one of her former admirers, a young gentleman named Thomas Culpepper. Culpepper was a junior member of the king's privy chamber, an ambitious womanizer with a ruthless and unpleasant streak in his personality. His intention seems to have been to establish a hold over the queen, with a view to marrying her when Henry's deteriorating health eventually carried him off. In the spring of 1541 that must have seemed fairly imminent. Catherine had little or no conventional morality, and understandably found the king a very unsatisfactory lover, however much she may have been in awe of him in other respects. She needed the gratification of Culpepper's advances, and may even have believed that she would be more pleasing to Henry if she kept herself in good practice.[26]

For whatever reason she may initially have taken up with Culpepper, Catherine soon became ensnared by her own emotions. She wrote passionate letters to her paramour, one of which has survived, and took into her confidence the principal lady of her privy chamber, Lady Jane Rochford, George Boleyn's widow. Whether it was devotion to her mistress, handsome financial reward, or simply a love of mischief and intrigue which prompted Lady Rochford into this dangerous course is not known, but her vigilance protected the queen's guilty secrets for some time; secrets because Culpepper was not the only gentleman admitted to intimacy. In August 1541 Catherine appointed as her private secretary no less a person than her former lover Francis Dereham. Nobody found it odd that she should find a position for an old friend, but then nobody at court knew what the nature of that friendship had been. Throughout the royal progress which took the king and queen to York in July and August, Culpepper continued his secret assignations with Jane Rochford's connivance, at exactly the time when Henry was congratulating himself upon his good fortune in finding so virtuous a wife. On 1 November, when they were back at Hampton Court, he even offered a solemn thanksgiving for the happiness which the queen had brought him. By that time the feckless Dereham was boasting of the same thing, and it could only have been a matter of time before the whole scandal was brought into the open.

Catherine was fatally vulnerable. Not only does she seem to have been unable to control her impulses, she also had many enemies. Some hated the Howards as factional rivals, and hated the queen particularly as the instrument and symbol of their ascendancy. Some also hated them for having brought about the fall of Cromwell, and apparently frustrated the advance of the Gospel since 1539. She was also open to blackmail. As early as 12 July 1540 one Joan Bulmer, a 'bedfellow' of Catherine's during the days of her youthful indiscretions at Horsham, wrote to her effectively demanding a place at court, which was duly provided.[27] Francis Dereham could also have ruined her if he had not been given a profitable preferment. Catherine had simply given too many hostages to fortune, and the remarkable thing is that Henry's self-deception was allowed to continue for as long as it did. There was plenty of gossip during the progress, and the king must have been almost the only person at court who did not harbour some suspicion of the queen. The pebble which eventually dislodged this inevitable avalanche was a man called John Lascelles. Lascelles was a Protestant, whose life was to end at the stake five years later, and he seems to have been motivated entirely by religious zeal. His sister, Mary Hall, had been in the service of the Dowager Duchess of Norfolk, and was one of a number of young women who must have known a lot to Catherine's discredit. Joan Bulmer turned her knowledge to profit, Mary Hall placed hers at the service of her brother's convictions. On 1 November, ironically at the same time that the king was celebrating his thanksgiving, Lascelles sought out the Archbishop of Canterbury and told him all that he had heard.[28]

The surviving letter from Catherine Howard to Thomas Culpepper, 1541. She says, 'I never longed so much for [a] thing as I do to see you and to speak with you, the which I trust shall be shortly now.'

His story was so circumstantial and convincing that Cranmer realized immediately that it would be his unpleasant task to break this news to the king. What Lascelles knew, of course, related entirely to the time before Catherine's marriage to the king, so it did not convict her of adultery. What it did was to prove conclusively that she was no innocent rose when the king married her, and to raise the possibility that she had actually been contracted to Dereham. On the following day, 2 November, Cranmer passed a discreet note to the king during mass, with a request that he read it in private. By this time he had also shared his knowledge with two other members of the council, the Lord Chancellor Sir Thomas Audley and the Earl of Hertford. Both were antipathetic to the Howards, but neither had the courage to confront the king. If they feared an explosion of wrath, however, they need not have worried. Henry's first reaction was to shrug off the report as a slanderous forgery. He ordered a secret enquiry, but believed it to be for no other purpose than to protect his wife's good name against calumny. The Earl of Southampton was sent to examine Lascelles, who repeated his story, and then down to Sussex to interview Mary Hall. Meanwhile Sir Thomas Wriothesley arrested Francis Dereham, allegedly on suspicion of piracy, and also detained Henry Mannox. Under pressure both Mannox and Dereham confessed, while Mary Hall confirmed her brother's story in every particular. The king was still not convinced, but Catherine was ordered to keep to her chamber and await his pleasure. On 6 November he returned to London without seeing her, and met his privy council in emergency session at the Bishop of Winchester's residence in Southwark. By this time several of the queen's ladies had also been arrested, and Dereham under interrogation had implicated Culpepper, so the story spread from pre-nuptial indiscretion to actual adultery. Henry was not only a dupe but also a cuckold.[29]

Under the weight of this evidence, the king's delusions finally collapsed. He raged, swearing to torture the ungrateful girl to death and then collapsed into an embarrassing orgy of weeping and self-pity. This time he had been really hurt, as he had probably never been hurt before. The last flickers of his youthful zest disappeared. He was old and tired. The days of courtly 'amours' were over, and there was no point in deluding himself any further about a Duke of York. But he could still hunt, and while his council turned to the distasteful task of unravelling the full story of Catherine's infidelities, Henry took himself off 'for the purpose of diverting his ill humour'. On 7 November Cranmer and Norfolk went to Hampton Court to interrogate Catherine, and to ensure that she remained confined to her chambers. His niece's behaviour had placed the duke in a very difficult situation, far more than the fall of Anne Boleyn, from whom he had already distanced himself. He had recovered his influence with the king on the strength of Henry's love for Catherine, and if he did not act circumspectly her folly would also be his downfall. At first she wept industriously and denied that she had ever been guilty of any offence, but the following day Cranmer got the full story out of her, in the intervals between fits of hysterics. The council was then faced with a problem. Dereham admitted intercourse, but claimed that there had been a contract of marriage. If that could be established it would absolve him of guilt for anything which had happened before July 1540, but meant that

Catherine was guilty of bigamy. If that had been the case her marriage to the king was invalid, but it could have been a defence that would have saved her life. However, the queen herself denied any such contract, either out of family pride or a sheer inability to understand the consequences. A few days later she wrote what purported to be a full and abject confession to the king, and threw herself upon his mercy. She described her indiscretions with both Mannox and Dereham in graphic detail, but claimed that her relationship with the latter had ended '. . . almost a year before the King's Majesty was married to my lady Anna of Cleves'. She then went on to explain,

> I was so desirous to be taken unto your grace's favour and so blinded with the desire of worldly glory that I could not, nor had grace, to consider how great a fault it was to conceal my former faults from your majesty, considering that I intended ever during my life to be faithful and true unto your majesty after. . . .[30]

The council was not quite sure how to respond to this. For the time being they were still concentrating upon the pre-contract, for which much of this confession was irrelevant. However, by 12 November reports of the queen's post-nuptial infidelities had overtaken that problem in importance, and a new agenda was being set. Dereham's allegations against Culpepper led to the latter's arrest, and he confessed to a sexual relationship with Catherine since her marriage. This the queen herself strenuously denied, but her familiar, Jane Rochford, in an attempt to dig herself out of the mire, confirmed that she believed intercourse to have taken place.[31] This made Catherine's confession appear not only inadequate, but also hypocritical, and the possibility that she might escape with her life began to disappear. She was removed to the suppressed monastery of Syon, and modestly but comfortably housed, with four ladies and a dozen servants. On 13 November her household at Hampton Court was closed down, and her jewellery was inventoried, which was always a bad sign. Cranmer and Wriothesley then made a further attempt to persuade the queen to confess to adultery, but the most she would admit to was indiscreet nocturnal meetings which, she claimed, never went beyond dalliance and talk. Culpepper, she claimed, had sought these meetings and Jane Rochford had arranged them, making the latter appear in the unlikely role of *agent provocateur*. Culpepper denied full sexual intercourse, but admitted that he had intended it. The truth of what happened cannot now be recovered, but full carnal knowledge would not have been necessary for the relationship to have been described as adulterous, and it may be that Catherine's denial was disingenuous. Culpepper alleged that the desire for intercourse had been mutual, and that may well have been an honest opinion since it did nothing to ameliorate either his position or the queen's.

The violation of a queen was ancient treason, but the desire to do so, without any overt act proven, could hardly be so described. On the other hand the Treason Act of 1534 had declared that if any person should '. . . by craft imagine, invent, practise or attempt any bodily harm to be done or committed to the King's most royal person, the Queen's or their heir apparent's . . .' then that person was guilty of treason.[32] Culpepper had certainly 'by craft imagined' bodily harm to

Catherine, and the fact that she may have condoned it was neither here nor there. The queen was similarly guilty of conspiring her own bodily harm, just as she had been guilty of deceiving the king at the time of their marriage. Such misconduct was treasonable by construction because of the threat which it presented to the legitimacy of the king's children – an extremely sensitive issue in Henry's case. The interrogations proceeded intensively through the third week in November, and it is probable that both Culpepper and Dereham were racked. By the 22nd the council was satisfied of the guilt of all three, and it was proclaimed at Hampton Court that Catherine had forfeited the honour and title of queen, and was to be known only as the Lady Catherine Howard. On 1 December the two men were arraigned, and both pleaded guilty, realizing the futility of any other course. Dereham's treason was actually much more problematic than Culpepper's, because he never seems to have had any intention of resuming his relationship with Catherine. However, the fact that the relationship had existed, and that he had gratuitously been given the opportunity to resume it, were deemed to be sufficient. Moreover, it was Dereham rather than Culpepper for whom the king reserved his bitterest hatred, probably because it was he who had spoiled what Henry believed to have been his innocent bride. On 10 December both were taken to Tyburn, where Culpepper was beheaded by the king's mercy, while Dereham suffered the full penalty of hanging, drawing, and quartering. Both made 'a good end', confessing their faults, and their heads were displayed on Tower Bridge.

The Howard ascendancy at court had been destroyed. Servants and minor members of the family were rounded up in large numbers. On 10 December the Dowager Duchess of Norfolk was arrested, and on the 13th Catherine's aunt, Lady Bridgewater. The duke at first scuttled around in a frenzy of penitent humility, and then tactfully retired to his estates. On 22 December the whole family with the exception of the duke were found guilty of misprision of treason for concealing Catherine's offences, standing to lose all their property and to suffer perpetual imprisonment. It did not come to that, because most of them were pardoned within a few months, but the shock was paralysing. For a while it seemed as though it would go hard with the dowager, especially when it was discovered that she had destroyed some of Dereham's papers, but she was eventually released in May 1542. Apart from Catherine herself, the only member of the family to suffer the full penalty was the unfortunate Lady Rochford. The ex-queen could have been tried by her peers, as Anne Boleyn had been, but instead it was decided to proceed against her by act of attainder. The reason for this is not clear. Lord Chancellor Audley seems to have had some qualms about it, faring that justice might not be seen to be done,[33] but perhaps it was felt that the spectacle of another queen on trial for substantially the same offence might have brought ridicule upon the English Crown. After an extremely cheerless Christmas, parliament convened upon 16 January, and the Bill of Attainder was introduced into the House of Lords on the 21st. This confirmed the attainders of those already condemned, and declared Catherine and Jane Rochford to have been guilty of treason. There was no proof in the modern sense that either of them had committed any offence worse than extreme indiscretion and stupidity, but since two men had already been executed for their dealings with the queen, her own guilt was in a sense presumed. It could also be argued that if Jane Rochford had been an unsuccessful pander, it had not been for want of trying.

On 8 February the Bill of Attainder passed its final reading, and on the 11th it receive the royal assent. This was given by letters patent rather than in person, to spare the king's feelings, which seem to have been real and sombre enough. The previous day Catherine had been transferred by river from Syon to the Tower, where she was honourably but securely lodged. Her time was now very short, and the violent fluctuations of mood to which she had been subject since November gave way to constant weeping and lamentation. It had seemed at first that she was unable to grasp the seriousness of her situation, and in spite of occasional hysterical outbursts, as late as Christmas had seemed more concerned over her clothes than over her impending fate. On Sunday 12 February she was warned for death, and subsided into a kind of numb acquiescence, asking only that she be allowed to die swiftly and secretly. The former request was granted, but not the latter. There had to be witnesses to what was, after all, an important act of state, and a large crowd gathered on Tower Green in the bleak dawn of 13 February. According to Charles de Marillac, the French ambassador, who was present, the wretched girl was almost too weak to walk to the block, and could do no more than confess in a few words the gravity of her (unspecified) offences. Everyone agreed that she made a very godly and Christian end, '. . . desiring all Christian people to take regard' to her 'worthy and just punishment'.[34] The agony of the occasion affected Jane Rochford differently. In her agitation she became excessively voluble, her confession and exhortation rambling on until it tried the patience of some of the onlookers. Both ladies died cleanly under the axe, and were interred in the nearby chapel of St Peter ad Vincula.

If ever a butterfly was broken on the wheel, it must surely have been Catherine Howard. She was only twenty when she died, having been guilty of little more than adolescent irresponsibility. The confessional would have been a more suitable expiation for her sins than the block. However, two factors elevated her indiscretions to the level of high politics. The first was that she inflicted serious psychological damage upon the king, and the second was that she was the instrument of a powerful aristocratic faction. As Lacey Baldwin Smith pointed out thirty years ago, Henry would have grown old anyway, and Catherine could hardly be blamed for that. However, that was not the real point. The king had fortified himself with illusions of virility for many years, and like many such men in middle age he had made a fool of himself over a pretty girl. The virility of a king was a part of the well-being of the realm, and Henry's disillusionment sapped the vitality of England. It is usually said that the wars of 1542–7 were partly occasioned by the king's desire to recapture his lost youth, and there is an element of truth in that. Catherine deprived Henry of the chance to grow old gracefully. That was perhaps not her fault, but the circumstances of her rise and fall determined the pattern of both domestic and foreign policy in the last five years of the reign, not least the eclipse of the Howards and the conservative policies which they represented. It was in 1541 that they became vulnerable to the *coup de grâce* which was to be administered in 1546.

# SIX

# The Final Haven: Catherine Parr, 1543–7

The traumatic events leading up to the execution of Catherine Howard had exhausted the king's emotional energies. By March 1542 the court was returning to life, and Henry was feasting with at least a show of enjoyment, but for the first time there was no talk of marriage. Once he had recovered from the shock caused by the discovery of her infidelities, Henry was less distressed by the loss of Catherine than he had been by that of Jane Seymour. On that occasion, however, the council had plunged straight into the search for a successor, even in the letters which had broken the news of the king's loss. This time, although only five years had passed, there was no point, and in any case the whole matter had become a political minefield. The act which had condemned Catherine had taken elaborate precautions against any repetition of her deception. The penalties of treason now awaited anyone who might conceal the indiscretions of a future bride, and so wide-ranging were the provisions of the statute that anyone responsible for introducing the king to an attractive young woman could be putting his (or her) head upon the block.[1] In 1542 there was an understandable lack of enthusiasm for the road which had brought power and success to the Boleyns, the Seymours and the Howards in turn, but which only the Seymours had survived. At the same time, although the subject was too dangerous to discuss openly, there was little prospect of the king begetting more children, and therefore even less incentive to run the risk of springing a nubile damsel into his bed.

It was to be war rather than sex which kept Henry's flagging energies alive over the next few years. Although there had eventually been no anti-English crusade for Scotland to join, James V had shown no desire to cooperate with his uncle. He had taken Marie de Guise from under Henry's nose, and his council was dominated by clergy, led by Cardinal Beaton. Henry thought that he had persuaded James to meet him at York during his extended progress in the summer of 1541, but his councillors did not trust English assurances, and there was never any serious chance that he would venture south. James' non-appearance gave Henry the pretext for a display of righteous indignation, and the perennial violence of the Anglo-Scottish borders flared up in consequence. An exchange of recriminations then followed, which continued throughout the king's matrimonial crisis, and into the summer of 1542. The international situation, which had seemed so threatening to England's security only two years before, was now running strongly in Henry's favour. On 10 July Charles and Francis renewed their intermittent warfare. Both had been angling for English support over the preceding months, and, as had happened before, Charles had been the more successful. Francis had pretended an interest in a marriage between his second son and Princess Mary, but Henry had called his bluff by refusing to have her declared legitimate, in spite of the fact that she was high in his favour and presiding at court in the absence of a queen consort. In June 1542, just before the outbreak of hostilities, a secret agreement was reached with the Regent Mary of Hungary, acting on the emperor's behalf, for a joint campaign against France in the spring of 1543.[2] Henry therefore had a good reason to force a show–down with Scotland, in order to secure his northern border before he was obliged to turn his attentions south.

James was in no mood for hostilities, but the relative complaisance of the Scottish commissioners who came to York in September did not suit Henry's purposes at all. The king may have been apprehensive of the way in which the Scots had served him in 1513, or he may simply have been cynical. His commissioners made unreasonable demands, and attempted to extract pledges that James would come either to York or to London at Christmas. Without waiting any reasonable time for a response, Henry then fired off instructions to the Duke of Norfolk, who was working out his disfavour as Lieutenant of the North, to carry out a devastating raid into the Scottish Lowlands. The duke's campaign lasted less than a week, but did a formidable amount of damage. The king was highly gratified, and sent further orders and reinforcements north in anticipation of the counter-attack which he hoped he had succeeded in provoking. Unprepared as he was, James could not afford to ignore so blatant a challenge. If he failed to respond his own authority would be seriously undermined, and he therefore walked straight into the unsubtle trap which Henry had prepared. On 21 November he launched twenty thousand ill-armed and untrained men into the Debatable Land, north of Carlisle. Two days later, at Solway Moss, they were defeated by a smaller but much better equipped English force. By comparison with Flodden, or Pinkie Cleugh a few years later, the casualties were light, but a large number of prisoners were taken, including a substantial number of Scottish lords. More significantly, three weeks after this not very humiliating defeat, James V suddenly died. His death may well have been unconnected with the battle, but rather the result of that illness which had prevented him from being present, but it was inevitably represented by the English as arising from shame and grief. The important thing was that it left the Scottish Crown in the hands of his week-old daughter, Mary, and appeared to present Henry with an unrivalled opportunity to order the country to his own liking.

Had the English pressed their military advantage, there could have been little serious resistance, but it was no part of the king's plan to continue a large-scale operation in the north when there was clearly no further danger from that direction. Within a few months his armies were due to march against France, and the Scottish situation would have to be resolved by political means. An obvious strategy lay ready to hand in the shape of a marriage between the infant queen and his own five-year-old heir, Edward, and a useful means could be found in the large number of noble Scottish prisoners presently kicking their heels in London. As a condition of their release, they were required to swear an oath committing them to support the English marriage. They were then entertained to a lavish

Christmas at court, and sent home.[3] In theory the English plan was foolproof, because hostages were demanded and given for the satisfaction of the conditions, and ten of the Scots who were considered to be the most trustworthy were also sworn to an additional secret clause, whereby the Scottish Crown would come to Henry in the event of Mary's death.[4] However, no one in England could hope to control events in the north unless an English army was actually sitting in the lowlands, and on 3 January 1543, before the 'assured' lords had even returned home, the Scottish council had named James Hamilton, Earl of Arran, as protector of the realm. Arran was the queen's cousin, and not her nearest blood relation, but he was also recognized as heir to the throne. Henry was confident that his party would succeed in overturning this arrangement, but once they had been reabsorbed into the Scottish political scene, there was little to hold them to their word. Aware of his military weakness, Arran wisely temporized. He had Cardinal Beaton, the leader of the pro-French clerical party, arrested, and spoke of reforming the Church. In February he negotiated a three-month truce with the English, and Henry offered a marriage between the Princess Elizabeth and Arran's son, in the hope of aligning him with the 'assured' party.

Perhaps the prospect of success in Scotland was invigorating, or perhaps he was becoming lonely, but while these events were unfolding, speculation began to revive that the king would marry again.[5] This time there was no unseemly haste, no passionate letters (or at least none that we know about) and no international complications. Unlike his father, or Ferdinand of Aragon, Henry VIII did not contemplate remarriage late in life to secure a diplomatic advantage, nor even to strengthen the succession, but simply to obtain that 'heart's ease' which had consistently eluded him since the early days of his reign. The lady of his choice was Catherine Neville, Lady Latimer, usually known by her maiden name of Catherine Parr. Catherine had been born in about 1512, and was the oldest child of Sir Thomas Parr of Kendal in Westmorland. Sir Thomas had been a courtier whose connections with his northern base had become tenuous. His own father, Sir William, had died while he was still young, and his mother's second marriage had brought him south, where his stepfather, Sir Nicholas Vaux, had established court connections. The young Thomas had already become sufficiently known to be knighted at Henry VIII's coronation, and married, probably in 1510, a lady named Maude Greene, who was the heiress to a modest estate in Northamptonshire.[6] Sir Thomas Parr was similar in status and antecedents to Sir Thomas Boleyn or Sir John Seymour – a companion in arms to the young king – and he might have emulated the success of the former if he had not died in 1517, leaving his widow with three young children to provide for. Maude Parr never remarried, and Catherine's upbringing and education are obscure. In common with most girls of her class, she was probably placed in the household of a trusted kinsman, but it is not known who that was, or where he lived. It is clear from later evidence that she was not brought up in scholarship, and such natural aptitude as she had was not developed during her youth. Her mother maintained contact with the court, but concentrated her main efforts on securing a good marriage for her son, William, who was a year younger than Catherine. In 1527, at the age of fourteen, he was wedded to Anne Bourchier, the only child of the Earl of Essex.

Maude's contacts and resources did not enable her to repeat this feat for her daughter, but she did well enough, in a sense. In 1529 Catherine married Edward Borough, the son of Thomas, Lord Borough, who was later to be Queen Anne's lord chamberlain.[7]

Edward was a man of substance and prospects – a satisfactory if not a brilliant match – but his health was consistently poor and he died in 1532 leaving his twenty-year-old widow childless. It is not even certain that the union was consummated. By this time Maude Parr was also dead, but it was obvious that the only future for the young widow was remarriage, and her family seem to have rallied round to provide it. In 1533 she wedded John Neville, Lord Latimer of Snape, already twice a widower, a man of about forty with two grown children. As Lady Latimer, Catherine was a distinct success, but it was a trying time. She ran her husband's great Yorkshire household with skill and determination, and was a tactful and accommodating stepmother. Lord Latimer was deeply involved in the Pilgrimage of Grace, not because he had any desire to be but because he was there, and in December 1536 Catherine had been held under house arrest by the rebels as a hostage for her husband's return from the court. Unavoidably implicated by Robert Aske's confidences, John Neville escaped any formal proceedings in the early part of 1537, not so much for lack of evidence as through the lack of any will to pursue him. His health, however, was broken by the experience, and for the second time in her young life, Catherine found herself wedded to an invalid. This was a life in which duty greatly exceeded gratification, but there were compensations, not least long periods spent at Lord Latimer's London residence in Charterhouse Yard. Good physicians were more common in London than in Yorkshire, and the opportunity to repair the Neville fortunes by discreetly renewing contacts at court was too good to be missed.

Catherine became friendly with the Princess Mary, and also with several members of the Seymour family.[8] The ascendancy of the Howards during the brief reign of Henry's fifth queen, and their penchant for traditional orthodoxy, had driven their political opponents into the arms of the reformers, and by 1542 the Seymours were becoming distinctly interested in evangelical humanism. During her husband's protracted final illness, Catherine began to learn Latin. She also developed a relationship with Thomas Seymour, the Earl of Hertford's younger brother, although it is not known whether there was any connection between these two things. By the beginning of 1543 her life was becoming distinctly complicated. Lord Latimer might, or might not, die in the near future, but for the time being both conscience and common prudence dictated that she should preserve the face of a good and upright wife. On the other hand two men other than her husband were becoming emotionally interested in her. The first was Thomas Seymour, who may have been in love, and who was certainly on the look out for a rich widow; the second was the king. The nature of her attraction for Henry can only be deduced. It was certainly not a sophisticated intellect, nor the responsive wit which he had found so fascinating in Anne Boleyn. Nor was it the kind of animal magnetism which had drawn him to Catherine Howard. The king's fires were spent, and his once magnificent body a corpulent wreck. Catherine was in many ways the antithesis of her predecessor, and it may well have been her dignity and self-possessed calm which first aroused his interest. It was not her availability, because when Henry made his first advances Lord Latimer was still alive, and his first recorded gift was dated 16 February, some two weeks before her husband's death.[9] Nor was this another courtly charade, because even if Henry had still been inclined to such advances, no woman would have dared to respond as Anne or Jane had responded in the past.

This potentially difficult situation was partly resolved on 2 March by John Neville's death. In other circumstances, after a seemly interval Catherine would probably have married Thomas Seymour, who seems to have kindled in her the fire which two unsatisfactory marriages had dampened down but not extinguished. As it was, however, the king inevitably claimed precedence. At what point Henry made the nature of his intentions clear is not known, but it was probably before the middle of June, when it was noted that Lady Latimer and her sister, Anne Herbert, were maintaining a rather conspicuous presence at court. Whenever it was, it impaled Catherine upon a cruel dilemma. In one sense the

*The marriage of Henry VIII and Catherine Parr, 12 July 1543*

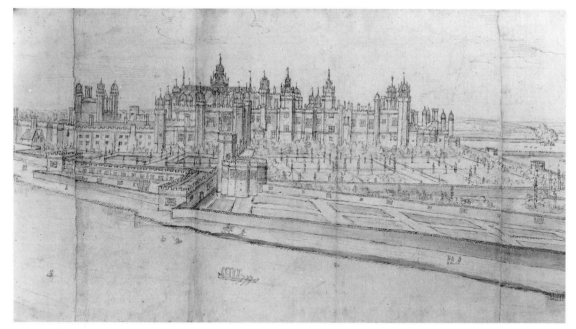

*Hampton Court Palace from the south, where Henry and Catherine Parr were married (from
A. van Wyngaerd's drawing of c. 1557)*

last thing she needed was a third unsatisfying marriage and the king had become
by this time a grotesque caricature of the ardent lover of ten years before. In most
respects Seymour was a much more attractive prospect, but it would have been
impossible to marry him in defiance of the king's wishes. She could have refused
them both, but marriage to the king clearly had a fascination all of its own. At
thirty-one Catherine had herself well in hand, and as a twice-married widow no
one would have expected her to be a virgin, so she had little to fear from the perils
which had undone two of her predecessors. At the same time she seems to have
convinced herself that Henry represented her true vocation. Four years later,
when the king's death had freed her for a fourth marriage, she wrote to Seymour,

> . . . as truly as God is God, my mind was fully bent, the other time I was at
> liberty, to marry you before any man I know. Howbeit God withstood my will
> therein most vehemently for a time, and through his grace and goodness made
> that possible which seemed to me most impossible; that was made me renounce
> utterly mine own will, and to follow his will most willingly. . . .[10]

What she said at the time we do not know, but Seymour effaced himself, and on
12 July Henry married the Lady Latimer in the Queen's Closet at Hampton
Court, to the great advantage of the Parr family, and of the evangelical party.
    The religious conservatives were not the only people to be disconcerted by this

KATHARINE PARRE

*Catherine Parr (1512–48) (portrait attributed to Wilhelm Scrots, c. 1545). This portrait is the only authentic likeness of Catherine*

development. Anne of Cleves, who had accepted her own displacement three years earlier with such apparent equanimity, was furious. She seems to have expected the fall of the Howards to be the signal for her own reinstatement, a misunderstanding which perhaps helps to explain her earlier complaisance. She seems never to have understood the true reasons for her dismissal, and no one wished to face the distasteful task of explaining. In venting her indignation to Chapuys, Anne complained that Catherine was far less beautiful than herself, a judgement with which most contemporaries would probably have agreed.[11] The fact that no observer commented upon the nature of the new queen's charms may mean that she was considered to be extremely plain, or possibly that her looks were recognized as irrelevant. Only one authentic portrait survives, attributed to Wilhelm Scrots, and that shows a bland, rather child–like face, not in any way less pleasing to a modern eye than those of her predecessors. Her personality, on the other hand, attracted general approbation. She was described as lively, friendly and gracious, and both her stepdaughters attended the ceremony when she married their father, which was recognized as a good omen for domestic peace. Only Anne, increasingly marginalized both by Henry's new marriage and by the diplomatic catastrophes which had overtaken her brother, could find no good word to say.[12]

As queen, Catherine was a benign presence rather than a power. Many years later, when historians were seeking an explanation for why Henry, who retained many orthodox Catholic views to his death, allowed his son to be educated by Protestants, they decided that this must have been brought about by the queen, either directly or through her influence over her husband. However, it now appears that this was a mistaken view.[13] Catherine certainly had pronounced evangelical opinions, which she was not afraid to discuss with Henry, but she was quick to defer to his authority if he insisted. Moreover, the education of the heir to the throne was far too important a matter to be dealt with by anyone except the king himself. Paradoxical as it may seem, it was Henry who appointed tutors such as Richard Fox, John Cheke, and Jacques Belmain, all of whom were later to emerge as strong Protestants. Part of the explanation for this lies in the fact that the borderline between evangelical humanism and Protestantism could be very indistinct. Catherine herself wrote two works of pious meditation, similar in their approach, but different in their doctrinal implications. The first, *Prayers or Meditations wherein the Mind is Stirred Patiently to Suffer all Afflictions*, was published by the king's printer, Thomas Berthelet, in 1545. It is clearly evangelical, but within the bounds of Henry's definition of orthodoxy. The second, *The Lamentation of a Sinner*, although written in Henry's lifetime, was not printed until 1548 and contains unambiguous passages of Lutheran doctrine. It seems very likely that a number of the evangelical party, including the queen herself, had embraced at least some Lutheran views before 1547, but they concealed them discreetly and with reasonable success. It cannot be proved that Edward was taught any heretical doctrine during his father's lifetime, although the speed with which it emerged thereafter makes such instruction a reasonable supposition.

Catherine was not a great scholar. She continued to work painstakingly at her Latin, and that fact, combined with her genuine evangelical convictions, earned her praise from the humanists which she did not really deserve.[14] Unlike

Catherine Howard, she was also sufficiently intelligent and well read to sustain a serious conversation, but her principal delights were in clothes, music and dancing. She also loved animals and flowers, kept jesters both male and female, and generally gave the impression of enjoying the simple things in life. Mirth and modesty are two of the words which her contemporaries regularly used in their descriptions of her, and the amiability which these words imply was clearly demonstrated in her relations with her second family of stepchildren. Mary by this time was twenty-seven, and her unmarried state was an anomaly. This was more the result of her indeterminate status than of any lack of attractiveness. She retained her father's favour from 1536 until his death, and intermittent negotiations continued for her hand, but even after she had been formally restored to the order of succession in 1544, no husband was found for her. This situation caused her great distress, and she was driven to observe that as along as her father lived she would be '. . . only the Lady Mary, and the most unhappy lady in Christendom'.[15] A warm relationship with a stepmother who was only four years older than herself was some consolation, and the much-married Catherine was in a good position to understand some at least of her frustrations. Scholarship formed another bond between them, although in that world the well-educated Mary was the teacher, and the queen the learner. In spite of their later

*Princess Mary aged twenty-eight (portrait by Master John, 1544)*

*Prince Edward (after Hans Holbein, c. 1542)*

reputations, the piety of the two women was not at this stage very far apart. Mary had been brought up in the humanist tradition, and like her father shared many of the evangelical priorities. Only when it came to justification by faith alone, or attacks upon the sacraments did she draw back, and Catherine concealed the steady progress of her private convictions in that direction. Although Mary had her own chamber servants, she had no independent income and lived at court under the broad umbrella of the queen's household until Henry's death dissolved that establishment in February 1547.

Neither Edward nor Elizabeth saw as much of their stepmother as Mary did, for the simple reason that they shared a separate establishment, with its own residences and its own itinerary. They met frequently, and the family was normally together for major festivals, such as Christmas or Easter. At the time of their father's last wedding Elizabeth was nearly ten and her brother nearly six, so their relationship with Catherine was quite different from that of their older sister. They were children for whom she was an affectionate but intermittent presence, like a favourite aunt. They wrote her occasional letters, Edward in schoolboy Latin and Elizabeth (on one occasion at least) in Italian. What mattered was less the closeness of the relationship than the fact that it was harmonious. Catherine treated the two younger children very much as if they had been her own, and protected them from their father's unpredictable temper. This was

*Princess Elizabeth (artist unknown)*

perhaps made easier by the fact that she was herself childless by any of her marriages, and that the Neville stepchildren had grown up. Edward and Elizabeth therefore had no rivals in her affections. Officially it continued to be stressed that any offspring begotten between the king and the queen 'that now is' would take precedence over both Mary and Elizabeth in the succession,[16] but in practice this was recognized as increasingly unlikely. Casual gossip about a Duke of York died away, and no coronation ever seems to have been contemplated. In this respect, Henry's last queen was uniquely fortunate. Not for her the agonizing wait for pregnancy, and the even more agonizing uncertainty about the outcome.

Catherine had given few hostages to fortune, and her political role was low key. She lacked Anne Boleyn's capacity to lead a family faction, and unlike Catherine Howard was not a member of an already powerful family. The Parrs, like the Seymours, became an important court family in the wake of her marriage, but they were not an effective force. Both William and Anne had established themselves before 1543, William enjoying the almost unique distinction of being commended both by Cromwell and the Duke of Norfolk. He was a cheerful cultivated man, who earnestly desired to be a successful soldier, but seems to have lacked the necessary ability. In 1539 he was created Baron Parr of Kendal for no very obvious reason, except perhaps the great estates which came to him via his wife on the death of the last Bourchier Earl of Essex.[17] The fact that he was estranged from Anne, who had abandoned him for a life of scandalous independence, did not affect his right to her inheritance. In April 1543 he was elected to the Order of the Garter, and in December of the same year, when his sister was already well established in the royal bed, he was elevated to his father-in-law's title, and became Earl of Essex. Few men can have risen so far, or so fast, for so little reason. William was neither a soldier nor a politician of any substance, and his promotion did not indicate any significant shift in the political forces at court. Over the next few years he became loosely aligned with the Seymours on the evangelical side of the religious divide, but he does not seem to have exerted himself very hard in the promotion of the cause. Catherine's sister, Anne Herbert, her cousin, Maude Lane, and her stepdaughter, Margaret Neville, all became members of her household. Her brother-in-law, William Herbert, was knighted and appointed to the privy chamber, and her uncle, William, became her lord chamberlain as Lord Parr of Horton.

All this was the normal patronage of a queen, and had no particular significance for the balance of power at court, but it is nevertheless likely that Catherine's advent coincided with a period of delicate evolution. In March 1543 conservatives in the council, probably led by Stephen Gardiner, had begun a drive against heresy. The fall of Catherine Howard and her family had revived the hopes of the evangelicals, still reeling from the Act of Six Articles and the fall of Cromwell, and Gardiner undoubtedly hoped to check that revival. The Dean of Exeter, Simon Heynes, was sent to the fleet for his 'evil opinions', and a few days later five members of the privy chamber (including the musicians Sternhold and Marbecke) were denounced by Dr John London for their attacks upon the sacrament of the altar. All five were committed to prison, and three of their wives were also implicated.[18] Encouraged by this success, the conservatives then decided to strike higher, and early in April charges were brought against Archbishop Thomas Cranmer. The background to the so-called 'Prebendaries' plot' lay in the factional politics of the Kentish gentry, and the infighting of the cathedral chapter, but it presented a formidable challenge to the great survivor of the reforming party.[19] Once the charges had been placed in the king's hands the accusers could only await his pleasure, but the omens at that time seemed favourable. However, according to an account written some twenty years later by Cranmer's secretary, Ralph Morice, Henry sent for the archbishop to join him in his barge on the Thames, and cheerfully observed that he now knew who was the greatest heretic in Kent. Not only did the king insist that Cranmer should investigate the charges against himself, but he also indicated that he knew a great deal about his archbishop (including the fact that he was secretly married) and did not propose to do anything about it. If this story is true, and Morice did not have anything to gain by inventing it, it casts a very interesting light upon Henry's state of mind at the time when he had already determined upon his sixth wife. While allowing his council to carry out a persecution which extended into his own household, he seems to have had little personal commitment to the defence of orthodoxy. Always unpredictable, his reaction to any particular situation may have depended upon nothing more stable than the mood of the moment.

How much Cranmer's enemies knew about this episode at the time is not clear.

*William Parr (1513–71), Marquis of Northampton, Earl of Essex and Baron Parr, brother of Catherine Parr*

Presumably they soon discovered that their purposes had been thwarted, but they may well not have known why, or how. Discussions then ensued, which certainly involved Norfolk, Gardiner and Lord Russell, and it was decided to try again. In the circumstances such pertinacity indicates a clear failure to read the king's mind, but they seem to have concluded that the tactics had been wrong, rather than the strategy. A week or two later, probably about the end of April, they prepared a new ploy.[20] This time, instead of relying upon charges prepared by an obscure group of provincial clergy, they would go to the king themselves, insisting upon their status as loyal councillors that the archbishop was guilty of heresy, but that his accusers were too nervous to come forward until he was under arrest. This was a tactic similar to that which had been employed against Cromwell, and depended upon Henry's well-known suggestibility when in the company of those whom he knew well. Ostensibly, the king agreed to Cranmer's arrest at the council board the following day, but later that night sent a principal gentleman of his privy chamber, Anthony Denny, to summon the archbishop to his presence. The conversation which then ensued, according to Morice, was remarkably similar to that which had taken place in the king's barge a short while before. Henry demonstrated that he knew perfectly well how the mechanics of such a coup would work, and may even have been aware of his own weaknesses. Once Cranmer was in the Tower, the charges would fly thick and fast, and Henry could not trust himself to check them.

. . . if they have you once in prison, three or four false knaves will soon be procured to witness against you and condemn you, which else now being at your liberty dare not once open their lips or appear before your face . . . I have a better regard unto you than to permit your enemies so to overthrow you. . . .[21]

Thereupon he gave the archbishop a ring, which he was to produce when challenged at the council, thereby appealing directly to the king. The following morning the prepared scene was duly played out, ending in a sharp lecture from the king on the subject of factious enmity, and a somewhat forced reconciliation.

Henry's motive in setting up this scene is unclear, and it has been suggested that he actually changed his mind between agreeing to Cranmer's arrest and sending for him. That is possible, given his propensity for being bounced into decisions, but it is more likely that he wished to administer a sharp lesson to a group of advisers whose zeal he was beginning to find tiresome. He probably also wished to demonstrate in the most dramatic fashion that he was not prepared to tolerate any further attacks upon his favourite prelate. Cranmer's convictions made him almost the perfect archbishop for the king's purposes, and in this case at least Henry knew where his true interests lay. Consequently Catherine and her evangelical friends found themselves from the start in a court which was more sympathetic to their views than they could reasonably have expected. Cranmer had won the critical battle on the eve of her marriage, and thereafter they were allies in a war which generally went in their favour. The final victory was not won, however, until the queen herself had come into serious danger, and the evangelicals could not afford to be complacent. As if to warn them of the delicacy of the situation, three sacramentaries were burned in Windsor Park within a few days of the wedding.[22] One of the secrets of Cranmer's immunity was that he was not a sacramentary, and by the autumn of 1543 no reformer had any excuse for not understanding where the king drew the line.

Throughout his reign Henry had periodically displayed a compulsive need to demonstrate that he was in charge, and his brinkmanship over Cranmer's arrest may have been another example of that unlovable trait. If so, then the conservative position may have been less damaged by the débâcle than at first appeared. In 1545 a Yorkshire gentlewoman named Anne Askew was arrested on suspicion of being a sacramentary. Her views were extreme, and pugnaciously expressed, so she would probably have ended at the stake in any case, but her status gave her a particular value to the orthodox. This was greatly enhanced in the following year by the arrest of Dr Edward Crome, who, under interrogation, implicated a number of other people, both at court and in the City of London. Anne had been part of the same network, and she was now tortured for the purpose of establishing her links with the circle about the queen, particularly Lady Denny and the Countess of Hertford. She died without revealing much of consequence, beyond the fact that she was personally known to a number of Catherine's companions, who had expressed sympathy for her plight. The queen meanwhile continued to discuss theology, piety and the right use of the bible, both with her friends and also with her husband. This was a practice which she had established in the early days of their marriage, and Henry had always allowed her a great deal of latitude, tolerating from her, it was said, opinions which no one else dared to utter. In taking advantage of this indulgence to urge further measures of reform, she presented her enemies with an opening. Irritated by her performance on one occasion, the king complained to Gardiner about the unseemliness of being lectured by his wife. This was a heaven-sent opportunity, and undeterred by his previous failures, the bishop hastened to agree, adding that, if the king would give him permission he would produce such evidence that '. . . his majesty would easily perceive how perilous a matter it is to cherish a serpent within his own bosom'.[23] Henry gave his consent, as he had done to the arrest of Cranmer, articles were produced and a plan was drawn up for Catherine's arrest, the search of her chambers, and the laying of charges against at least three of her privy chamber.

The greatest secrecy was observed, and the unsuspecting queen continued with her evangelical sessions. Henry even signed the articles against her. Then, however, the whole plot was leaked in mysterious circumstances. A copy of the articles, with the king's signature on it, was accidentally dropped by a member of the council, where it was found and brought to Catherine, who promptly collapsed. The king sent one of his physicians, a Dr Wendy, to attend upon her, and Wendy, who seems to have been in the secret, advised her to throw herself upon Henry's mercy. No doubt Anne Boleyn or Catherine Howard would have been grateful for a similar opportunity, but this was a different story. Seeking out her husband, the queen humbly submitted herself '. . . to your majesty's wisdom, as my only anchor'. She had never pretended to instruct, but only to learn, and had spoken to him of Godly things in order to ease and cheer his mind.[24] Henry, so that story goes, was completely disarmed, and a perfect reconciliation was affected, so that when Sir Thomas Wriothesley arrived at Whitehall the following day with an armed guard, he found all his suspects walking with the king in the garden, and was sent on his way with a fearsome ear-bending. Had the conservatives walked into another well-baited trap? As related by Foxe, the whole story has an air of melodramatic unreality about it, but it bears a striking resemblance to the two stories of Cranmer, which come from a different source. Whether Henry was playing games with his councillors in order to humiliate them, or with his wife in order to reassure himself of her submissiveness, or whether he was genuinely wavering between two courses of action, we shall probably never know. In outline the story is probably correct, and we may never be able to disentangle Foxe's embellishments. The consequences, in any case, were real enough. Gardiner finally lost the king's favour, and did not recover it, so that he was deliberately omitted from the regency council which Henry shortly after set up for his son's anticipated minority.[25] Before the end of the year, as the king was declining to his end, the great house of Howard, which had survived so many crises, was finally destroyed, and the Duke of Norfolk barely survived the reign as a prisoner in the Tower. Protestant historiography may have improved all these stories in the interest of establishing Henry as a Godly prince, but it is worth remembering that the conservatives, too, could sometimes benefit from the king's mercurial changes of mood. In 1544 Germain Gardiner, the Bishop of Winchester's nephew, was suddenly arrested and executed on a charge of upholding the papal supremacy. Gardiner's enemies persuaded the king that the

*Henry VIII reproving Sir Thomas Wriothesley for attempting to arrest the queen (engraving from the painting by William Hamilton)*

bishop was behind his nephew's treason, but, warned in time, he obtained an audience and diverted the danger.

Meanwhile, there was a war to be fought. In Scotland the Earl of Arran continued to spin out the time during the spring of 1543, Cardinal Beaton was released and nothing was done about the reformation of the Church. On the other hand, on 1 July Scottish ambassadors signed at Greenwich a treaty of peace which included clauses providing for the marriage of Mary and Edward. This was rather less than Henry's full objective. The Scots did not renounce their friendship with France, and Mary was not to come to England until she was ten years old, but it gave the king the substance of what he wanted. Time was to show that Henry was self-deceived over this treaty, because although hostages were given, there were no adequate safeguards for its implementation. Despite accumulating evidence to the contrary, he insisted on believing that the assured Scots would keep their devious Regent to his word. The reason for this was that

Scotland had already distracted him far too long from his main business of war with France. A fresh agreement had been signed with the emperor on 11 February, but it was not made public until the end of May, when the Greenwich negotiations were sufficiently advanced for the outcome to be taken for granted. On 22 June an ultimatum was delivered to the French ambassador, which was very revealing of Henry's state of mind. There was really no good political reason for England to aid the emperor in this conflict, and the king simply resorted to his ancestral claim to the Crown of France.[26] In other words, he was fighting, as he had done thirty years before, because he wanted to. To ride again at the head of a victorious army, and to enter captured cities as he had once entered Tournai – by such means he could reassure himself that he was still a great king. With his body in rebellion against his will, and his wife more a sick-nurse than a bedfellow, war was a medicine against despair and advancing death. However, thanks to the Scottish complication, he had already delayed too long to launch his army royal in the summer of 1543 as had originally been intended. Hostilities commenced almost at once, when an expeditionary force of about five thousand men was sent across to assist in the defence of the Low Countries, but the major offensive was postponed to the following year.

Before that could happen, his fragile ascendancy over Scotland collapsed. Arran ratified the Treaty of Greenwich, but was helpless to implement it, even if he had really wished to do so, because political opposition led by Cardinal Beaton amounted to virtual rebellion, which the Regent lacked the resources to suppress. Ralph Sadler's reports from Edinburgh became increasingly depressed and by the end of August he was convinced that civil war was inevitable.[27] Arran appealed to Henry for financial support, but before it could arrive he had changed sides, joining Beaton in opposition to English interests. The king threatened savage reprisals for Scottish perfidy, and actually seized some Scottish ships, ignoring the existence of official peace. More constructively, however, he identified two new allies thrown up by the turbulent complexities of northern politics, the Earls of Angus and Lennox.[28] On 11 December the Scottish parliament solemnly repudiated the Treaty of Greenwich, and the results of Solway Moss had been completely annulled. Thereafter Henry wavered between two policies. The temptation to violent direct action was irresistible, but that would do nothing to help Angus and Lennox, and might well result in making their position untenable. By March 1544 he seems to have decided to work through his allies, provided that Lennox could secure control of the queen and promote religious change in Scotland. Within a few weeks it was clear that such a task was beyond him, and the king reverted to direct action. Ignoring the advice of his own commander, the Earl of Hertford, Henry decided to launch a punitive expedition, rather than to seize a bridgehead as a base for future operations. In the spring of 1544 a temporary expedient to prevent the Scots from interfering in the coming French campaign was more important to him than a solution to the Scottish problem itself. Early in May Hertford carried out his master's orders, against his better judgement but with ruthless efficiency. Edinburgh and Leith were sacked, and a great deal of damage done, but the only political consequence of any significance was the replacement of Arran as Regent by the Queen Mother, Mary of Guise. The only advantage gained was the one specifically aimed at; the Scots would be in no position to launch a major attack on England while the king was absent in France.

The emperor regarded the prospect of a personal appearance by his ally with dismay. Henry would be nothing but an encumbrance to an army on campaign. Moreover, the king's own councillors, via Chapuys, were doing their best to solicit Charles's good offices to dissuade him. Such efforts were a waste of time, because the whole point of the campaign from Henry's point of view was that he should lead it. Strategy and tactics were negotiable, but the king's personal presence was not. Unfortunately by the end of May logistical preparations had run ahead of strategic planning, so while the king and the emperor were still arguing about whether to launch a direct attack against Paris, an English army of some forty thousand men had landed at Calais, and was stuck, aimlessly and expensively, just outside the Pale. By the middle of June, in response to the Duke of Norfolk's urgent representations, Montreuil had been besieged, but the siege was not going well, and Norfolk was complaining of innumerable shortages. There may have been an element of calculation about this, because Henry had not yet joined his army, and when he did so a dramatic improvement in its performance would be expected. His uncertain health may well have been to blame for the delay, because there is some evidence to suggest that Catherine was working overtime, beside the royal physicians, to prepare him for the ordeal of campaigning. She vacated her own apartments and moved into a small bedroom next to the king's in order to be available, not for his pleasure but for her ministrations. Her apothecary's bills show long lists of remedies of which she herself was in no need, and contemporaries commented upon her solicitude. By the beginning of July, through good luck or skill he was as ready as he was ever likely to be, and on the 7th it was recorded by the privy council that,

> The Queen's Highness shall be regent in his grace's absence; and that his highness' progress shall pass and bear test in her name, as in like cases heretofore hath been accustomed.[29]

No clearer demonstration could have been given of Henry's confidence in Catherine; the only precedent was when her namesake had been given a similar responsibility in 1513. Perhaps it was hoped to induce a repetition of that successful year. The queen travelled to Dover to see her still-ailing spouse on his way, and was to bombard him with affectionate letters throughout his absence. These letters, encouraging, dutiful, and full of small domestic cares, give the measure of the woman. Unlike Catherine of Aragon, she was not a royal princess with a mind of her own in matters of state, but a good wife keeping the home fires burning. The queen's didacticism (if it really existed) seems to have been confined entirely to matters of religion.

On 15 July Henry landed at Calais, and within a few days the campaign obtained the strategic direction which it had hitherto lacked. Although the Dukes of Norfolk and Suffolk were his generals in the field, this was going to be the king's operation, and his reluctance to issue clear instructions in advance of his

*Dover harbour, drawn by Vincenzo Volpe in 1532. This scene cannot have changed much by 1544 when Catherine saw Henry leave Dover for the campaign in France*

arrival is quite consistent with that intention. Five days after he reached the camp, the larger part of his army moved off to besiege Boulogne, while the remainder under the Duke of Norfolk, stayed around Montreuil. The emperor was indignant. What had happened to the joint attack on Paris? Henry blandly replied that it was necessary to take the two besieged towns in order to secure his communications, but it soon became apparent that he had no intention of campaigning outside Picardy. Charles considered this to be a breach of faith, which absolved him from the terms of the alliance. His own army being in considerable difficulties, he accepted peace overtures from the French, and signed the Treaty of Crespy on 14 September. This left Henry to continue the war alone, a situation which it had always been one of the chief objectives of his foreign policy to avoid. Fortunately, Boulogne capitulated four days later, and the king did at least have something to show for his efforts. Henry had hugely enjoyed the siege, supervising every aspect of the work, and he equally enjoyed his triumphal entry. Observers remarked this his health and spirits appeared to be better than they had been for years.[30] The capture of Boulogne meant a great deal to Henry, and English propaganda, both at the time and subsequently, gave it the status of a

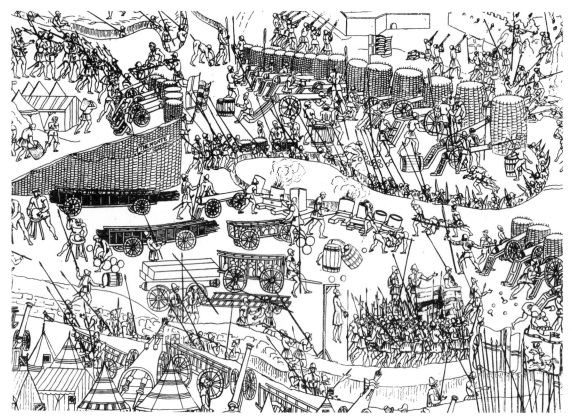

*The siege of Boulogne, 1544 (detail from an engraving of a wall painting at Cowdray House –
now destroyed)*

major victory but in fact it was a conquest of dubious value acquired at vast
expense. Quite apart from the offence which it had given to the emperor, the
campaign had been mismanaged in many ways, and the only unquantifiable bonus
was the new lease of life which it appeared to have given the king.

Catherine's only contribution to these events had been the suitable one of
writing a prayer for men going into battle, which had petitioned '. . . turn the
hearts of our enemies to the desire of peace'. When Henry returned quietly to
England on 30 September, there was little sign of that happening. Indeed there
was every sign that Francis, now having the advantage against his old sparring
partner, would press him hard in 1545. Meanwhile the queen had discharged her
responsibilities as Regent unobtrusively but competently. She had kept the king
informed of the satisfactory progress which the Earl of Lennox seemed to be
making in Scotland, and had written gracious letters of thanks to those who had
been involved in supporting him. It also seems that she had grown closer to her
fellow councillor Archbishop Cranmer, and that may not have been without
relevance for her evangelical activities over the next two years. Having survived

the crisis which these activities provoked in 1546, the last few months of Catherine's marriage to Henry were more concerned with easing his physical health and his temper than conducting theological debates. The improvement noted in the autumn of 1544 did not last, and even then his ulcerated leg, which he had probably acquired from years of heavy falls in the lists and the hunting field, continued to trouble him. Even at the siege of Boulogne he had been unable to endure armour below the thigh, and had been hoisted onto his horse with a crane. The last crisis of the reign had nothing to do with the queen, but a lot to do with the story of sexual politics which we have been unfolding. On 2 December 1546 Henry Howard, Earl of Surrey, was arrested and charged with treason. Technically his crime had been the assumption of part of the royal arms, which in view of the state of the king's health, could be construed as a claim to the Regency, if not to the Crown itself. Surrey was a reckless, arrogant man, who made no secret of his contempt for the 'upstart' families, such as the Seymours and the Parrs, with whom the king had chosen to surround himself. Moreover, under interrogation his sister, Mary, widow of the Duke of Richmond, had declared that both her brother and her father had pressed her to become the king's mistress in the interest of furthering Howard influence over the court.[31] Mary, of course, professed her virtuous refusal of such a role, and there is no proof that the suggestion was ever made, but it would have been consistent with the family's tactics in the period 1540–1, bearing in mind the success which Catherine Howard briefly achieved. True or not, the charge took Henry on the raw, demonstrating the way in which his servants and subjects had believed that they could exploit his weaknesses for their own ends. Surrey was rushed to his death on 19 January 1547.

King Henry VIII spent his last Christmas in London, a very sick man and preoccupied with the treason of the Howards. Catherine, along with Mary and Elizabeth, left Westminster on Christmas Eve to spend the festival at Greenwich. As late as 16 January the king was still transacting business, but a week later he was only intermittently conscious. By the time that he finally accepted that he was dying, it was probably too late to send for either his wife or children. So Catherine was not with him during his last illness, nor at the time of his death. We have no evidence of her reaction to the news. No commentator spoke of her grief, nor of any lament made, and it may well be that her overwhelming emotion was one of relief.[32] Her role had not been an easy one, and although as a respectable widow and a remarkably self-controlled person, there had never been any breath of scandal attached to her, she had apparently come within a stone's throw of disaster for not knowing exactly where to draw the line in expressing her religious views. Everyone who dealt with the king walked on a tightrope, and as she had probably never felt any great emotional attachment to him, her release from a position of duty can only have been welcome. At the age of thirty-five, she was now free to find a more meaningful relationship.

Because she was the last of Henry's queens, and because of the importance of the minority government which followed his death, Catherine remains in some ways a controversial figure. Until after the king's return from France she was regarded by all as a model spouse. She promoted her own family as and when possible, and patronized reforming clergy and scholars. She had taken as her motto 'To be useful in all I do', and her role in caring for the king's children was a practical example of that precept. She was no bluestocking, and occasionally disclosed a disconcerting streak of anti-intellectualism, but there is no sign that she was anything other than pleased by the arrangements which Henry made for his son's education. During the first year of her marriage she seems to have had few pretensions, and a recent commentator has noted that her letters to the king during the Boulogne campaign lacked that touch of the didactic which had been very evident in the letters which Catherine of Aragon had written in similar circumstances.[33] However, in the latter part of 1544 there seems to have been a subtle change. Perhaps the responsibilities of the Regency had aroused in Catherine a political animal which had hitherto lain dormant. Moreover, her religious views seem to have been getting stronger. She made at least one attempt to interest Henry in a Protestant alliance once the emperor had signed a unilateral peace with France. In February 1545 her secretary, Walter Bucler, accompanied the king's agent, Christopher Mont, on a tour designed to create a league between England, Denmark, Holstein and Hesse. This was not necessarily the queen's idea, because a similar scheme had been mooted in 1539, but the use of her secretary is suggestive of her involvement.[34] The mission was a closely guarded secret, but was aborted after about six months, when no progress had been made. The year 1545 was largely taken up with defensive preparations against the French, who attempted to mount a large-scale invasion during July. This armada was turned back in the Solent without serious fighting because England's naval defences were fully mobilized. Having also failed to recover Boulogne, by the autumn Francis was ready for peace negotiations, and it may have been for that reason that the search for a new alliance was abandoned. It was also during this year that Catherine began to step up her evangelical activities, and probably crossed that shadowy border zone between orthodox reform and Protestantism. The second of her two works of piety, the *Lamentation*, was written either late in 1545 or early in 1546, and shows an animus against the Catholic Church which had not been evident in the *Prayer and Meditations*. The *Lamentation* is a positive, almost aggressive piece of proselytizing, and if it reflects the tone of her discourse in the spring of 1546, it is not difficult to see why the king could be persuaded that she had overstepped the mark.

The crisis of 1546 frightened Catherine badly, and in restoring amicable relations with her increasingly sick and ill-tempered husband, she abandoned all further attempts to convert him. How important her role was in the development and eventual triumph of the evangelical party in court and council must therefore remain a matter for some speculation. Always sympathetic to reform, she seems to have undergone a personal conversion at some point between the summer of 1544 and the end of 1545, but her specific doctrinal position was never made clear during Henry's lifetime. As the person best placed to influence the king, her part was a very conspicuous one, but she was not necessarily a leader. How much Henry really listened to her, as opposed to being flattered and diverted, may be questioned, and eventually her over-enthusiasm came close to wrecking the whole enterprise. The king's reasons for favouring the evangelical party, and eventually destroying their opponents, probably had little to do with sympathy for their religious programme. Hertford, Cranmer, Lisle and Denny were men whom he trusted in the last months of his life, and it was to them that he eventually entrusted the management of his heir. His widow was given no role, and should probably be seen as no more than a useful member of the winning team. The old king may have been erratic, and intermittently gullible, but he could not be tamed to anyone else's purpose, even by a woman who was prepared to lavish such dutiful care upon his decaying body.

Henry died on 28 January 1547, and was interred at St George's chapel, Windsor on 16 February. By that time Edward Seymour, Earl of Hertford, had been created Protector of the Realm, Governor of the King's Person, and Duke of Somerset.[35] Somerset had sufficient allies in the Regency council which Henry had decreed to control the government, and within a few weeks a policy outline began to appear, which involved a renewal of war against the Scots and a radical change in the practices of the Church. In all this, however, Catherine was to play no part, which suggests that her importance had always rested more on Henry's conceit of her than in any political talent which she might possess. Although now the queen dowager, and an immensely wealthy woman, her aptitudes were seen to be domestic rather than public. At the same time, she seems to have entertained no ambition for power, and instead began to look for that personal satisfaction which her three marriages had so far failed to provide. Within a few weeks Thomas Seymour, now Lord Seymour of Sudeley and Lord High Admiral, renewed the suit which he had been forced to abandon in 1543. Catherine responded as she had always been inclined to respond. The cool self-controlled discretion of eighteen years of chaste matrimony was forgotten as she threw herself into a torrid romance. Seymour may well have made the running, but it is clear from the reaction of Catherine's close friends that they approved of the affair, and did everything in their power to promote it.[36] The couple seem to have become lovers by early May, and have married secretly some time in June. Somerset was strongly opposed to what he saw as his brother's bid for self-aggrandisement, but Edward, who liked both his stepmother and his tearaway uncle, was persuaded to bless the match on 25 June, some time after it had taken place. This did not appease either the Duke of Somerset or his wife, but it did make it impossible to take any action against the offenders.

Undeclared war ensued between Catherine, who claimed precedent at court by right of her status as queen dowager, and the Duchess of Somerset, who claimed it as wife of the first subject. These skirmishes were sufficiently ludicrous in themselves, but unfortunately they contributed to the growing animosity between the two Seymour brothers, and fed Thomas' paranoid jealousy of his elder. He began to sulk, neglecting his responsibilities as admiral, and even entering into clandestine relationships with some of the pirates he was supposed to bring to justice. In due course this would lead to his dramatic downfall, but Catherine did not live to mourn the only man who had ever offered her the kind of love she craved. At the end of 1547 when she was nearly thirty-six, she conceived her first child. In spite of her husband's antics, both public and private, her pregnancy proceeded smoothly, and the intimate letters which passed between them give a vivid picture of her happiness at this time.[37] The indiscreet romps with the Princess Elizabeth, then living in their household, in which they both indulged, were probably no more than a reflection of the same high spirits. However, happiness seems to have robbed Catherine of her habitual good sense, and only when it was too late, and her husband's reputation further compromised, was Elizabeth sent to live elsewhere. At the end of June 1548 Catherine retired to Sudeley Castle to await her confinement, and on 30 August gave birth to a daughter, who was named Mary. The child thrived, but the mother did not. Like Jane Seymour before her, she contracted puerperal fever, and died six days later. Her husband of fifteen months was with her at the end, and she was buried with Protestant rites under the auspices of her almoner, the biblical scholar, Miles Coverdale.

Catherine would no doubt have been delighted by the way in which her young stepson's reign was to develop, and if she had lived Lord Thomas might not have died in disgrace. However, she was not the midwife of a Protestant England. Her brief marriage to Henry was significant in many ways, but more for the peace and contentment which she managed to bestow on her extremely difficult and irascible husband than for any influence which she had over him or his court. At the end, as at the beginning, Henry was the master in his own house, and in his kingdom, and however foolishly he behaved from time to time, he made the decisions which shaped the future. Whether his sixth wife was ever more to him than a comfortable piece of furniture may be doubted, because Henry was only truly influenced by passionate relationships, and when she came to him his passion was spent. Hers was not, but it could not be given to him. Instead it was reserved for a charming rogue, who gave her a year of happiness to compensate for a barren crown.

# EPILOGUE

# The Much-married King

Henry VIII was larger than life in every respect. Physically he was a giant who came close to ending as a monster. Politically he sustained a role in Europe to which neither his lineage nor the resources of his kingdom entitled him. England and Wales had a population of barely three million in the early sixteenth century, compared to some fourteen million in France, and over thirty million in the various territories of the Emperor Charles V. Henry's revenues were a fraction of those of his principal rivals, less than Portugal and a little more than those of Denmark.[1] And yet he played in the premier league throughout his reign, invaded France three times without effective reply, and defied the whole of Catholic Europe for fifteen years. To some extent the reasons for this were historical, and had little to do with Henry himself. The English Crown was institutionally strong, and better able to mobilize its resources than any of its contemporaries. The English people, moreover, were xenophobic and fiercely independent, so that foreign intervention was always likely to be rejected, no matter what the circumstances. However, the king should also receive his share of the credit. It was he who created a navy, as large and well-armed as those of his rivals, and far better organized, which largely controlled the Narrow Seas, and effectively withstood the one serious French attempt to invade in 1545.[2] It was he also who created a court which in many respects outshone that of the emperor, and rivalled that of France in everything except size. Circumstances conspired to favour him. The rivalry between Francis I and Charles V, which was partly inherited and partly the result of the imperial election of 1519, enabled him to play one off against the other. Through no contrivance of his own, his quarrel with the Pope also coincided with the rise of the Lutheran movement in Germany, which distracted attention from his activities. Yet much of his success must be attributed to bluff, both at home and abroad. His honour, his magnanimity, even his towering rages, all were to some extent fraudulent. This was not done deliberately, because he deceived himself as assiduously as he deceived others, but was the product of his charasmatic and exceedingly complex personality. It is because so much of that personality is revealed by his successive marriages that they so richly repay investigation.

Each marriage was, in its own way, a political and personal statement. No one expected Henry to marry Catherine of Aragon in 1509, and in doing so he declared his independence of his father's councillors, and his confidence in his own ability to manage a woman both older and more powerfully connected than himself. Had their second child, Prince Henry, lived, it is highly unlikely that the marriage would ever had broken down, and the whole subsequent history of England would have been different.[3] However, it would be equally true to say that if Edward IV had lived another ten years the Tudors would never have come to the throne at all; or if one of Queen Anne's numerous brood had survived there would have been no Hanoverian succession. Young Henry did not live, and what was in every other respect a normal and successful royal marriage had foundered on the lack of a male heir. Such dynastic misfortunes were commonplace, and the king was altogether exceptional in refusing to accept his alloted fate. Whether this was a result of his sensitivity to the needs of his realm, or of his own colossal ego can be debated. Neither Henry nor his subjects wanted a female heir, but his decision to contest the judgement on grounds of conscience was highly eccentric, and left everyone puzzled and wrong-footed. Catherine, for all her intelligence and strength of character, was a profoundly conventional woman, and unable to understand the passions which motivated her husband in that crisis. From about 1525 Henry was seeking to bend the will of God to his own purposes, and in the process he demonstrated that others were doing the same, and had done so for centuries. As God can only work through human agents, the interpretation of His will was subject to the normal dynamics of political power.

It was this discovery, felt rather than articulated, which set the king's agenda over the next ten years. Martin Luther expressed it succinctly and disapprovingly when he said 'Junker Heintz will be God and do whatever he lusts'. That was not how Henry saw it. In his own eyes he was an heroic figure, striving to free his realm from the toils of an ancient conspiracy, and give it an independent future.[4] To do that it was necessary to establish his own undisputed control over the Church within his realm, and the royal supremacy became his masterpiece. So convinced did Henry become of the rightness of this course of action, and of its conformity with the Divine purpose, that it became the touchstone of loyalty and morality among his subjects. It is in this context that the king's second marriage must be viewed. In one sense Anne Boleyn was a complication he could have done without, because his relationship with her enabled Catherine's numerous friends and supporters to represent him as no more than a traditionally unfaithful husband. On the other hand, without her support, to say nothing of his desire for her, it is quite possible that his will to solve his dynastic and political problems might well have collapsed. She held him to his purpose because she was part of it, but she was not the whole of it, as subsequent events were to reveal. Anne represented freedom, not merely from Catherine, or even from the papal jurisdiction, but from a whole framework of political thought.[5] Law was no longer a question of finding the best way to express accepted norms; it was a question of identifying a legislative will between the king and the political nation, in which no outsider had any right to interfere. Henry's second marriage, therefore, was the one which affected the most profound changes. The fact that it did not endure was much less important. Anne fell, not because of the changes which she had helped to bring about, but because of the dynamics of court politics and the fact that her power over the king was based upon nothing more durable than sexual chemistry. Had she borne a son, no doubt she would have survived, but her survival was not necessary to protect the achievements which her rise had brought about. The king's behaviour during the summer of 1536 demonstrated that his self-deception was capable of taking the form of a monstrous and amoral credulity, but it also demonstrated that the new agenda was his own, and not that of Anne and her friends.

Jane Seymour represented no new policy, and Henry's third marriage was probably the least significant in political terms. Her half-hearted attempts to persuade the king to retreat from some of the positions which he had adopted were totally unsuccessful. Jane, on the other hand, finally brought the crowning glory of a son, and her relationship with Henry probably brought out the best in him. She was a desirable woman and an unchallenging companion, and her brief incumbency of the crown matrimonial represents its retreat into domesticity. Henry loved her, and described her as his 'only true wife', but he did not take any steps to make their union legitimate in the sight of the Catholic Europe. Given her conservative religious views, if she had lived and borne the king more children, it is possible that he might have been tempted to renegotiate his relations with the papacy. However, since it was during her reign that the dissolution of the monasteries was decreed, and the campaign against pilgrimage shrines reached its peak, that seems unlikely.

The Cleves marriage, although in most repects the least successful of Henry's unions, as well as the shortest, was nevertheless important. Cromwell certainly, and the king probably, embarked upon the negotiation on the assumption that the woman was less important than the policy which she represented. If Jane Seymour had been wedded for purely personal reasons, Anne of Cleves was the symbol of a foreign policy which was trying to get off the Franco-Imperial roller-coaster without being enveigled into the Confession of Augsburg. How she would have fared if the international situation had not changed must remain a matter for speculation. Henry was fairly public with his expressions of distaste, although his manners to Anne herself remained good.[6] The issue remained low key, partly because Anne was not another Catherine of Aragon (nor Duke William another Charles V), and partly because the royal supremacy gave the king of England the jurisdiction to settle all such matters to his own satisfaction without recourse to outsiders. Anne had not represented a Protestant alliance, so her repudiation did not represent its abandonment. Nor was it the principal cause of Thomas Cromwell's fall, which was the most seismic event of 1540. The loud expressions of disgust in many European courts which greeted the news of the dissolution of this marriage were conventional noises, but they were partly provoked by a renewed awareness of just how far the king of England had stepped ouside the conventions of normal royal behaviour. Kings had occasionally repudiated their wives in the past, but Henry had now done so three times in less than a decade, and this time, as it was generally appreciated, upon a mere whim of sexual taste. How much more irresponsible could a monarch become? At the same time Anne's treatment, including her continued residence in England, was yet another example of how completely Henry had become master in his own house. Nevertheless, in another sense it was a deeply undermining experience. In confessing to his physician, Dr William Butts, that he felt no desire for his wife, he felt constrained to add that he was sure that he could do 'the deed' with another, but not with her.[7]

Who that other might be soon became apparent, but the charms of Catherine Howard were an afterthought as far as the repudiation of Anne was concerned. They also snared Henry into what was probably his worst matrimonial blunder. On the rebound from one humiliation, he leapt straight into another, without any apparent thought for the political consequences. Catherine, like Jane Seymour, represented no policy higher than a search for personal gratification, unless it was an increasingly desperate hope for further offspring. In political terms she was no more than a piece of factional bait, dangled under the king's nose by her Howard kindred with a fine disregard for the possible consequences. If she represented anything at all, it was an attempt to consolidate the conservative religious successes which had culminated in the overthrow of Cromwell. However, that conservatism was relative. Neither Norfolk nor Gardiner was seeking to bring about a papist reaction, knowing perfectly well which options were open and which closed. Catherine herself had neither the intelligence nor the maturity to sustain a political role, and although the reformers were on the retreat during this period, they were never defeated or removed from the council and privy chamber. In advancing a young woman with a shady past, and little control over her emotions, the Howards took an appalling risk which came within an ace of destroying them, but they also inflicted serious psychological damage upon the king. It was not so much that he suddenly grew old as that his growing fears about his sexual impotence were suddenly confirmed. Not with all the puissance of his Crown could he hold the affections of a wayward girl.

By 1543, when his political power was at its height and all challenges had been defeated, the king had become a pathetic figure. He was enormously fat, crippled with what was probably osteomyelitis, and a martyr to continual colds and colics.[8] A portrait engraving of him by Cornelius Matsuys, executed at about this time, shows a figure of brooding menace, with a face which has been compared, not unfairly, to a giant potato. We do not know how, or why he selected his last bride. She may have been brought to his attention by some trusted courtier who understood his needs, she may have been put forward by the reforming party, as Catherine Howard had been by the conservatives. We can be reasonably sure that she did not draw attention to herself, because she had already set her cap at Thomas Seymour before Lord Latimer died. She was in many respects Henry's best choice, and she fulfilled her brief better than any of her predecessors. It was a simpler brief, because the explosive sexual element, which had made and unmade most of the king's relationships, was almost entirely absent, but it must have been a demanding and in some ways distasteful one. Most of what we know about Catherine Parr relates to her domestic virtues and her general amiability, but her political role should not be neglected. Whether she intended it or not, her evangelical activities gave her a party affiliation. In other words she was very much a part of the power struggle which was going on at court in the last four years of Henry's life – a power struggle which was aimed at the control of an increasingly imminent minority.[9] If Catherine had any ambitions for herself in that struggle, they did not appear. She made no protest, either at the time or subsequently, at being ignored in the establishment of the Regency, and her priority after the king's death was obviously and very urgently personal. In spite

HENRICVS DEI GRA REX ANGLIE ·

*Cornelius Matsuys' portrait engraving of Henry VIII at the age of fifty-three, 1544*

of her innocent reputation, Henry's last queen was exceedingly good at concealing her real feelings, and her behaviour in the last year of her life raises some questions about the apparent selflessness of her years as the king's companion and sick-nurse.

To his own subjects Henry VIII eventually became a great king, whose shadow dominated the twenty years after his death, and whom his long-lived and successful daughter Elizabeth delighted to honour.[10] To his European contemporaries he was a monster who had torn apart the fabric of the universal Church in order to gratify his unlawful lust, and had repudiated four wives, killing two of them when they failed to please him sufficiently. Catherine of Aragon became a saint, Anne Boleyn a demon (in which guise she still featured in Spanish carnivals to the present century), and Anne of Cleves became a bad joke. There was truth both in the icon and in the caricature. Whatever views we may embrace about the mechanics of English government during his reign, it cannot be denied that he wrought a major transformation in the legislative process. His establishment of the royal supremacy in partnership with parliament turned out to be a major development in the evolution of the realm.[11] It could have been a dead end, but it is not quite sufficient to say that if his daughter Mary had lived longer his achievements would have been consigned to oblivion. By the time that Henry died the royal supremacy had become 'an English thing', and Mary's repeal of the statutes in which it was embodied did not end its appeal. Elizabeth rather than Henry made it a permanent feature of the English state, but it may well be doubted whether she could have created it from scratch in the circumstances of her succession in 1559. We are, in fact, perfectly entitled to regard Henry as one of the major political architects who transformed medieval England into the dominant partner of a modern nation state. And although he was never a Protestant, he was also mainly responsible for the fact that England had become a Protestant state by the end of the sixteenth century, and a Protestant world power by the end of the seventeenth. Whatever judgement we may pass on his faith or his morals, his political achievements justified his historical stature.

However, Henry was a man who did not live his life in separate compartments. Despite some theories to the contrary, medieval kings did not normally keep the affairs of Church and State in different pockets, and Henry similarly did not distinguish between his public and private life. However unfortunate the consequences may have been, he took his women seriously. All of them, except Anne of Cleves, played boudoir politics to secure the promotion of their own families or favourites, but there was far more to their roles than that. Catherine of Aragon was an ambassador, first for her father and then for her nephew. She was also an active champion of strict religious orthodoxy. Consequently far more was involved in her repudiation than the king's search for an heir. That was certainly the occasion, but the causes were more complex, and the consequences extended far beyond the limits of dynasticism. By the same token Anne Boleyn was far more than a seductress who stole Henry's heart from his lawful wife. She was a political leader of skill and determination, with a programme which involved much more than the elevation of her kindred. Anne understood the significance of the royal supremacy, and the uses to which it could be put, which raised far wider issues than the security of her own position. Because of her sex, and her relationship to the king, her fall had to be choreographed in emotional and salacious terms, but she was executed for the same reason that Thomas Cromwell was to be executed, because she was too dangerous to be rusticated. In spite of the spectacular nature of the charges against her, Anne was at least as much a rejected councillor as an adulterous wife. Those who considered Henry to be a mere barbarian who cut off his wife's head if she displeased him, chose not to notice that the one woman whose death would really have solved his problems, namely Catherine of Aragon, survived to die in her bed. The execution of a royal spouse was almost unprecedented, and it must be seen as a reflection of the quite exceptional role which Anne had come to play in her husband's affairs.

Later generations, on both sides of the confessional divide, represented Anne as the foster mother of English Protestantism, but that is certainly incorrect. She was a reformer whose patronage extended to many who later became Protestants, but there is no evidence to suggest that her own views on such central issues as justification or the eucharist were anything but orthodox. Nor was she ever accused of heresy, even when her enemies were on the look out for any possible way of damaging her reputation. The woman who could, perhaps, have been so charged, and against whom a case was at least made, was Catherine Parr. After Anne she was the queen who had the most courage. However we may view her personal influence over Henry, she represented a religious culture which emerged into a position of dominance in the last months of the reign, with incalculable consequences for the future. In this context Jane Seymour hardly counts, being by far the most 'normal' of Henry's queens. Perhaps it is hardly safe to describe any of them as a 'mere woman', but her importance depended entirely upon her physical appeal to the king, and her success in bearing him the much needed son. The political convulsion which attended her rise was none of her making, and her death caused scarcely a ripple, except of personal grief. Catherine Howard enhanced Henry's reputation for 'frightfulness', and no doubt her fate confirmed Christina of Denmark in her low opinion of the king of England as a prospective mate.[12] Catherine was not dangerous in the sense that Anne had been, and there seems in retrospect very little justification for her death. In a previous generation she would very probably have been incarcerated in a nunnery, but by 1541 there were no nunneries in England. Her execution can only be interpreted as an act of revenge, Henry's enraged reaction to disillusionment and humiliation, dressed up in a quasi legal form.

Passion and sexuality are thus interwoven with the politics of Henry's reign from the first until almost the last. War and procreation are both ways in which a king can demonstrate his prowess, and he longed for success in both with all his heart. Instead his performance in both was unsatisfactory, and consciousness of this wore away the self-esteem upon which he needed to build. Jousting and courtly love were really no substitute for foreign conquests and a full nursery. Edward, and finally Boulogne, were precious trophies, but not a great deal to show for such an enormous investment of time, money and emotional energy. Henry's final war with France, concluded in the summer of 1546,[13] cost him well over £2,000,000 and left the realm heavily in debt. Without the fiasco of his relationship with Catherine Howard it might never have been fought. His greatest triumph was the establishment of the ecclesiastical supremacy, and we may well doubt whether that would ever have come about had his fascination with Anne Boleyn not held him to his purpose against what must have seemed enormous odds. Personal monarchy was always full of such complex interpenetrations, but nowhere were passion, ambition and conscience so curiously and dangerously juxtaposed as in Henry VIII. Contemporaries found it remarkable that he chose to marry his women, no matter what the cost, instead of using them and casting them aside as his fellows did. One of the reasons for this was his need for legitimate children, but another was his belief, curiously enough, in the sanctity of marriage. He was offended by loose sexual morality, and upbraided his sister, Margaret, when she abandoned her second husband, the Earl of Angus. He took both his known mistresses while his first marriage still seemed to be secure. Until 1525 he was a conventional Renaissance prince, but thereafter his political and sexual imperatives drove him into uncharted waters, with extremely constructive results for the future of England. Over half a century after his death William Shakespeare was to write,

> . . . what infinite heart's ease
> Must Kings neglect that private men enjoy!
> And what have kings that privates have not too,
> Save ceremony, save general ceremony?[14]

and, of course, the facility to change their wives when personal or public necessity might require it.

# Notes and References

## Introduction

1. Duke Francis II of Brittany had died in 1488, leaving his twelve-year-old daughter, Anne, as his heir. Charles VIII claimed her wardship, as her father's feudal overlord, and married her three years later, in spite of strenuous objections from both Henry VII and Maximilian. The marriage was childless, and when Charles died in 1498 he was succeeded by his cousin, Louis XII. In order to preserve the union, Louis was permitted to set aside his existing wife, Jeanne, in order to marry the twenty-two-year-old widow. In October 1499 she bore him a daughter, Claude. In January 1514, when Anne died, Claude technically became Duchess, but Brittany remained under the control of her father. In May 1514 Claude married Francis of Angoulême, the heir to the throne, and became his queen later in the same year, when her father died. In June 1515 Claude was persuaded to make over the administration of the duchy to the French Crown in perpetuity, and after her death, in 1532, it was formally and finally annexed.

2. Henry's interest in a Scottish marriage sprang originally from James IV's support of Perkin Warbeck in 1495/6. The Scots invaded England on Warbeck's behalf in September 1496, but the pretender had no support south of the border, and James concluded the Truce of Ayton with Henry in 1497. Bishop Richard Fox of Durham continued his diplomatic efforts and the truce was renewed in 1499. By that time Warbeck was no longer a factor, but Henry desired a long-term settlement, and a peace treaty, sealed by the marriage, was concluded in 1502.

3. Elizabeth Grey was the daughter of Richard Woodville, Lord Rivers, and the widow of Sir John Grey of Groby, the son of Lord Ferrers. Her mother was Jaquetta of Luxembourg, the widow of John, Duke of Bedford. Charles Ross, *Edward IV*, 85–93.

4. Anne was descended on her father's side from the Butler Earls of Ormonde, and her mother was Elizabeth, the daughter of Thomas Howard, 3rd Duke of Norfolk, but none of this cut much ice when one of her chief disparagers was the king's sister, Mary. E.W. Ives, *Anne Boleyn*, 206–7.

5. Baldesar Castiglione, *The Book of the Courtier*, trans. George Bull, 211.

6. Juana's madness may in fact have been more apparent than real, because it suited her father, and later her son, to keep her out of the way. However, it is hard to accept S.B. Chrimes' view that Henry had 'no reason to suppose' her deranged when he sought a marriage. *Henry VII*, 291.

7. Arthur (1486–1502), Henry (1491–1547), Edmund (1499–1500), Margaret (1489–1541), Mary (1496–1533).

8. R.A. Griffiths, *The Reign of King Henry VI*, 868.

9. J. Gairdner, *Letters and Papers Illustrative of the Reigns of Richard III and Henry VII* (Rolls Series), I, 233–4.

10. Edward was survived by Elizabeth, who married Henry VII, Cecily, who married John, Viscount Welles, Anne, who married Thomas Howard, 2nd Duke of Norfolk, Catherine, who married William Courtenay, Earl of Devon, and by Edward, Richard and Bridget, who died unmarried. Had he lived it seems very likely that one or more of them would have been matched to secure foreign alliances.

11. D.M. Loades, 'Philip II and the Government of England' in *Law and Government under the Tudors*, eds. C. Cross, D. Loades and J. Scarisbrick, 177–94.

## Chapter One

1. This had been provisionally agreed at the Treaty of Medina del Campo in 1489, and although it was not finally concluded for another ten years Catherine seems to have been referred to as 'Princess of Wales' thereafter. Jeromino Zunita, *Anales de la Corona de Aragon* (Saragossa, 1610), IV, 358–9; G. Mattingly, *Catherine of Aragon*, 21.
2. Edward Hall, *Chronicle*, 493. For a full discussion of this pageantry and its significance, see S. Anglo, *Spectacle, Pageantry and Early Tudor Policy*, 56–97.
3. Mattingly, op. cit., 40–1.
4. Polydore Vergil, *Anglica Historia*, ed. D. Hay (Camden Society, LXXIV, 1950).
5. *Calendar of State Papers, Spanish*, I, 267.
6. Catherine's early widowhood seems to have been very secluded, first because of her mourning, and then because of the fierce protectiveness of Dona Elvira, but she would have known Henry by sight, and known that his name was being linked with her own. Mattingly, op. cit., 51–2.
7. Ibid., 57.
8. Roderigo de Puebla was a man of humble, and what was worse, Jewish origins. He must surely have been one of the most misused as well as one of the most dedicated diplomats of the period. Ferdinand trusted him but kept him perpetually short of money, so that he became dependent upon subsidies from Henry VII. Catherine was typical of the Spanish aristocracy in general in despising him. G. Mattingly, 'The Reputation of Dr de Puebla', *E(nglish) H(istorical) R(eview)*, LV, 1940, 27–46.
9. *Correspondencia de Gutierre Gomez de Fuensalida*, ed. Duke of Berwick and Alba, 490.
10. B(ritish) L(ibrary), Additional MS 7099, ff. 18, 19, 36, 41; which record the king's expenditure on a tennis professional and equipment.
11. Hall, *Chronicle*, 507.
12. *Correspondencia*, 515–17.
13. For a full account of this tournament, see Hall, *Chronicle*, 510–12.
14. *Cal. Sp.*, II, 44.
15. Francesca, an incorrigible gossip, had quit Catherine's service early in 1509 and married an Italian banker resident in London, named Grimaldi. Mattingly, *Catherine*, 110–12.

16. Hall, *Chronicle*, 532. Hall has a full and circumstantial account of this campaign. See also J.J. Scarisbrick, *Henry VIII*, 29–31.
17. *Letters and Papers . . . of the Reign of Henry VIII* (BL Cotton MS Vit. B IV, ff. 107). Scarisbrick, *Henry VIII*, 52–3. P.J. Gwyn, *The King's Cardinal*.
18. Andrea Badoer to the Doge and Senate, 8 January 1515, *Calendar of State Papers Venetian*, II, 555.
19. BL Harleian MS 3504, f. 232. David Loades, *Mary Tudor: a Life*, 14–15.
20. T. Rymer, ed., *Foedera, conventiones . . . etc.* XIII, 624 ff. Scarisbrick, *Henry VIII*, 71–3.
21. *Cal. Ven.*, II, 1103.
22. Mattingly, *Catherine*, 135–6.
23. Ibid. An eye-witness description of the events of Evil May Day was given by the Venetian envoy, Chieragato. *Cal. Ven.*, II, 385.
24. Maria Dowling, *Humanism in the Age of Henry VIII*, 223–4.
25. On 2 July 1520, before Henry got back from Calais, three of Francis' gentlemen paid a formal call upon the princess at Richmond and were able to confirm in their report that her absence had not been caused by any illness or hitherto unsuspected defect. Loades, *Mary Tudor*, 19–20.
26. *Letters and Papers*, III, 1508, 1571.
27. *Letters and Papers*, III, 1150.
28. Hall, *Chronicle*, 635.
29. Ives, *Anne Boleyn*, 19. *Letters and Papers*, XII(2), 952.
30. Hall, *Chronicle*, 696. For a full discussion of the Amicable Grant and its circumstances, see G.W. Bernard, *War, Taxation and Rebellion in Early Tudor England, passim*.
31. Giovanni Batista Sangi to the Bishop of Capua, *Letters and Papers*, IV, 843.
32. H. Ellis, *Original Letters Illustrative of English History*, II, 19.
33. There is a long-running disagreement about the relative ages of Mary and Anne. I have here accepted the dating proposed by Ives (*Anne Boleyn*, 17–19). Retha Warnicke on the other hand (*The Rise and Fall of Anne Boleyn*, 8–10) argues that Anne was the elder, but since she also appears to accept 1507 as Anne's year of birth, Mary would have been no more than twelve on her marriage, and possibly less when she became the king's mistress. If Anne was born in 1507, then Mary was certainly the elder, but I am convinced

that Anne was born in 1501, and that she was the younger.

34. Ives, op. cit., 32–4.
35. S.J. Gunn, *Charles Brandon, Duke of Suffolk, 1484–1545*, 28–30.
36. G. Ascoli, *La Grande-Bretagne devant l'Opinion Française*, lines 55–8, cited Ives, 36–7.
37. Ives, *Anne Boleyn*, 43–6.
38. *Letters and Papers*, III, 1559; Hall, *Chronicle*, 631; Ives, 47–8.
39. Ibid., 77–110; D. Loades, *The Tudor Court*, 96–113.
40. George Cavendish, *The Life and Death of Cardinal Wolsey*, ed. R.S. Sylvester (Early English Text Society), 243, 29–35.
41. Hall, *Chronicle*, 707.

## Chapter Two

1. Sir Thomas Wyatt, *Collected Poems*, ed. J. Daalder, VII.
2. BL Cotton MS Otho C X, f. 185. *The Divorce Tracts of Henry VIII*, eds. J. Sturtz and V. Murphy, xiii.
3. George Wyatt (normally a source sympathetic to Anne) supports this story, saying that she 'having had crafty counsel did thus overreach the king with show of modesty'. BL Sloane MS 2495, f. 3. Ives, *Anne Boleyn*, 104.
4. Francis was a notorious womanizer, and the unsuitable nature of the match was widely commented on, particularly by the queen's friends.
5. *Letters and Papers*, IV, 3148, 3232.
6. Mattingly, *Catherine*, 185–6. For Henry's attempt to impede Felipez, see the confidential letter from William Knight to Wolsey, dated 14 July 1527. *Letters and Papers*, IV, 3265.
7. Henry's first intention had been to apply for a licence to commit bigamy, but Wolsey got wind of that and managed to scotch it. The fact that he did not discover about the second request is a measure of the extent to which he had lost the king's confidence. Scarisbrick, *Henry VIII*, 159–60.
8. *Letters and Papers*, IV, 3757, 3783: Scarisbrick, op. cit., 198–9.
9. BL Cotton Otho C X, f. 220. *Letters and Papers*, IV, Appendix 197. Ives, *Anne Boleyn*, 133.
10. Hall, *Chronicle*, 754.
11. Ibid., 755.
12. Ibid., 756.
13. George Cavendish, *The Life and Death of Cardinal Wolsey*, ed. R.S. Sylvester (Early English Text Society), 243, 35–6.
14. J. Dauvillier, *Le Marriage dans le Droit Classique de l'Eglise*; Scarisbrick, 214.
15. *Letters and Papers*, IV, 3844; *Cal. Sp.*, III, ii, 845.
16. *Letters and Papers*, IV, 5797.
17. Ibid., 574; Ives, *Anne Boleyn*, 145.
18. Ibid., 154.
19. Ibid., 170–3.
20. For a discussion of these views and their influence, see Jasper Ridley, *Thomas Cranmer*, 24–8; D. Loades, *Cranmer and the English Reformation*, 4–9; G.D. Nicholson, 'The nature and function of historical argument in the Henrician Reformation' (Cambridge University Ph.D, 1977) *passim*.
21. *The Papers of George Wyatt*, ed. D. Loades (Camden Society, 4th series, vol. V, 1968), 24.
22. Edward Herbert, *The History of England under Henry VIII*, ed. White Kennett, 446–51.
23. 'I say I am his lawfull wyfe, and to hym lawfully maryed and by the ordre of holye Churche I was to hym espowsed as his true wyfe. . . .' Mattingly, *Catherine*, 241.
24. *Cal. Ven.*, IV, 682; 25 August 1531.
25. Ives, *Anne Boleyn*, 190.
26. A. Ogle, *The Tragedy of the Lollards' Tower*, 340.
27. Only one other woman was so honoured during the sixteenth century. Margaret Pole was created Countess of Salisbury in her own right in 1513, but she was the daughter of the Duke of Clarence, and her maternal grandfather had held the title.
28. Hall, *Chronicle*, 793–4. Francis was negotiating for a marriage between his second son, Henri, and the Pope's niece, Catherine de' Medici, which took place in October 1533.
29. Henry also seems to have believed that Francis would join him in appealing his cause to a General Council. Ives, *Anne Boleyn*, 202.
30. Cranmer held strongly Erastian views from his first appearance in a public forum. J. Foxe, *Acts and Monuments of the English Martyrs*, eds. S.R. Cattley and George Townsend, VIII, 9.

## Chapter Three

1. Printed by Wynkyn de Worde for John Gough, in 1533 (STC 656). Reprinted in A.F. Pollard, *Tudor Tracts* (London, 1903), 9–29.
2. Loades, *Mary Tudor*, 69.
3. *Letters and Papers*, VI, 568.
4. *Cal. Sp.*, IV, ii, 510. Mattingly, *Catherine*, 258.
5. A view of Catherine's expenses from 19 December 1533 to 30 September 1534, after the second reduction of her household, showed an income of £3,000 and an expenditure of £2,950. *Letters and Papers*, VII, 1208.
6. Ascoli, *l'Opinion*, lines 111–27.
7. Ives, *Anne Boleyn*, 230–1.
8. *Letters and Papers*, IX, 477 (PRO SC6 Henry VIII 6680). An incomplete *valor* for the 5th Earl of Shrewsbury in 1538–9 gives a landed income of £1,735, which would suggest a total of about £3,500; PRO C54 412. In 1560 the earl was alleged to be worth £4,000 a year.
9. Mattingly, *Catherine*, 258–61.
10. *Letters and Papers*, VI, 1186.
11. Ibid., VI, 1296.
12. Loades, *Mary Tudor*, 82–3.
13. Ibid.
14. *Letters and Papers*, VII, 296; Ives, *Anne Boleyn*, 248.
15. Thomas Cromwell had been perfectly well aware of this argument since at least 1533, and had noted it in April of that year, at the time when Catherine's marriage had finally been declared void. *Letters and Papers*, VI, 386 ii.
16. BL Arundel MS 151 f. 194; *Letters and Papers*, VI, 1126. For the dating of this letter, see Loades, *Mary Tudor*, 78 n. 5.
17. Ascoli, *l'Opinion*, lines 209–13.
18. BL Wyatt MS 18, f. lv. Loades, *George Wyatt* (Camden Society, 4th series, vol. V 1968), 22.
19. *Letters and Papers*, IX, 271, 326. Ives, *Anne Boleyn*, 336–7.
20. Hall, *Chronicle*, 818. In public Anne was as triumphant as Henry, but there are some suggestions that in private she was troubled by the death of her old rival; *Letters and Papers*, IX, 199.
21. The record of this rebuke is in his instructions to his own ambassador with the emperor, delivered in September 1534 '. . . we think it not meet that any person should prescribe unto us how we should order our own daughter, we being her natural father'. *Letters and Papers*, VII, 1209.
22. George Wyatt, 'The Life of Queen Anne Boleigne' in *The Life of Cardinal Wolsey by George Cavendish*, ed. S.W. Singer, 443. For a full account of the 'sexual heresy' theory of Anne's fall, see Warnicke, *Rise and Fall*, 191–233.
23. Warnicke, *Rise and Fall*, 195.
24. There is no explicit reference to this deformity before Sander, and the thesis of its importance depends upon psychological reconstruction.
25. Ives, *Anne Boleyn*, 347–8.
26. *Letters and Papers*, X, 351, 699. An important meeting was held between the king and Chapuys at Greenwich on 18 April.
27. *Letters and Papers*, X, 908, 1069. Ives, *Anne Boleyn*, 355–6.
28. Warnicke, *Rise and Fall*, 204–5.
29. *Letters and Papers*, X, 726.
30. Ives, *Anne Boleyn*, 359.
31. *Letters and Papers*, X, 908; P. Friedman, *Anne Boleyn: a Chapter of English History, 1527–1536*, ii, 176 n. i, 267 n. ii.
32. Singer, *Wolsey*, 458–9; Baynton to Sir William Fitzwilliam; both were commissioners investigating the charges against Anne and Norris.
33. The poisoning charges were not included in the indictment, but were made in the course of the trial. The numerous accounts of the trial are listed in Ives, *Anne Boleyn*, 386 n. 6.
34. Singer, *Wolsey*, 451, 457.
35. Warnicke, *Rise and Fall*, 203–4: *Letters and Papers*, X, 876; Charles Wriothesley, *A Chronicle of England during the Reigns of the Tudors, 1485–1559*, ed. W.D. Hamilton (Camden Society, 2nd series, vol. XI), 189–226.
36. Warnicke, *Rise and Fall*, 219. The sixteenth-century horror of homosexuality was very strong, and if there had been any viable suspicion that Rochford had engaged in such activities, it would surely have emerged at his trial. The evidence is tenuous and circumstantial.
37. *Letters and Papers*, X, 908.
38. Ibid., X, 866. Nearly all the witnesses against Anne were female members of the privy chamber, notably Lady Worcester, but none were charged with collusion, or with concealing her offences. Ives, *Anne Boleyn*, 397–8.
39. Ives, op. cit., 404–6.

## Chapter Four

1. Scarisbrick, *Henry VIII*, 335, n. 3.
2. *Letters and Papers*, X, 1161, 1227.
3. Ibid., 1047.
4. Ibid., 384.
5. Loades, *Mary Tudor*, 98–9.
6. BL Cotton MS Otho C X, f. 283; *Letters and Papers*, X, 968.
7. Loades, *Mary Tudor*, 100.
8. BL Cotton MS Otho C X, f. 278; *Letters and Papers*, X, 1022.
9. Loades, *Mary Tudor*, 101.
10. *Letters and Papers*, XI, 7; Chapuys to the emperor, 1 July 1536.
11. Ibid.
12. *Historical Manuscripts Commission*, Twelfth Report, Rutland MSS, Part IV, i, 309–11.
13. John Strype, *Ecclesiastical Memorials*, vol. I, pt. ii, 304.
14. M.H. and R. Dodds, *The Pilgrimage of Grace and the Exeter Conspiracy*; C.S.L. Davies, 'The Pilgrimage of Grace reconsidered', *Past and Present*, 41, 1968, 54–76; G.R. Elton, 'Politics and the Pilgrimage of Grace', in *Studies in Tudor and Stuart Government*.
15. BL Cotton MS Vespasian C XIV, f. 246; *Letters and Papers*, X, 1187. Loades, *Mary Tudor*, 105.
16. Ibid., 107.
17. *Letters and Papers*, XII, 254, 286.
18. Scarisbrick, *Henry VIII*, 345–6.
19. It is not quite certain why the plans for Jane's coronation were dropped, although all the points mentioned here are relevant. Some evidence suggests that the plan might have been revived if Jane had survived Edward's birth. *Letters and Papers*, Addenda I, pt. i, 430–1.
20. *Letters and Papers*, XII, pt. i, 600.
21. *Cal. Sp.*, Further Supplement, 453.
22. Helen Miller, *The English Nobility in the Reign of Henry VIII*, 233 ff.
23. *State Papers of King Henry VIII*, I, pt. ii, 551.
24. Ibid.
25. Hall, *Chronicle*, 825.
26. Miller, *English Nobility*, loc. cit.
27. Hall, *Chronicle*, 825.
28. The arrangements for the funeral were made by the Duke of Norfolk as Earl Marshall and Sir William Paget as Treasurer of the Household. Antonia Fraser, *The Six Wives of Henry VIII*, 280–1.
29. *Letters and Papers*, XII, ii, 1004; Scarisbrick, *Henry VIII*, 356.
30. *Memorials of King Henry VII*, ed. J. Gairdner (Rolls Series), 223–39.
31. *Letters and Papers*, XIII, i, 387, 695, 1132–3; Scarisbrick, *Henry VIII*, 357–8.
32. Ibid.
33. *Letters and Papers*, XIV, ii, 400.
34. *Letters and Papers*, XIII, ii, 1087; Scarisbrick, *Henry VIII*, 361.
35. D.B. Fenlon, *Heresy and Obedience in Tridentine Italy*, 27–8.
36. Loades, *Mary Tudor*, 120–1.
37. *Letters and Papers*, XIV, 37; Chapuys to Charles V, 9 January 1539.

## Chapter Five

1. *Letters and Papers*, XIV, i, 345, 365. Scarisbrick, *Henry VIII*, 361–2.
2. Ibid., 362. H.M. Colvin, *The History of the King's Works*, IV, *passim*.
3. S.E. Brigden, 'Popular disturbance and the fall of Thomas Cromwell and the Reformers, 1539–40', *H(istorical) J(ournal)*, 24, 1981, 257–78.
4. *Letters and Papers*, XIV, i, 441–3, 955.
5. *Letters and Papers*, XIII, i, 1198.
6. Ellis, *Original Letters (*1st series, II), 122ff.
7. *State Papers*, I, 605. Fraser, *Six Wives*, 299–300.
8. There had been a negotiation in 1527 for Anne, then aged twelve, to marry the ten-year-old Francis of Lorraine, and it was not quite clear when that negotiation had been broken off. In 1539 the Cleves negotiators were adamant that Anne was free to marry where she chose. Ellis, *Original Letters* (1st series, II), 121.
9. Fraser, *Six Wives*, 303.
10. Strype, *Ecclesiastical Memorials*, I, 459.
11. Hall, *Chronicle*, 832–6.
12. Strype, *Ecclesiastical Memorials*, II, 462.
13. Fraser, *Six Wives*, 313.
14. The best recent summary of this conflict is set out in J.A. Guy, *Tudor England*, 185–8.
15. M. St Clare Byrne (ed.), *The Lisle Letters*, VI, 61–6.
16. PRO SP1/167 ff. 135–6. *Letters and Papers*, XVI, 1321.
17. PRO SP1/168 f. 155. *Letters and Papers*, XVI, 1339.
18. *Original Letters relative to the English Reformation*, ed. H. Robinson, II, 205.
19. Fraser, *Six Wives*, 326–7.

20. The first of these visits occurred at New Year 1541, when Anne appeared in the guise of the king's 'good sister'. She seems to have borne no malice against Catherine for having supplanted her. Mary, in spite of her poor personal relations with Catherine, was living more or less permanently on the 'Queen's side' of the household by this time.

21. H.A. Kelly, *The Matrimonial Trials of Henry VIII*, 261. This act also declared that any consummated marriage would supersede an unconsummated marriage, no matter what the state of the contract, which was clearly aimed at the Cleves union.

22. *Narratives of the Days of the Reformation*, ed. J.G. Nichols (Camden Society, LXXVII), 260.

23. It was believed at the time that Catherine would have been crowned if she had become pregnant, and that was also Marillac's opinion, although nothing was said to that effect. *Letters and Papers*, XVI, 550.

24. *Historical Manuscripts Commission Reports*, Bath Papers, II, 8 ff. Whether this was a sign of credulous naïvety or a shrewd comment on the clergy as a royal secret service is not clear.

25. *Letters and Papers*, XVI, 1426. *Proceedings and Ordinances of the Privy Council of England*, ed. H. Nicholas, VII, 355.

26. L.B. Smith, *A Tudor Tragedy: the Life of Catherine Howard*, 188–92.

27. PRO SP1/161 ff. 101–2. *Letters and Papers*, XV, 875.

28. Ridley, *Cranmer*, 220. *Proceedings . . . of the Privy Council*, VII, 352–4.

29. It was never proved that Catherine did have intercourse with Culpepper after her marriage, but the king was right to believe that any such omission would have been purely technical. Smith, *Tudor Tragedy*, 181–2.

30. *HMC*, Bath Papers, II, 8–9.

31. PRO SP1/167 f. 160. *Letters and Papers*, XVI, 1339.

32. Statute 26 Henry VIII, c. 13; *Statutes of the Realm*, III, 508–9.

33. Smith, *Tudor Tragedy*, 200.

34. Ellis, *Original Letters* (1st series, II) 128–9.

## Chapter Six

1. 33 Henry VIII, c. 21. *Statutes of the Realm*, III, 859.

2. *Letters and Papers*, XVII, 441, 447. Thomas Thirlby, Bishop of Westminster, was sent as a special envoy to conclude this negotiation.

3. Hall, *Chronicle*, 856–7. Scarisbrick, *Henry VIII*, 436.

4. Ibid. *Letters and Papers*, XVIII, i, 22.

5. Ibid., 44.

6. Susan James, 'The Making of a Queen; the Life and Times of Queen Kateryn Parr and William Parr, Marquis of Northampton' (forthcoming), 1–13.

7. James, op. cit., 35. The Boroughs of Gainsborough were an old Lincolnshire family.

8. The connection with Mary was the result of Maude Parr's service to her mother. Mary never failed to honour an obligation of that kind. Fraser, *Six Wives*, 366.

9. Ibid.

10. *Letters and Papers*, XX, i, 266.

11. *Letters and Papers*, XX, i, 65.

12. Duke William had been roundly defeated by the emperor in the summer of 1543, and in September, by the Treaty of Venloe, he had been forced to abandon his intended French marriage and surrender his claims to Zutphen and Guelderland. He later married Charles's neice, Maria of Austria, and became firmly attached to the Catholic and Habsburg interest.

13. Maria Dowling, *Humanism in the Age of Henry VIII*, 234–7; Susan James is inclined to take a more positive view of Catherine's influence, on the basis of her known patronage of humanists such as John Parkhurst and Anthony Cope, but the evidence for her intervention is purely circumstantial.

14. Dowling, *Humanism*, 47–8.

15. *Letters and Papers*, XVII, 371.

16. 35 Henry VIII, c. 1; *Statutes of the Realm*, III 955–8.

17. *Letters and Papers*, XIV, i, 651 (20).

18. Hall, *Chronicle*, 858–9; Ridley, *Cranmer*, 234–5.

19. M.L. Zell, 'The Prebendaries plot of 1543; a reconsideration', *J(ournal) of E(cclesiastical) H(istory)*, 27, 1976, 241–53; Glyn Redworth, *In Defence of the Church Catholic: a Life of Stephen Gardiner*, 176–207.

20. Redworth, 200–1, where the role of Gardiner in these machinations is played down.

21. Nichols, *Narratives*, 254–8.

22. Ridley, *Cranmer*, 243.

23. The only source for the story of the plot

against Catherine is Foxe, *Acts and Monuments*, V, 553–6. For a recent discussion, and particularly of Gardiner's role in it, see Redworth, *In Defence*, 232–7.

24. Foxe, *Acts and Monuments*, V, 564.
25. Redworth argues that Gardiner's loss of favour was not the direct result of the failed attack on Catherine, but of a much more mundane failure later in the year to read the king's mind correctly over a land transaction; *In Defence*, 237–41.
26. *Letters and Papers*, XVIII, i, 754, 759.
27. Ibid., 880, 897, 905, etc.
28. Scarisbrick, *Henry VIII*, 442–3. Mathew Stewart, Earl of Lennox, had recently returned from exile in France, having apparently decided that the English interest would serve him better. Before Henry left for France he married the young earl to his niece, Lady Margaret Douglas.
29. *State Papers*, I, 736.
30. *Letters and Papers*, XIX, ii, 174, 424.
31. *State Papers*, I, 891, ns 1, 2. Fraser, *Six Wives*, 393.
32. Fraser (395) says 'her feelings of grief were no doubt sincere', but I have been unable to find any expression of such feelings.
33. Mattingly, *Catherine*, 120–1.
34. James, 'The Making of a Queen . . .', 140–2.
35. *Acts of the Privy Council of England*, ed. J.R. Dasent, II, 34–5.
36. Fraser, *Six Wives*, 400.
37. S. Haynes and W. Murdin, eds., *Collection of State Papers . . . left by William Cecil, Lord Burghley*, I, 62 etc.

# Epilogue

1. The ordinary revenue of England (that is without taxation) amounted to about £150,000 in 1530. The revenue of the French Crown at the beginning of Francis I's reign in 1515 was some 4.9 million *livres*, or about £950,000.
2. D. Loades, *The Tudor Navy*, 74–138.
3. Henry would have been thirty-six when his father died, so there would have been no minority, and probably no female succession.
4. This can be seen, not only in the preambles to the relevant statutes such as the Act in Restraint of Appeals (24 Henry VIII, c.12), but also in propaganda works such as Thomas Starkey's *Exhortation to the People* (1536).
5. Quentin Skinner, *The Foundation of Modern Political Thought*, II, 90–108.
6. Strype, *Ecclesiastical Memorials*, I, ii, 462.
7. Ibid., 460.
8. L.B. Smith, *Henry VIII: the Mask of Royalty*, 231–3.
9. James, 'The Making of a Queen . . .', *passim*. Smith, *Henry VIII*, 238–59.
10. Contemporaries affirm that Elizabeth 'gloried' in her father, and Philip's envoy, the Count of Feria, noted that she 'has her way absolutely in everything, as her father did . . .'. D. Loades, *The Reign of Mary Tudor*, 390–2.
11. A point discussed thoroughly in G.R. Elton, *The Tudor Constitution*, 338–78.
12. *State Papers of Henry VIII*, 142–6.
13. By the Treaty of Camp (June 1546): Guy, *Tudor England*, 191–2.
14. *Henry V*, IV.i.

# Bibliography

A comprehensive bibliography of this subject would be a volume in itself. The following suggestions are designed to aid those who wish to investigate further, and they are highly selective:

## Primary Sources

'A Diary of the Expedition of 1544', *E(nglish) H(istorical) R(eview)*, 16 (1901).
*Acts of the Privy Council of England*, ed. J.R. Dasent et al. (London, 1890–1964).
*Anglica Historia of Polydore Vergil*, ed. Denys Hay, Camden Society, LXXIV (1950).
Byrne, Muriel St Clare, ed., *The Letters of Henry VIII* (London, 1968).
Byrne, Muriel St Clare, ed., *The Lisle Letters* (Chicago, 1981).
*Calendar of State Papers, Spanish*, ed. R. Tyler et al. (London, 1862–1964).
*Calendar of State Papers, Venetian*, ed. R. Brown et al. (London, 1864–98).
Cavendish, George, *The Life and Death of Cardinal Wolsey*, ed. R.S. Sylvester, Early English Text Society (London, 1959).
*Chronicles of London*, ed. C.L. Kingsford (London, 1905).
Dowling, Maria, 'William Latymer's Chronickelle of Anne Boleyn', Camden Miscellany, XXXIX (1990).
*Foedera, conventiones etc.*, ed. T. Rymer (London, 1727–35).
Foxe, John, *Acts and Monuments of the English Martyrs*, eds. S.R. Cattley and George Townsend (London, 1837–41).
Gardiner, Stephen, *The Letters of Stephen Gardiner*, ed. J.A. Muller (Cambridge, 1933).
Hall, Edward, *The Union of the two Noble and Illustre Houses of York and Lancaster, (Chronicle)* ed. H. Ellis (London, 1809).
*Letters and Papers, Foreign and Domestic . . . of the Reign of Henry VIII*, ed. J. Gairdner et al. (London, 1862–1932).
Nichols, J.G., ed., *Narratives of the Days of the Reformation*, Camden Society, LXXVII (1859).
Nicholas, Sir Harris, ed., *Proceedings and Ordinances of the Privy Council of England* (London, 1837).
Nicholas, N.H., ed., *The Privy Purse Expenses of King Henry VIII* (London, 1829).
Ridley, Jasper, *The Love Letters of Henry VIII* (London, 1988).
Sander, Nicholas, *The Rise and Growth of the Anglican Schism*, ed. D. Lewis (London, 1877).
*State Papers of King Henry VIII*, (London, 1830–52).
*Statutes of the Realm*, ed. A. Luders et al. (London, 1810–28).
Strype, J., *Ecclesiastical Memorials* (Oxford, 1822).
Sturtz, J. and Murphy, V., eds., *The Divorce Tracts of Henry VIII* (Angers, 1988).
*The Noble Triumphant Coronation of Queen Anne*, in A.F. Pollard, *Tudor Tracts* (London, 1903), 9–51.
*Tudor Royal Proclamations*, eds. P.L. Hughes and J.F. Larkin (New Haven, 1964–9).
Wriothesley, C., *A Chronicle of England during the Reigns of the Tudors, 1485–1559*, ed. W. Hamilton Douglas, Camden Society, new series, XI, XX (1875, 1877).
Wyatt, George, *The Papers of George Wyatt*, ed. D. Loades, Camden Society, 4th series, vol. V (1968).

## Secondary Works

Anglo, S., *Spectacle, Pageantry and Early Tudor Policy* (Oxford, 1965).
Auerbach, E., *Tudor Artists* (London, 1954).

Behrens, Betty, 'A Note on Henry VIII's Divorce Project of 1514', *B(ulletin of the) I(nstitute of) H(istorical) R(esearch)*, 11 (1934).

Bernard, G.W., 'The fall of Anne Boleyn', *EHR*, 106 (1991).

Carles, Lancelot de, *'Poème sur la mort d'Anne Boleyn'*, in Georges Ascoli, *La Grande-Bretagne devant l'Opinion Française depuis la guerre de cent ans jusqu' à la fin du XVIe siècle* (Paris, 1927).

Coleman, C. and Starkey, D., eds., *Revolution Reassessed* (Oxford, 1986).

Colvin, H. M., *A History of the King's Works*, IV, ii (London, 1982).

Dowling, Maria, 'Anne Boleyn and Reform', *Journal of Ecclesiastical History*, 35 (1984).

——, *Humanism in the Age of Henry VIII*, (London, 1986).

——, 'The Gospel and the Court; Reformation under Henry VIII', in *Protestanism and the National Church in the Sixteenth Century*, eds. M. Dowling and P. Lake (London, 1987).

Elton, G.R., *Policy and Police* (Cambridge, 1972).

——, *The Tudor Constitution* (Cambridge, 1982).

——, *The Tudor Revolution in Government* (Cambridge, 1953).

Fraser, Antonia, *The Six Wives of Henry VIII* (London, 1993).

Friedman, Paul, *Anne Boleyn: a Chapter in English History, 1527–1536* (London, 1884).

Gamon, S.R., *Statesman and Schemer: William, first Lord Paget* (Newton Abbott, 1973).

Garnett, F.B., 'Queen Catherine Parr and Sudeley Castle', *T(ransactions of the) C(umberland and) W(estmorland) A(ntiquarian and) A(rchaeological) S(ociety)* (1894).

Gunn, S.J., *Charles Brandon, Duke of Suffolk, 1484–1545* (Oxford, 1986).

Guy, J.A. and Fox, A., *Reassessing the Henrician Age* (Oxford, 1986).

Guy, J.A., *Tudor England* (Oxford, 1988).

Gwyn, Peter, *The King's Cardinal: the Rise and Fall of Thomas Wolsey* (London, 1990).

Harris, Barbara, *Edward Stafford, third Duke of Buckingham, 1478–1521* (Stanford, Calif., 1986).

——, 'Women and Politics in early Tudor England', *H(istorical) J(ournal)*, 33 (1990).

Haugaard, W.P., 'Katherine Parr; the Religious Convictions of a Renaissance Queen', *Renaissance Quarterly*, 22 (1969).

Hume, Martin, *The Wives of Henry VIII and the Part they Played in History* (London, 1905).

Ives, E.W., *Anne Boleyn* (Oxford, 1986).

James, Susan, 'Queen Kateryn Parr, 1512–1548', *TCWAAS*, 88 (1988).

——, 'The Devotional Writings of Queen Catherine Parr', *TCWAAS*, 82 (1982).

——, *The Making of a Queen* (Bangor, forthcoming).

Jones, Michael and Underwood, Malcolm, *The King's Mother: Lady Margaret Beaufort* (Cambridge, 1992).

Kelley, H.A., 'Kingship, Incest and the Dictates of Law', *American Journal of Jurisprudence*, 14 (1969).

——, *The Matrimonial Trials of Henry VIII* (Stanford, Calif., 1976).

Levine, Mortimer, 'The Place of Women in Tudor Government', in *Tudor Rule and Revolution*, eds. D.J. Guth and J.W. McKenna (Cambridge, 1982).

Loades, David, *The Chronicles of the Tudor Kings* (London, 1990).

——, *Mary Tudor: a Life* (Oxford, 1989).

——, *The Tudor Court* (Bangor, 1992).

McConica, J., *English Humanism and Reformation Politics* (Oxford, 1965).

MacLean, J., *The Life of Thomas Seymour*, (London, 1869).

Martiensson, A., *Queen Katherine Parr* (London, 1973).

Mattingly, Garrett, *Catherine of Aragon* (London, 1963).

——, 'The Reputation of Dr de Puebla' *EHR*, LV (1940).

Miller, H., *Henry VIII and the English Nobility* (Oxford, 1986).

Mueller, Janet, 'Katherine Parr's Prayers and Meditations', *Huntington Library Quarterly*, 53 (1990).

Muir, Kenneth, *The Life and Letters of Thomas Wyatt* (Liverpool, 1963).

Paget, Hugh, 'The Youth of Anne Boleyn', *BIHR*, 55 (1981).

Parmiter, G. de C., *The King's Great Matter* (London, 1967).

Paul, J.E., *Catherine of Aragon and her Friends* (London, 1966).

Redworth, Glyn, *In Defence of the Church Catholic: the life of Stephen Gardiner* (Oxford, 1990).

Richardson, W.C., *Mary Tudor, the White Queen* (Baton Rouge, 1970).

Ridley, Jasper, *Thomas Cranmer* (Oxford, 1962).

Russell, Jocelyn, *The Field of Cloth of Gold* (London, 1969).

Scarisbrick, J.J., *Henry VIII:* (London, 1968).

Smith, L.B., *Henry VIII: the Mask of Royalty* (London, 1971).

——, *Tudor Prelates and Politics* (Princeton, NJ, 1953).

——, *A Tudor Tragedy: the Life of Catherine Howard* (London, 1961)

Starkey, David, *Henry VIII: a European Court in England* (London, 1991).

——, *The Reign of Henry VIII: Personalities and Politics* (London, 1985).

——, ed., *The English Court from the Wars of the Roses to the Civil War* (London, 1987).

Strong, Roy, *Holbein and Henry VIII* (London, 1967).

——, *Tudor and Jacobean Portraits* (London, 1969).

Warnicke, Retha, 'Sexual Heresy at the Court of Henry VIII', *HJ*, 30 (1987).

——, *The Rise and Fall of Anne Boleyn* (Cambridge, 1989).

Williams, Neville, *Henry VIII and his Court* (London, 1971).

# Index